Sexuality in World History

This book examines sexuality in the past, and explores how it helps explain sexuality in the present. The subject of sexuality is often a controversial one, and exploring it through a world history perspective emphasizes the extent to which societies, including our own, are still reacting to historical change through contemporary sexual behaviors, values, and debates.

The study uses a clear chronological structure to focus on major patterns and changes in sexuality – both sexual culture and sexual behaviors – in the main periods of world history, with comparison and discussion across cultures and societies. Topics covered include:

- Issues involved in studying the history of sexuality
- The sexual implications of the transition from hunting and gathering economies to agricultural economies
- Sexuality in classical societies
- The post-classical period and the spread of the world religions
- Sex in an age of trade and colonies
- Changes in sexual behaviors and sexual attitudes between 1750 and 1950
- Sex in contemporary world history.

The book is a vital contribution to the study of world history, and is the perfect companion for all students of the history of sexuality.

Peter N. Stearns is Provost and Professor of History at George Mason University. He is co-author of *Premodern Travel in World History* (2008), and author of *Gender in World History* (2nd edition 2006), *Consumerism in World History* (2nd edition 2006), *Childhood in World History* (2005), and *Western Civilization in World History* (2003), all in this series. His other recent publications include *The Global Experience* (2005) and *World History in Brief* (2007).

Themes in World History
Series editor: Peter N. Stearns

The *Themes in World History* series offers focused treatment of a range of human experiences and institutions in the world history context. The purpose is to provide serious, if brief, discussions of important topics as additions to textbook coverage and document collections. The treatments will allow students to probe particular facets of the human story in greater depth than textbook coverage allows, and to gain a fuller sense of historians' analytical methods and debates in the process. Each topic is handled over time – allowing discussions of changes and continuities. Each topic is assessed in terms of a range of different societies and religions – allowing comparisons of relevant similarities and differences. Each book in the series helps readers deal with world history in action, evaluating global contexts as they work through some of the key components of human society and human life.

Gender in World History
Peter N. Stearns

Consumerism in World History: The Global Transformation of Desire
Peter N. Stearns

Warfare in World History
Michael S. Neiberg

Disease and Medicine in World History
Sheldon Watts

Western Civilization in World History
Peter N. Stearns

The Indian Ocean in World History
Milo Kearney

Asian Democracy in World History
Alan T. Wood

Revolutions in World History
Michael D. Richards

Migration in World History
Patrick Manning

Sports in World History
David G. McComb

The United States in World History
Edward J. Davies, II

Food in World History
Jeffrey M. Pilcher

Childhood in World History
Peter N. Stearns

Religion in World History
John Super and Briane Turley

Poverty in World History
Steven M. Beaudoin

Premodern Travel in World History
Steven S. Gosch and Peter N. Stearns

Premodern Trade in World History
Richard L. Smith

Sexuality in World History
Peter N. Stearns

Sexuality in World History

Peter N. Stearns

Routledge
Taylor & Francis Group

LONDON AND NEW YORK

First published 2009 by Routledge
2 Park Square, Milton Park, Abingdon, Oxon OX14 4RN

Simultaneously published in the USA and Canada
by Routledge
270 Madison Ave, New York, NY 10016

Reprinted 2010

*Routledge is an imprint of the Taylor & Francis Group,
an informa business*

© 2009 Peter N. Stearns

Typeset in Garamond and Gill Sans by Swales & Willis Ltd, Exeter, Devon
Printed and bound in Great Britain by TJ International,
Padstow, Cornwall

British Library Cataloguing in Publication Data
A catalogue record for this book is available
from the British Library
Library of Congress Cataloging in Publication Data
Stearns, Peter N.
Sexuality in world history / Peter N. Stearns.
p. cm.—(Themes in world history)
1. Sex—History. I. Title.
HQ12.S698 2009
306.709—dc22
2008041590

ISBN 10: 0–415–77776–3 (hbk)
ISBN 10: 0–415–77777–1 (pbk)
ISBN 10: 0–203–88032–3 (ebk)

ISBN 13: 978–0–415–77776–6 (hbk)
ISBN 13: 978–0–415–77777–3 (pbk)
ISBN 13: 978–0–203–88032–6 (ebk)

Contents

Acknowledgments

I have always enjoyed teaching about the history of sexuality, mainly because I deeply believe that history in a complex subject area like this really helps us understand contemporary issues by showing how they have emerged from the past, but also because students enjoy the chance to talk about the subject in a scholarly context. So I welcomed the chance to do this book and to broaden my own knowledge through the global framework. My thanks to Vicky Peters, Eve Setch, and Elizabeth Clifford from Routledge, who encouraged the project. Huge gratitude to Clio Stearns, who did a great deal of research for the book, and to Deborah Stearns, who provided a critical reading. I benefit tremendously from the intelligent organization of Laura Bell, who processed the manuscript. My wife, Donna Kidd, put up with my recurrent chatter about a topic that is truly important but also, sometimes, quite amusing.

Chapter 1

Introduction

The whys and hows of sex history

This is a book about sex in the past, and how sex in the past helps explain sex in the present. It deals with a variety of societies around the world, while talking about how sexual attitudes and behaviors are affected by larger global forces like the advent of agriculture or, later, urbanization.

A study of sexuality in history can understandably evoke several skeptical responses, and these are best discussed explicitly and in advance:

(1) This is a frivolous topic, not worthy of historical attention compared to the really important features of human society in the past. *Response*: to an extent, of course, this is a matter of personal taste. Serious work on the history of sex is only a few decades old; traditionally, historians devoted themselves mainly to work on politics, diplomacy, great ideas, and possibly economic patterns. But understanding patterns of sexuality in the past helps illuminate a major aspect of human behavior, which should be justification enough for this expansion of history's topical range. Sex history connects also to other topics— like differences among social classes or gender patterns. Governments often seek to regulate sexual behavior (not always with great success), and sex certainly figures in the impact of armies or colonial authorities—linking sex history directly with conventional historical topics. We increasingly realize how much rape plays into war and civil strife, another if particularly horrible linkage. So the topic is not really a frivolous aside in the history enterprise.

(2) This is an inconceivable topic (no pun intended), for sex is a basic behavior, biologically determined, so it has no real history. *Response*: this one is easy to disprove. Attitudes toward sexuality vary widely according to different social contexts—some societies in some periods disapprove vigorously of masturbation, to take one example, but then, later, ease off into greater permissiveness. Sexual culture, the values and beliefs applied to sex, obviously change over time, and this is an important part of the larger history. Actual behavior has a history too. Rates of adultery vary, depending on time period and larger social conditions. Ages of puberty change (which means that even biology is not an absolute constant), depending on nutrition and social context. Average age of menopause can vary and change as well. Basic features of sex figure into sexual history, which is what makes the topic interesting, significant, and sometimes surprising.

(3) This is a disgusting topic, certainly not fit for student audiences. *Response*: again, to an extent this is a matter of personal taste. The history of sex unquestionably involves issues that some people, even in our permissive society, still prefer not to discuss. I have deliberately referred to masturbation already; it's an important aspect of sex history in some societies and times, but it's not something usually discussed in history classes. My own belief is that it's better to talk about sex, using history in fact as a way to explore key issues, than to cover it up. But there is no intention of being gratuitously shocking. Some sex histories have focused on exotic behaviors that don't necessarily shed much light on what sex has involved for most people, and that's not the approach taken in this survey. Sex is an important aspect of the human condition and its history can and should be explored in this framework, and not deliberately either to titillate or to offend.

(4) All well and good, but sex is such a private behavior that its real history is impossible. *Response*: there are, without question, aspects of the history of sex that cannot be as clearly studied as one might like, because accurate data are simply not available. Behaviors that a society disapproves of are particularly resistant to history probes. Homosexual practices in some times and places are not easy to get at, to take an obvious example. While historians can deal with attitudes toward masturbation, and some aspects of their impact, we will never be able to talk about rates of masturbation from one period to the next; this is almost always a concealed practice. Another current challenge is intriguing. The massive promotional campaign for drugs to improve male sexual functioning—Viagra and the like—makes one wonder if male dysfunction has been increasing. New health issues, like higher rates of diabetes or high blood pressure and its medication, might cause new problems; and/or growing desire for sexual pleasure and a need to demonstrate sexual masculinity even in later age could account for the new interest. Or the whole thing may be a function of drug company hype. Great questions, but the fact is we can't know for sure: there is no tidy census of male erectile capacities in previous decades. There are, in other words, real limitations in what we can know historically (or even about sexual habits in our own times). But historians have discovered a great deal, and it is possible to talk about significant historical changes and continuities. Public attitudes, important in their own right, are easier to get at than behaviors; but even many of the latter lend themselves to serious historical description and analysis. The subject is important enough that even a somewhat constrained historical treatment is worth the effort.

Casting a history of sexuality in world history terms heightens the problem of documentation. Different societies generate different types and amounts of relevant records. All societies have values that apply to sexuality—the subject is too essential not to generate both laws and cultural commentary. So we can get at sexual cultures as soon as significant historical materials of any sort become available. The first known law code, from Babylonia, spent a great deal of time on sexual regulation, and early art also had strong sexual content—to take two examples. But material on sexual practice is much more varied. At least as important, for our purposes, is the fact that historians have studied sexuality far more extensively for some societies than for others, which means that not all the comparisons one might wish to develop are possible. Indeed, there is real opportunity for further work on the history of sexuality seen as a global and comparative topic, with strong potential for serious advances in historical knowledge (of the sort that have already paid off in research on several societies).

Still, the world framework, though not commonly applied to sexuality, and certainly challenging, has its merits already, even in the present state of scholarship. All three of the main approaches developed for world history apply readily to sexuality, and gain additional richness when patterns of sexual culture and behavior are factored in. Different societies have different standards, so that comparison can reveal a great deal about how particular civilizations operated. Even the sensual content of art could differ greatly, as a comparison between statues of Hindu goddesses and women in Chinese art reveals quite easily. Contacts between societies—the second world history approach, after comparison—could also strongly affect sexual culture and practice. Spanish colonists frequently fathered illegitimate children with Native American women, helping to establish a widespread incidence of sex outside of marriage that has a continuing impact in Latin America. British colonial control of India, at the nineteenth-century peak of prudery back home, necessitated special exemptions from British law for the use of Hindu art on Indian postage stamps, revealing an unexpected complexity introduced by contact between two societies with very different public sexual values. Finally, both culture and practice reflected some of the larger forces in world history. Global trade patterns, in our own day, help explain a new incidence of sex trafficking in several parts of the world. Diffusion of agriculture, much earlier in time, had dramatic impact on sexuality. Sex, not surprisingly given its importance, has been a vital part of the panorama of world history, and helps translate world history patterns into an understanding of ordinary human behavior and daily life.

*   *   *

The history of sexuality begins with the fact that, as many anthropologists have noted, the human animal has some distinctive characteristics. Sex is, after all, a matter of animal behavior, though with human beings more is involved. Compared to many mammalian species, humans have an unusual number of erogenous zones on their bodies, which obviously can encourage sexual stimulation. Although women of the species are fertile only a few days each month, their fertile periods are more frequent than those of many other mammals and they can be stimulated sexually even at non-fertile times, or after fertility has ended with menopause; their sexual activity is thus less dependent on a few annual points at which they are "in heat" than is true of many other animals. There's another interesting distinction from most mammalian species (except for some chimpanzees): humans gain capacity for and interest in sexual activity before most young women are regularly ovulating, which means that they can indulge in sex for a few years with less likelihood (NOT, be advised, no likelihood) of pregnancy resulting. Human children display certain kinds of sexual awareness, at least of their own bodies.

These simple but basic points mean that human sexual activity can be, and often is, rather frequent and may be less fully tied to reproductive effort than is true for many other species. The point about a partial gap between appetite and reproductive capacity almost builds in some possible experimentalism for adolescents and certainly some big societal issues about regulating these experimental impulses in turn. Indeed the whole human biological apparatus, where sex is concerned, quite literally inevitably imposes some needs for sexual regulation on the species, to make sure that sexual activity does not get out of control or become too disruptive either of individual lives or of social relationships. This is particularly true because humans have the capacity for more reproduction than most families or societies usually want. If a couple tries to maximize their reproductive behavior, having sex as early in life as fertility develops and continuing until it ends, they will have on average about 14 children. This is called the Hutterite formula, for a religious sect in Canada that for several decades practiced this kind of unrestrained reproductive effort. And through history there have always been some couples that had family sizes at this level. But in most historical periods the Hutterite formula generates more children than can easily be raised or supported, so most societies develop some customs designed to encourage somewhat less reproduction, which in turn means either less sexual activity or some controls on sexual activity. Here too, the human sexual capacity quickly generates the need for social response. The precise nature of the response can, obviously, vary from one society to the next, and it can alter. This is part of the history of sexuality. But a tension between biological capacity and social needs is something of a constant, even though its specific manifestations change greatly over time.

Sociobiologists would add some other basics about human sexuality. They note that, like other animals, there are significant gender differences. Some have contended that males, constantly producing new sperm during their fertile years, are "naturally" bent on having as much sex with as many different partners as possible, to spread their genetic heritage; females, on the other hand, with a finite supply of eggs and the burden of actually carrying children before birth, find it important to limit their partners and work toward assuring stability for the offspring they have. There is, according to this argument, a built-in gender distinction that will also play out in social arrangements, with men more eager, women more reticent. This may also help explain, though not excuse, some of the deployment of sexuality for male gender dominance, as in abuses of women during wartime. Historians would urge that this biological gender imperative not be overdone, because individuals and cultures can introduce a number of variants on any basic pattern; but it is worth keeping in mind. Men's fertility usually lasts longer than that of women, which introduces some interesting issues for sexuality in later age. The overall point is clear: biology introduces important complexities into human sexuality, which in turn assure that the history of sexual attitudes and behaviors will be complex.

A few other biological issues should be noted. Some authorities argue that about 10 percent of the population is "naturally" homosexual. Others, who find homosexuality a matter of sin or psychological aberration, of course dispute this. A few people are born with unclear gender sexuality traits, which means that many societies face an issue of what to do in such circumstances, how to define and manage what is currently called inter-sex (or hermaphroditic). Here too, a standard phenomenon, in biological terms, calls for a whole variety of cultural responses, from one place and from one time to the next. Biology obviously dictates that fact that interbreeding among close relatives produces a higher rate of genetically defective children than is otherwise the case, and presumably early societies registered on these results; this explains the many efforts to prohibit sexual contacts among siblings and other primary kin. Again, biology intersects with human sexual history in many important ways.

*   *   *

Human sexuality has been changing a great deal in recent decades. New levels of population pressure—global populations tripled in the twentieth century, an unprecedented rate of increase—force new personal and social decisions about reproductive sex. New devices, like the pill, facilitate a growing separation between sex and reproduction, creating greater opportunities for recreational sex than ever before. Novel types of media, like movies and television, create opportunities for the visual portrayal of sexual stimuli never before experienced. Growing contacts among societies, thanks to global communication and commerce, inevitably create tensions as different sexual standards collide. New human rights ideas create debates over the treatment of certain kinds of sexual minorities, and while these debates are particularly vigorous in some societies they can have some global resonance. Changing work and coeducational schooling patterns, with more and more women studying and working outside the home thanks to global industrialization and urbanization, create opportunities for sexually-relevant interactions but also for concerns about appropriate regulation of behavior—the novel modern concept of sexual harassment is one important response. And amid these and other fundamental changes, many societies and individuals react with indignation, seeking to defend against undue innovation in one of the most intimate but potentially sacrosanct areas of human life. One of the reasons that the history of sexuality gains significance involves the opportunity to analyze current patterns of change and reactions to change—using recent history better to understand our contemporary global selves.

But the history of sexuality is not just a modern topic, and earlier patterns are interesting in themselves as well as providing vital backdrops to more contemporary concerns. Different regional reactions to common contemporary trends, for example, relate directly to sexual values systems often developed many centuries ago.

This book begins with a discussion of the sexual implications of the transition from hunting and gathering economies to agricultural economies—a transition that had obvious impacts on behaviors and which, even more dramatically, encouraged development of new cultural norms. Inevitably this first exercise involves some effort to determine whether, in the past, some societies managed to express sexuality more successfully, with fewer personal and social hang-ups, than more complex societies would achieve; after some anthropologists thought they found superior sexual adjustments in some of the more "primitive" societies early in the twentieth century, the issue has been debated vigorously. There is no question, however, that agriculture changed the framework for sexual behavior considerably, in this first great transition in the human economy.

As agricultural societies matured, they developed various standards for sexuality, brought out by comparisons among the classical societies detailed in Chapter 3. Gender norms and approaches to homosexuality were among the key variables, but within agricultural civilizations differences of social class must also be considered.

The spread of the world religions introduced still further change, particularly during the post-classical period between about 500 and 1450 CE. Explaining the causes and impacts of change, and updating comparative findings, bring the history of sexuality closer to modern times. This post-classical period also saw an unprecedented surge of extensive travel, and many accounts dealt with sexual issues.

Between 1500 and 1750, the big story is the development of new contacts and migration patterns (including the forced migration of the Atlantic slave trade), and the results on sexual behaviors. Criticisms of the sexual practices of various societies become clearer amid accelerating interaction, and these could have significant results.

Beginning definitively in the eighteenth century, initially particularly in the Western world, forces of urbanization, early industrialization and rising consumerism had important results in changing both sexual behaviors and sexual attitudes. Historians begin to talk about "sexual revolutions," with the later eighteenth century marking a crucial first step. At the same time, growing Western influence and outright imperialism saw new efforts to impose sexual standards on other societies, sometimes with unintended consequences. The period 1750–1950 was a complicated one in the global history of sexuality—evidenced among other things by frequent gaps between professed standards and actual behaviors. Two chapters cover, first, the complex Western transformation and, second, global patterns and reactions.

The final part, dealing with the past several decades, focuses on the interaction between new global pressures affecting sexuality, building on the increasingly intricate contacts among different parts of the world, and regional reactions ranging from revolutionary innovation to traditionalist resistance to change. Global trends include the influence of new media, such as the movie industry; the spread of birth control devices and practices; and the ongoing acceleration of urban and industrial growth. They also include new scientific claims and findings, affecting, for example, the definition of homosexuality. Feminism also developed some global outreach, and while feminism expressed complicated thoughts about sexuality it could shape new attitudes to issues like rape, female circumcision or prostitution, or legitimate new expectations among women themselves. More recently still, gay rights movements strive for global response. Global trends did not, however, create a single global model for sexual culture or sexual practice. Key societies responded to regional forces, like the surge of communist revolutions that gripped several nations, or the impact of wars and civil strife; while religious leaders attempted to reassert their role in guiding sexual propriety. Comparison remains essential as global factors encounter varied mixtures of accommodation, resistance, and enthusiastic embrace. Arguments about sexuality, within and among global societies, constitute a significant global reality in the early twenty-first century.

The big point, and the key reason to study the history of sexuality, involves the extent to which societies, including our own, are still reacting to historical change through contemporary sexual behaviors, values, and often bitter debates. Older traditions, launched, for example, by major religions, continue to shape reactions. Even more important is the extent to which virtually all societies have been confronted with huge alterations in the factors affecting sexuality—including birth control and media representations—and are still trying to adjust. Not surprisingly, the process generates deep-seated divisions and controversies, within and among societies, on issues ranging from premarital sex to homosexuality to how many body parts should be easily visible on television or beaches. The subject is a vital one to human life; it has been in active motion for upwards of two centuries almost everywhere; it colors contacts among societies. And all of this is best understood through the discipline that combines the study of change with comparisons among different societies—that is, through history. The history of sex is arguably interesting in itself, and it is truly inescapable as it sheds light on a complex and contested set of changes that directly connects present to past.

Further reading

J.W. Howell, W.E. Burns, V.L. Mondelli, and C.A. Gottsleben, eds., *Greenwood Encyclopedia of Love, Courtship, and Sexuality*, 6v (Greenwood, CT: Greenwood, 2008), is a valuable reference work, though frustratingly selective from a global standpoint.

Part I

Sexuality before modern times

Sexuality, not surprisingly, was a vital part of human life and society from the long hunting and gathering phases of human existence, to the rise of agriculture, and the centuries-long agricultural period of history. The special characteristics of particular civilizations show clearly in distinctive approaches to sexual standards, representations, and (to a degree) behaviors. The advent of major religions had a definite impact on sexuality, in some cases providing new justifications and norms for patterns that had already been established, in other instances introducing considerable change—for example, in approaches to homosexuality.

There is no such thing as "traditional" sex, to be contrasted with modern sex. Too much change occurred before modern times; too much variety existed to permit this kind of generalization. The great transformations in sexuality, and the reasons for these transformations, with the rise of agriculture and then (though to a lesser degree) the impact of new religions, form a key theme in the chapters that follow. Differentiation is vital as well. Both early societies and classical civilizations varied widely in what they believed about sex, how they regarded female sexuality, and how—and how frankly—they represented sex in art. At the same time, the arrival of agriculture introduced certain characteristic themes and problems in sexuality that can be traced beneath the surface of the various major civilizations and religious formulations. These commonalities deserve attention also, and they do contrast with what more modern conditions have generated more recently—while also clearly reflecting basic biological and psychological constants in a species whose fundamental characteristics were set by the time *Homo sapiens sapiens* emerged around 100,000 BCE.

Change, diversity, commonalities—all these conflicting patterns can be identified even in an overview of major sexual developments in the long premodern phases of the human experience. An underlying question cannot be avoided as well: did human sex display greater freedom and openness in early societies, only to encounter greater constraint and repression as economies became more complicated, formal governments emerged, and more systematic religions took hold? The answer, frankly, is not clear-cut, and the question merits serious debate. Some early attempts to generalize about this kind of contrast between carefree indulgence and later deterioration have been shot down. Probably a more accurate picture flows from a realization that different societies, over time, identified different kinds of problems, to which sexuality had to be adjusted. Merely because the question is undeniably complicated, however, does not mean that it should be sidestepped entirely.

Chapter 2

Sexuality and the rise of agriculture

Two (frankly contradictory) images may spring to mind when thinking of sexuality and "primitive" peoples. The first is the brutal caveman, batting women over the head or dragging them off by the hair, prior to forcible sex. The second invokes the carefree sexuality of people before the rules of civilization and the burdens of trying to maintain a more sophisticated economy. Both images are off the mark. While some implications of male sexual dominance exist, particularly at the symbolic level, there is also ample sign that women were active participants in sexuality in early societies, with bargaining power of their own. And while sexual standards in early human societies were in some ways less restrictive than those that would come later, and there was clear if implicit acknowledgement of sexual enjoyment, there were definite rules and constraints. Human sexuality was different in early societies from what it has become today; a number of important, even fundamental, changes have altered the picture. These changes have been far more complex than any idea of taming the aggressive caveman or disrupting the sexual idylls of blissfully primitive teenagers can convey. Along with change, however, we can, not surprisingly, see some underlying continuities: early human societies contended with the tension between recognition of sexual pleasure and interest and the need, for the sake of social order and even economic survival, to introduce key regulatory standards.

*   *   *

For hundreds of thousands of years, humans lived in a hunting and gathering economy, with small bands of people spread widely over most of the inhabitable portions of the globe. Our knowledge of daily life in the long period before agriculture is limited: there are archaeological remnants, artistic representations where several sexual emphases are marked, and evidence from the scattered remaining hunting and gathering groups in different parts of the world. What we do know, while sometimes tantalizingly sketchy, suggests the close relationship in human sexuality between biological imperatives and possibilities and the constraints of particular economic frameworks.

While great variety prevailed in specifics, not surprisingly since hunting and gathering bands were small and widely scattered, it is clear that hunters and gatherers placed high value on certain kinds of sexual symbolism. Their societies were not concerned about certain aspects of sexuality that would be vigorously contested by more recent kinds of human groups. But they experienced severe limits in key aspects of sexuality because of the constraints a hunting and gathering economy and lifestyle placed on the numbers of children that could be sustained. Birth control needs, and the absence of devices that could help meet these needs, contended with considerable erotic interest. The result was a pattern of sexual expression that would change considerably when agriculture emerged to replace hunting and gathering, beginning (depending on region) between 9000 and 5000 BCE. Sexuality in hunting and gathering societies indeed provides a fascinating baseline against which to assess later developments, challenging historical analysis not only to document but also to explain why some features of sexuality encountered such dramatic transformations.

Two tensions seem to have operated in hunting and gathering societies overall: the first, expressed in art but also in certain kinds of practical arrangements, involved a fascinating combination of emphasis on male sexuality and prowess with an equally common tendency to blur gender lines in sexual matters. The second, centered on actual sexual expressions, attempted to combine a clear delight in sexual pleasure with the birth control needs of the same societies.

Primitive art—on which so much of our speculation about early human sexuality depends—periodically featured female forms. Venus, or love-goddess, figurines have been found from groups during the ice age and immediately thereafter. They tend to seem rather passive, and are usually faceless—raising all sorts of questions about how these societies viewed female sexuality. They are also usually rather fat, and it is assumed that plumpness was seen as erotic because it signified good health and capacity for childbearing. Female clothing sometimes stressed sexual features, displaying breasts or cleavage, sometimes also with slits to show pubic hair. Ochre found off the Cape coast of South Africa from 70,000 years ago is thought to be remnants of lipstick, designed to make women's mouths look more like vaginas to signal sexual availability.

Male figures, often with pronounced phallic apparatus, are far more common than female. Symbols of male sexual potential were clearly important. Sometimes they were associated with animals; a famous carving from France features a lioness licking an enormous human penis, and other representations clearly highlight the dominance of the penis. Phallic sticks were shaped, and probably used in sexual rituals. Some groups manufactured jewelry to adorn the penis, and ornaments of this sort have been found in grave sites. Stone monuments also frequently stressed the penis, sometimes with womb imagery as well, but implying male sexual dominance. An Egyptian creation myth from 2600 BCE featured Atum, a sun-god, masturbating in the water, his ejaculation creating the river Nile; a Sumerian myth has a god's semen filling the Tigris River—all indications of the strength and creativity attributed to male sexual power.

At the same time, however, hunting and gathering groups also generated a great deal of ambiguous sexual imagery, and it is sometimes difficult to tell, in carvings, whether male or female anatomy is being depicted—or possibly some combination. Rituals of cross-dressing or transvestism were common, for example in a Siberian bear ceremony in which everyone, priests included, dressed in clothing from the opposite sex. Many groups attached spiritual meaning to people who could transcend gender boundaries.

Some priests or healers were transvestites or used tools associated with the opposite gender. In some groups, on the same basis, priests or shamans had intercourse with both sexes. Again, the idea was that a certain dose of what is often called "two-spirit" behavior was healthy and normal. In some tribes as well, particularly in North and South Americas but also in parts of southern Africa like present-day Mozambique, certain males were systematically dressed and treated as women. Sometimes this expressed an excess of males, with a need to provide people for characteristic "female" work even though they had been born male. But sexual and spiritual significance attached as well. In Mozambique some of the boys treated as female adorned wooden breasts to entertain males, and were seen as having magical powers. More rarely, girls might be designated to dress and act as men. Outright bisexuality was also common. Among Native Americans, certain tribes featured (and still feature) an initiation rite where boys were taken to sleep in the men's house at the first sign of puberty, with a maternal uncle supposed to penetrate each boy to make him strong and imbue him with semen so that he could be a fertile male. Again, there was great variety from one region to the next, complicating any generalizations. But it seems that many hunting and gathering groups did not place firm boundaries between what we would call heterosexual and homosexual characteristics and behaviors, even as they displayed a fascination with sexuality and with the power that accompanied the capacity to combine sexual features from both genders. While relevant art most commonly features heterosexual activity there are also rock engravings in places like Sicily with homoerotic scenes.

The kind of sexual prowess emphasized in art carried over into actual behaviors. Some societies—for example, among the Inuit communities in North America—established lovers' camps, along with more normal residential and hunting camps, where couples could go for sexual activity. Successful hunters were probably regarded as the most appealing sexual partners and were most likely to attract a number of women and to father the largest numbers of children. At least some hunting and gathering societies seem to have placed no special value on female virginity or any sort of defined sexual purity. Some tribes, for example in the South Pacific, developed a ritual where young women who had just reached puberty had to have sex with male relatives of their first sexual partner. Relatively early sexual activity and plural partners seems to have been common. Some hunting and gathering groups probably developed monogamy or serial monogamy (loyalty to one partner for a while, but then movement to a new partner); there seems to have been relatively free choice for people in finding a mate, which could allow the emphasis on desirable physical characteristics as well as hunting prowess.

Against this obvious interest in sexual expression and enjoyment, the demands of birth control offered a stark contrast. The nomadic lifestyle and limited food resources precluded any desire to have many babies, and also imposed a real need to space children at several-year intervals. The importance of sex for procreation was obvious, as suggested in much primitive art; but too much procreative sex was a danger.

Three methods of limiting the number of births were widely practiced, and all had implications for frequency and pleasure in sexual expression. First and most obvious: women nursed their babies for long periods, up to six years of age or beyond. This provided food but also constrained the ability to conceive a new child. Breastfeeding does not absolutely prevent conception, but its chemical impact on the female body makes conception less likely. On the surface, this method of birth control suggested an interest in combining pronounced spacing of children with continued access to sexual pleasure. There was no particular taboo, as would develop later in many societies, on having sex with a nursing mother. On the other hand, breastfeeding a child several times an hour, even through the night (when infants slept with mothers) could easily distract the mother herself and discourage potential male partners, reducing, though not eliminating, sexual activity. The gap between a period of youth sexuality and pregnancy-induced adulthood could be considerable.

A second method involved what would in modern times come to be known as fertility awareness, or the rhythm method, in which women would try to keep track of their menstrual cycle in order to prevent sex during days of peak fertility. Evidence from incisions in bones or antlers suggests that women were tracking their menstrual cycle for birth control purposes, but also that they hoped to be sexually active when conditions were safe. On the other hand, rhythm methods are inherently unreliable and many early societies were unclear about when fertility occurred in any event (some wrongly believed that it was during menstruation), so it is not clear how much this approach allowed sexual desire and the need to limit births to coexist. For example, some aborigine groups in Australia did not associate sex with conception, believing instead that sex throughout pregnancy was what permitted a fetus to grow properly. This kind of belief would encourage intercourse once pregnancy was discovered, but might constrain it in other times when the need to limit and space births might require abstention.

Finally, couples might simply abstain from sex, or at least from intercourse, for long periods. Sexual activity may well have declined after first youth, in part because of the increasing realization of how important it was, for the family food supply and nomadic travel, to prevent many conceptions. Hard work and ageing might take their toll as well on sexual attractiveness, even in what we would call relatively early middle age. One reason that some alternative sexual forms developed in certain cases, such as sexual access to young men on the part of older relatives, or some sharing of young women just past puberty, might have reflected a recognition of the limits on heterosexual activity with an older partner.

The point was that, along with a seeming absence of certain kinds of restrictions, sex in hunting and gathering societies required some thought and calculation, some recognition of certain kinds of limits in timing and frequency, in order to combine expression with avoidance of unwanted children. This probably generated a reasonably clear distinction between sexual experimentation among young people before a first pregnancy, and the sexual regime that would describe subsequent adulthood. Art that celebrated sexual prowess may not only have celebrated the importance of sexual activity, but also provided some symbolic compensation for restrictions in the actual experience of normal adulthood.

Margaret Mead and the South Pacific

Some decades ago a pioneering American anthropologist, Margaret Mead, produced an elaborate study of adolescents in Samoa and other South Pacific societies, using her findings to claim a predominant role for culture in determining sexual behavior and, by comparing with what she saw as the damaging repression in the American society around her, drawing out moral implications for the contemporary United States. Her work, easily simplified in presentations to the public, seemed to paint a picture of sexual indulgence with which American standards contrasted unfavorably.

Mead particularly attacked any notion that men and women had different sexual needs or potentials for pleasure. Biology paled, she argued, before the power of culture, and it was a particular culture that was doing America wrong. In the South Seas, anxiety resulting from sexual constraint was kept to a minimum because of widely permitted and considerable promiscuity for young men and women, and the absence of any particular value ascribed to virginity. Samoan girls, in obvious contrast to their American counterparts, could freely seek sexual pleasure and express themselves openly, in ways that were mentally healthy and prepared a well-adjusted adulthood that would not be confined by rigid family rules and roles.

The picture was charming, and it surely stimulated some useful thinking about contemporary American habits; but, insofar as it purported to describe a carefree primitive society, it does not seem to have been correct. (Indeed, some other South Pacific islands, like Mangaia, seem to have had a more liberal approach than Samoa.) In recent times a variety of anthropologist critics, led by Derek Freeman, have discredited Mead on several counts. They argue that she did not systematically study the girls she generalized about, and that some of them deliberately lied to her by exaggerating their behaviors. Later research has shown a high valuation of sexual fidelity, with far less promiscuity in fact than Mead had claimed. Critics also worry about Mead's fascination with using norms from one culture as moral coaching for another, very different society.

The scholarly episode certainly highlights the complexity of generalizing about sex in any society, even when direct observation is possible, and the danger of assumptions that idyllic sexual standards should be associated with economically simpler societies. Early human groups did have values and behaviors different from those of later times—Samoa itself was already an agricultural society, though without elaborate formal government prior to the nineteenth century—but they already operated among sharply conflicting pressures where sex was concerned.

Agriculture

One of the great changes in human history involved the introduction of agriculture, which gradually replaced hunting and gathering in many key regions as the basic economic system for humankind. Agriculture first emerged around 9000–8000 BCE in the Black Sea region and Mesopotamia. It soon spread to North Africa, parts of India, and parts of Southern Europe; it was separately invented in Southeast Asia and south

China, and again in central America, and possibly elsewhere. Not every human group converted. Hunting and gathering continued in many regions, sometimes spiced with a bit of grain growing; and nomadic herding societies also sprang up, based on the domestication of animals like horses, cattle, and camels. In these cases, sexual patterns established earlier continued without great change.

With agriculture however—and agricultural economies did come to predominate in most key regions and for the largest populations of humans—the framework for sexuality shifted in many ways. Agricultural patterns of sexuality reflected a new set of economic needs and opportunities, and the responses demonstrate how adaptable human sexuality can become in the face of new frameworks. In turn, these patterns would persist for many millennia in much of Asia, Africa, Europe, and key parts of the Americas. Even today, when agricultural societies are yielding to more urban and industrial conditions, key remnants and traditions of agricultural sexuality hang on, making the movement toward these characteristic sexual forms not just a matter of historical interest.

We have no explicit records about sexuality from societies experiencing the transition from hunting and gathering to agriculture. Neither art nor archaeology provides a direct account of exactly when or how humans began to register on the sexual implications of their new way of life, or how they personally experienced the mixture of gains and disadvantages (judging from a pre-agricultural set of traditions) that sexual change entailed.

We do know, and can abundantly speculate about, the many changes in living conditions that could impinge on sexuality. For example, with agriculture most people began to settle in one spot and live in close-knit villages—there were cases of more transient agriculture or more widely-scattered dwellings, but they were not the norm. With settled residence, and most families living jointly in some kind of house, opportunities for collective supervision of sexual behavior increased—including supervision by parents and other older relatives. Of course, agricultural communities could have modified this change by a practice of separate lovers' areas, as some hunting and gathering camps had provided, but, revealingly, this did not occur. For thousands of years, sexual behavior would be strongly conditioned by small-group oversight, even when basic rules were established by larger societies. And while this oversight has weakened in the last two centuries, with urbanization, remnants of the agricultural pattern persist.

Agricultural housing and community life also made it normal for children to see their parents having sex, as most family members slept in close proximity. A hundred years ago many psychologists made a big deal about the disturbing effects of this kind of witnessing, but we can only speculate about the implications for rural societies. The fact that exposure was fairly routine may have reduced its impact on children.

With settled agriculture came some kinds of rules concerning property. No group would be willing to put in the effort to clear land, dig wells, or set up irrigation systems without assurances of ownership. Definitions here could vary widely—ownership might be by individual families, or by wealthy landlords, or by village collectives—but some form of property control would emerge. Historians have speculated that, with property, the importance of determining the fatherhood of children increased in turn.

A man would increasingly seek some assurance, before he passed on property to offspring, that the children involved were his. It is important to note that we cannot prove exactly how or why this connection emerged—and it would certainly be possible to conceive of other ways of approaching this issue. What is clear is that agricultural societies quickly began to adopt measures that would help assure paternity by developing new rules to govern female sexuality. This is turn would generate clear differences, at least at the level of official regulations, between the sexual standards applied to women and those applied to men. All agricultural societies became, in some fashion, patriarchal—that is, dominated by men (and for sons, by fathers); and a fundamental expression of patriarchy was the impulse to try to control female sexuality and to differentiate standards by gender. Here was a crucial change from characteristic hunting and gathering traditions. The same preoccupation with monitoring female sexuality helped generate intense emotions relating to sexual possessiveness—jealousy, in short—that most agricultural societies legitimated but many hunting and gathering societies, far more easy-going in this regard, did not produce. Jealousy would be a complicating factor in many sexual relationships from this point forward.

Agriculture put most people in closer regular contact with animals than had been the case with hunting and gathering. They could more regularly observe animal sexual behavior. This fact could of course generate diverse results: it might become newly possible to criticize sexual appetites as animal-like, and to contrast standards of human respectability and self-restraint. The obvious agricultural interest in having domestic animals reproduce could help focus attention on the reproductive purposes of human sexuality—which would mesh with new purposes for human children themselves. Availability of tamed animals unquestionably also produced new opportunities for bestiality, for human (mainly male) sexual intercourse with animals. Agricultural societies all passed firm rules against bestiality, if not immediately then ultimately; Islamic, Jewish, and Christian law proscribed it in the strongest terms. But there is no question that sexual contact with animals occurred anyway in rural conditions. Death penalties for bestiality were not uncommon, for example in early modern Europe or colonial New England—but there were many opportunities for sexual contact with animals that would not be detected. As late as the 1940s a study of American sexual habits disclosed that a quarter of all rural men had engaged in some sexual activities with animals. Animal sex existed in agricultural societies; it gave rise to all sorts of stories of mythical half-human, half-animal creatures and the sports of gods and goddesses with animals. We simply cannot know how common or significant this kind of sexuality was as part of the overall sexual patterns of agricultural peoples.

Most important was the fact that agricultural societies generated new needs and uses for children. As family economies came to depend more on farming, children became increasingly useful as a source of labor. Very young children were still an economic drain, but even six-year-olds could do some useful work, and by their teens children were an absolutely vital component of the overall labor supply. In turn, of course, more reliable food sources—the big advantage of agriculture over hunting and gathering—permitted larger family size. Birth rates went up quite dramatically, and the spacing between children narrowed—usually to about two years, though of course there were many variations. Breastfeeding might still continue for 18 months or so, but its duration declined notably as part of the overall change in family goals and strategies.

What did these huge changes mean for sexuality? Most obviously, the reproductive purposes of sex tended to gain greater attention. Even in art, for example, while attention to male sexuality hardly disappeared, new interest in agricultural societies focused on mother images and to links between human fertility and the fertility of the agricultural cycle. Infertility became a greater concern than had been the case before. In agricultural societies about 20 percent of all couples would not have children because of problems for at least one of the partners. Worry about assuring the desired birth rate could become an important part of family life, and indirectly at least of sex life, even after a first child was born. Some agricultural societies allowed marriages to be dissolved because of infertility and a few (for example, in early modern France) actually could punish infertile males. It was also a fact that women in agricultural societies would be spending more time preparing to give birth, recovering from delivery and tending to very young children than was true of their hunting-and-gathering counterparts, which could affect sexual interest as well.

A key result of new emphasis on reproductive sex may have been, at least in some societies, an emerging disapproval of masturbation as, at the least, a waste of time and potential (at least for men). Responses within this framework varied, however. Judaism castigated masturbation in the Old Testament. Other agricultural societies disparaged but did not label it as sin. Still, the reorientation was interesting and could affect behaviors or reactions to behaviors.

The opportunity—indeed the need and desire—to have more children could obviously promote heterosexual activity, even when the purpose was ostensibly reproduction rather than any particular pleasure. But agricultural societies also faced constraints. Too many children could be an even greater disaster than not having any at all—there would be too many mouths to feed, too many burdens on the land available to the peasant family. Generally, six to seven children during the fertility span of a couple would be ideal. In agricultural societies, up to half of all children born would die within two years, so six to seven in total would assure an adequate labor supply and a reasonable number of adult children to provide for—with, admittedly, a little margin for safety. (Excess surviving children could, among other things, be sent to childless families to provide labor there, reducing upkeep demands at home.) When a population disaster hit—like a war or major disease—higher birth rates might briefly be feasible, to fill out community ranks. But in normal times the goal was considerably higher than in hunting and gathering societies, yet not limitless.

This goal, in turn, was about half what an average couple will produce if no precautions are taken, as the Hutterite formula suggests. Obviously, some individual agricultural families, in other times and places, produced a Hutterite level of children, and it was always a possibility. Equally obviously, most farming families would have found this level an appalling prospect, and sought various means to avoid it.

Sexuality in agricultural societies was strongly conditioned, then, by a great desire to have children in some number but an almost equally great desire to make sure that maximum breeding did not occur. Different communities, of course, would introduce different mechanisms to achieve this delicate balance—and always there were families for whom, for whatever reason, the balance failed, and too many children resulted. Overall, however, several strategies were possible, all with direct impact on sexuality:

1   In general breastfeeding continued, as we have seen, for a relatively long period by modern standards, though far shorter than in hunting and gathering societies. This helped assure an average child spacing, during the early years of a marriage, of about two years, which in turn limited the total birth rate overall. This practice might now be accompanied by new beliefs about the inappropriateness of sexual activity soon after childbirth (the postpartum taboo) or during at least some stages of breastfeeding, with a restrictive culture supplementing natural constraints.
2   The age of first sexual activity might be limited by culture or law, backed by community monitoring and efforts to make sure sexual activity did not take place before or outside of marriage. Certain groups in the population might be encouraged to be permanently celibate, usually for religious reasons but with some impact on overall population levels and (it can be argued) with implicit birth rate concerns in mind. Some discouragement to sexual activity, in other words, might be part of the agricultural package.
3   Frequency of sexual activity might decrease in mature adulthood, but before menopause. Health issues or the burdens of demanding agricultural work might affect sexual appetites for people in their thirties in any event, but sometimes community norms encouraged a sense that it was inappropriate or unseemly for sexual activity to maintain the pace of the first years of marriage. The notion that sex should wane with age, plus the vigorous association of sex with reproduction, particularly for women, contributed to the widespread sense, in agricultural communities, that women should refrain some sexual activity entirely after menopause. Along with other considerations it might also promote beliefs that many widows should not remarry.

Sexuality in agricultural societies, strongly, though of course not exclusively, tied to reproduction, was thus also conditioned by the need to limit the birth rate, and a variety of devices might be introduced or combined to produce the desired result. Commonly, as well, there was interest in some artificial assistance. Most agricultural societies developed rituals designed to discourage, as well as encourage, fertility; sometimes these involved magical practices. Herbs might be used to limit fertility—not always to much effect—or to induce abortion. As we will see, a few artificial devices, including condoms made from animal bladders, were used in some cases, though it is unclear whether these efforts were widespread or how effective they were.

More generally still, the concerns about reproduction and its limitations tended to encourage a somewhat cautionary value system where sex was concerned, though each agricultural society had its own specifics in this regard. Whether this reduced interest and opportunity for sexual pleasure, compared with hunting and gathering conditions, is frankly unclear. Many modern experts, including Sigmund Freud, have speculated about the burdens of restrictive sexual culture as part of the advent of more complex societies and civilizations. It is important, as we have seen, not to over-glamorize the hunting and gathering precedent, and also not to ignore many pleasure opportunities in agricultural communities (including cases where cultural signals were cast aside). The most important point is the fact of change: the sexual systems of agricultural societies were shaped by different problems from those humans had previously faced, as they adjusted to new realities of work and property.

A final cautionary note became increasingly explicit in most agriculture societies: the interest in proscribing sex among close relatives. Many hunting and gathering societies developed customs here as well, as it was realized that sex between parents and children or among siblings often resulted in deficient offspring. But agricultural societies, with more resources to develop formal regulation and more emphasis on reproduction in any event, generated firm laws and moral precepts against what was now defined as incest (though close relatives were variously defined). Literature and art might still portray incest, either to titillate or to reinforce common values, and abuses surely continued in practice, but the basic approach became a standard part of sexual ethics and, usually, outright law, and unlike some regulation it applied equally to both genders.

There was one standard twist inherent in the rise of agriculture, though it built on patterns probably already present in hunting and gathering bands: sex varied by social class. Because they generated more surplus than earlier economies could manage, agricultural societies usually created conditions also for growing inequalities—a minority of people, as large landowners, merchants, priests, or officials, gained access to living standards that were impossible for ordinary peasants, though sometimes gradations emerged among peasants as well, based on size of land holdings. If successful hunters were probably seen as particularly sexually desirable, the same could prove true for upper-class individuals, particularly males, in agricultural conditions. In many agricultural societies, as we will see, upper classes enjoyed sexual opportunities quite different from those available to the mass of the population—including, again particularly for men, more sexual partners. The upper classes could also afford larger families than most peasants could contemplate, which meant that some of the constraints affecting ordinary people could be reduced or ignored. Often, for example, upper-class people married younger than most peasants did. Indeed, the importance of having offspring, particularly sons, to carry on the family line put a premium on reproductive sex for both men and women in the elite group, making birth rate constraints noticeably less rigorous than was true for average families. The upper classes still did not normally reach a Hutterite standard, but the tension between sex and desired family size was defined differently for these elite groups.

Variations on themes

The actual patterns of sexuality in agricultural societies—early ones, but also through later iterations as well—always reflected the basic conditions and problems that came into place with agriculture itself. The people involved were not always aware of the extent to which the agricultural framework conditioned sexuality, often assuming that values were conveyed by the gods or a God or from some other source; but in retrospect the fundamental issues were clear. Within the agricultural pattern, however, a host of variables were possible, in terms both of constraining sex and of exploring opportunities for enjoyment. While evidence for early agricultural societies is less rich than we might like, some sense of the variety forms a crucial part of the story.

Interest in birth control was widespread, but specific recourses depended on local beliefs and conditions. Early Greeks sometimes placed half of a lemon into the vagina as a birth control measure—a kind of natural spermicide. Egyptians used crocodile droppings for the same purpose. Early societies in India seem to have developed the most elaborate interests and capacities in the use of herbs for contraception. Again, the variety was striking, around a common theme.

Some agricultural societies developed requirements for the circumcision of males, presumably for reasons of health and hygiene, though almost always as a religious prescription. Some circumcision was practiced in Egypt as early as 4000 BCE, but evidence from mummies reveals that not all males were involved; the obligation may have applied to men destined for the priesthood. Jews and Phoenicians required circumcision (Jewish law stipulated on the eighth day after birth), but other peoples in the Middle East and Mediterranean did not; it would, however, later become part of Islamic law. Again, variety, even in the same basic region, was considerable.

In parts of northeastern Africa, a custom of female circumcision also developed, probably fairly early. Here, the purpose was surely not health but—by removing the clitoris or the labia at the onset of puberty—a limitation of female sexual pleasure and therefore a means of controlling female sexuality. There is no way to be sure when the practice began; the first fairly definite reference comes from a Roman traveler who visited Upper Egypt in 25–24 BCE; it seems to have been practiced on a limited basis. Female circumcision certainly at some point thereafter spread to, or independently developed in, agricultural communities in parts of northeastern Africa, and later still in other parts of Africa right below the Sahara. Ultimately, as well, it would take on religious as well as ritual significance. The practice continues in some places today, amid growing controversy; it was not, however, common in agricultural societies generally, but another symptom of the distinctive responses possible amid more generally shared concerns.

Agricultural societies developed an array of approaches toward homosexual or bisexual practices—there was no standard norm, despite the fact that a new emphasis on reproductive sex might lead to some new attention to such behaviors. Some priestly groups, for example among Mesopotamians, used anal sex as a connection to the gods: this reflected a common belief that orgasm had spiritual qualities and that homoerotic activities, particularly, reflected spiritual capacity. Some agricultural societies also maintained certain individuals whose sexuality was more consistently ambiguous. Mesopotamians, again, recognized a social group called sag-ur-sag that was probably bisexual or intersex. On the fringes of the agricultural Black Sea regions some Scythian men frequently drank urine from a pregnant mare to counter their male hormones and generally appear less male (the practice, among other things, retarded beard growth); presumably this expressed personal proclivities, but also gave some spiritual cachet.

Almost all, if not literally all, agricultural societies, as we have seen, developed a new level of concern about female sexual behavior and applied different rules to men and to women—the origins of the sexual double standard. Both early law codes and early religious formulations made clear the importance of female sexual fidelity. In Mesopotamia, the Hammurabic code around 1700 BCE, the first known legal compilation, devoted great attention to sexual regulations. The code stipulated that men might take concubines or mistresses, at least if their wives did not bear children, though the concubine should not rank as high as the wife in the household. Women were told to defend their sexual honor above all: "If a finger has been pointed at the wife of a man because of another man, even if she has not been caught lying with another man, for her husband's sake she shall throw herself in the river" (where presumably, if she were indeed innocent, she would not drown). Nothing similar was applied to male reputation. A man and a woman caught in adultery presumably should both be punished by death, but adultery was defined in terms of a man having sex with a married woman, not the other way around—as the permissibility of concubines already suggested. But while many societies would generate similar norms, applying a different standard to men and to women, specific rules varied, and the approach in the Middle East was unusually legalistic. It was also in the Middle East, probably during the second millennium BCE, that the practice of veiling respectable women began to be introduced in cities, another means of trying to shield them from sexual advances—but not one that was adopted in most other agricultural societies.

Quite early in the development of agricultural economies, differences also emerged over polygamy. Some societies strongly emphasized monogamy, as would be true in the Jewish religion for example; but others widely tolerated multiple wives. In many agricultural civilizations—as in both Mesopotamia and Egypt—prominent men were frequently buried with several women, wives or concubines, as a clear sign of status. Social factors were involved here as well, and not just regional differences: where multiple wives were permitted, men had to demonstrate the capacity to support them, which de facto distinguished between most situations where economic limitations compelled monogamy, and possibilities among the elites.

Most agricultural societies continued the practice of using art to represent sexuality, but specific styles and degrees of explicitness varied greatly. Among early agricultural civilizations, sexual expressiveness seems to have been particularly vivid in Egypt. Both art and literary texts described a variety of sexual positions, and depicted premarital sex, adultery, homosexuality, masturbation, and even incest. Both female and male sexual organs were used as artistic themes, amid a general openness toward erotic pleasures. Love poetry might refer to the power of orgasm, as when a woman rejoices in a man's "virility": "and love for him flowed through her body; your dew is all through my limbs." The frequency of public discussions of spells and recipes for contraceptives and abortificants also testifies to a wide and apparently fairly open interest in sexual pleasure independent of procreation. Wide use of cosmetics and perfumes suggests women's interest in proving sexually attractive to men. In contrast, Mesopotamian civilization, close by geographically and operating in the same time period, seems to have been considerably more prudish, characterized more by the regulatory approach than by a deep commitment to open expressiveness.

The variety of sexual specifics among agricultural societies, and some of the common if not universal constraints, generated another revealing symptom: the tendency of early travelers not just to report on sexual differences but also to project fanciful stories of the sexually bizarre. Accounts of this sort may have circulated in hunting and gathering societies, of course, without leaving a surviving record. But for many centuries after 600 BCE, when travelers did begin occasionally to write up their observations, attention to both sexual comparisons and fanciful inventions was quite frequent. Stories of societies where family members slept together constituted a way to draw reader interest, but also to insult other societies while perhaps reflecting some of the tension that formal constraints imposed back home. Tales of bestiality had the same ring: a way to run down foreigners but also let off steam. A common reference might also involve highly-sexed or menacing women. Beliefs in a tribe of one-breasted warrior women, the Amazons, which circulated widely in the eastern Mediterranean, though not necessarily explicitly sexual, showed a fear of female power that indirectly reflected the growing sexual subordination of women in agricultural societies themselves.

Violence and exploitation

Agricultural societies generated, or at least newly highlighted, two other features of human sexuality: rape and prostitution.

Rape may well have occurred in hunting and gathering situations, particularly during tribal wars; as always, there is the problem of deficiencies in available records. The rise of agricultural societies affected rape most clearly by producing more formal definitions, as part of religious or state law, but also by introducing some gendered responses. It is also possible that as agricultural societies extended the practice of slavery and enlarged social inequality, while also introducing some new constraints in respectable sexuality, they increased the phenomenon of rape as well.

Specifics varied, as we would expect by this point, but there were some common themes. Jewish law, ultimately incorporated in the Bible, made rape a crime but also made it evident that women would have an uphill battle to prove that they had not consented to sex—they must cry out and be heard to have any case at all. Proved rape of a married woman is to be punished by death (just as adultery is punished by death, though here for both parties); but rape of a single woman is a crime not against her but against her father who "owns" the daughter and so has his property defiled—the rapist must marry the woman (whether she wishes this or not). The Bible offers several stories about rape including some in which the rapist is excused because of his ties with officials in high places. In the case of Jewish law as in other early societies, concern about rape demonstrates that it did occur, and that it violated accepted norms; but it was also clear that women were often very vulnerable, and that rape was sometimes regarded more as a violation of family honor than as an attack on the woman herself.

Intriguingly, at least one artistic scene, from Letnitsa (Bulgaria) in the fourth century BCE, depicts two women about to pounce on a man, for either seduction or rape. Whether this merely expressed a social fear, of the sort often prevalent among dominant groups as they worry about some reversal of inequality, or an actual event cannot be determined.

Agricultural societies certainly generated the practice of prostitution. Sharper definitions of marriage—compared to hunting and gathering societies—and in some cases new restrictions on pre- and certainly extramarital sex created part of the context in which prostitution could emerge. New and usually harsh punishments for adultery, even for men when involved with married women, arguably created new room for a different kind of sex service—whether this should ideally have been the case or not. More basically, growing economic specialization, ultimately including the introduction of money, established conditions in which women (and occasionally also men, if only for homosexual purposes) could sell sexual services. Prostitutes could be the only women independent of specific male dominance, in control of their own sexuality. But equally obviously the status came with real costs.

Some early prostitution may have involved relatively high prestige, associated with connections to gods or goddesses; even in ancient Israel there is some evidence of "sacred prostitutes" who worked in the temples and re-enacted holy unions. The point is debated. Generally, however, prostitutes were regarded as low-status. Jewish law stipulated that a prostitute's wages were not suitable offerings for the temple, and prostitutes should not marry priests. Scythians marked prostitutes with a special tattoo. In many early societies, women captured in war or drawn from conquered groups were placed into prostitution, linking the activity with slavery. Assyrian law distinguished prostitutes from other women—they would not be veiled, whereas respectable women would be.

Prostitutes, whatever their status, did usually constitute a recognized group in agricultural societies, providing service. The Sumerian word for prostitution, *kar.kid*, appears on the first known written list of human professions, around 2400 BCE, along with priests and, later in the list, male prostitutes and transsexuals who are cited along with entertainers. This is the origin of the idea that prostitution is the oldest profession, though in fact several other occupations, including priests, can make the same claim. Hammurabi's code not only recognized prostitutes, but defined certain rights for them and their children. In China, brothels may have existed as early as the seventh century BCE, where they were legal and, through taxes, a way for the state to earn income. The rise of prostitution was also accompanied by a rise of venereal disease—a major development in its own right.

The ubiquity of prostitution in early cities reflected many of the key features of sexuality as it evolved in agricultural societies: unequal approaches to the genders, certainly, but also the strong emphasis on reproductive sex which would lead some men to seek a special outlet for various recreational urges—all in an economy which could afford some new kinds of professional specialties.

*   *   *

Early agricultural societies left many legacies to human sexuality later on, even to some extent to the present time. New distinctions between men and women in sexuality were vital. The heightened focus on reproductive sex but concomitant constraints because of birth control needs did not eliminate a sense of sex as pleasure, and certainly did not prevent a variety of responses according to particular regions and particular social classes; but it did, on balance, create some new tensions and uncertainties. The emergence of prostitutes as a group defined precisely because its members would operate quite differently from what was normally expected—sometimes, seeking greater independence from male family controls—was a key symptom of the new complexities. At the same time, early agricultural societies also demonstrated that basic patterns could be expressed in a host of specific ways, not only in artistic representations, but in actual behaviors. This, too, was a theme that would be embellished as agricultural civilizations further matured.

Further reading

J.W. Howell, W.E. Burns, V.L. Mondelli, and C.A. Gottsleben, eds., *Greenwood Encyclopedia of Love, Courtship, and Sexuality*, 6v. (Greenwood, CT: Greenwood, 2008) provides a good overview. A controversial analysis is G. Lerner's *The Creation of Patriarchy* (New York: Oxford University Press, 1986).

On sex and sexuality throughout history, see K. Mysliwiec and G.L. Packer, *Eros on the Nile* (Ithaca, NY: Cornell University Press, 2001); T. Taylor, *The Prehistory of Sex: Four Million Years of Human Sexual Culture* (New York: Bantam Books, 1996); M. Potts, *Ever since Adam and Eve: The Evolution of Human Sexuality* (New York: Cambridge University Press, 1999); R.A. Schmidt and B.L. Voss, *Archaeologies of Sexuality* (New York: Routledge, 2000); C. Spencer, *Homosexuality in History*, first US ed. (New York: Harcourt Brace, 1995); R. Schumann-Antelme and S. Rossini, *Sacred Sexuality in Ancient Egypt: The Erotic Secrets of the Forbidden Papyri* (Rochester, VT: Inner Traditions, 2001); J. Margolis, *O: The Intimate History of the Orgasm* (New York: Grove Press, 2004); L. Glick, *Marked in your Flesh: Circumcision from Ancient Judea to Modern America* (New York: Oxford, 2006); S. Ellen Jacobs, W. Thomas, and S. Lang, eds., *Two-spirit People: Native American Gender Identity, Sexuality, and Spirituality* (Urbana: University of Illinois Press, 1997); J. Archer and B. Lloyd, eds., *Sex and Gender* (Harmondsworth: Penguin, 1982); and G. Lerner, "The origin of prostitution in ancient Mesopotamia," *Signs*, Winter 1986.

Margaret Mead's groundbreaking work is explored in M. Mead, *Male and Female* (New York: W. Morrow, 1949) and *Sex and Temperament in Three Primitive Societies* (New York: W. Morrow, 1963). See also H. Fisher, "Introduction," in M. Mead, *Male and Female* (New York: Perennial, 2001); and D. Freeman, *The Fateful Hoaxing of Margaret Mead: A Historical Analysis of her Samoan Research* (Boulder, CO: Westview Press, 1999).

Chapter 3

Sexuality in the classical period

Between about 1000 BCE and 500 CE, great classical civilizations arose in the Middle East, the Mediterranean, China, and India. All expanded to embrace territories of unprecedented size. All developed cultural and trading systems designed to integrate and take advantage of the new expanse. This was the period, for example, when Indian religions and social systems began spreading through the whole subcontinent, and when the Chinese Middle Kingdom took shape. All the classical societies also, at various points, worked at political integration, developing large and mighty empires. In the process, each classical civilization began to generate a signature identity, a set of cultural and institutional characteristics that helped define the society at the time and that would survive, though always amid change, as part of a civilizational heritage long after the classical period had ended.

Not surprisingly, sexual values and representations figured strongly in these developments. Each classical civilization established a somewhat distinctive approach to gender, to the artistic expression of sexual beauty, and to particular behaviors such as homosexuality. As with other aspects of the civilizations, some of these formulations would last into later periods as well; to take an easy but significant example, contemporary Indian movies use sexual themes that link to the classical period, even as they also interact with Hollywood influences and other more modern developments. This chapter focuses on the particular sexual definitions that would form part of each major tradition, and on the comparative analysis that can bring these distinctive formulations into clearer understanding.

At the same time it is vital to recognize that this was not a period of fundamental change in sexuality. Each of the classical civilizations continued to work on the elements already introduced by the needs and opportunities of an agricultural economy. They refined these elements and added new specifics—as, for example, in the shifts in Greek and Roman approaches to homosexuality. But they did not innovate in any groundbreaking fashion. They all assumed major differences between male and female sexuality and sexual privileges, including the need for special regulation or oversight over female sexual behavior; they all reflected major social class distinctions; they all tried to balance some opportunities to express interest in sexual pleasure with a focus on reproduction and limitations of births. Because the classical civilizations generated much more surviving evidence than the river valley civilizations did, in art, literature, and official records, they allow us to gain a much fuller view of how sexuality operated in the context of agriculture. This greater detail, along with the special twist each civilization provided to its sexual standards as part of shaping a distinctive culture, and along with a few interesting though relatively minor new themes, forms the analytical targets in approaching sexuality in the classical period. In the process we deal, inevitably, with the interaction of major cultural systems—like Confucianism or Hinduism—with sexual issues, as this forms part of the story and the legacy that make this period such an important chapter in the global experience. Approaches toward sexuality, in other words, constituted a vital part of what each civilization was all about, and how each civilization formed some distinctive expressions within the common context of an agricultural economy.

*   *   *

China

Classical civilization first emerged in China, with the evolution of the Zhou dynasty from about 1050 BCE onward, and then the advent of stricter political forms with the emergence of the durable institutions of the Chinese empire and its bureaucracy. The introduction of Confucianism under the later Zhou, and then greater acceptance of Confucian values under the mature Han dynasty (202 BCE–220 CE) not only articulated clearer social and political values, but had direct implications for sexual standards. In general, the evolution of classical China suggests a clear movement from rather tolerant and expressive sexuality to increasing regulation in the interests of social hierarchy and family order. Indeed, of all the classical societies, China moved most directly from a rather early-stage river valley civilization to a full-fledged classical operation, becoming in fact the most highly organized of all: changes in sexuality during the classical period undoubtedly reflected and amplified this process. The classical Mediterranean, in contrast—the next case to be taken up—started with more sexual regulation already established on the basis of earlier Middle Eastern precedents.

Materials from the Zhou dynasty suggest a strong appreciation of sexual pleasure, not simply sex for reproduction. Sexual prowess, particularly for men, was widely appreciated, with husbands expected to have sex with multiple wives and, possibly, concubines. Women's desire was noted, though regarded as different from men's: an early writing from the twelfth century BCE described male and female orgasms in terms of fire and water, respectively. Links to religion were also prominent, as was common in early civilizations: many older poems used copulation as imagery for the relationship between humans and gods.

China generated the earliest known sex manuals, quite graphic in terms of body parts though with poetic names attached. Thus the penis was the heavenly dragon stem or jade stalk, the clitoris a jade pearl. Orgasm was described as a bursting of the clouds. The manuals, and also some explicit pornography, were written for women as well as men, again a sign of the considerable sexual latitude given women in initial Chinese formulations. Of course, written materials were available only to a literate minority;

we have no way of knowing if similar information was more widely transmitted by word of mouth.

Chinese thinkers also early linked sexuality to basic philosophical principles that would long operate in Chinese culture. Thus heterosexual activity helped men balance yin and yang: they used up yang in orgasm but absorbed yin from women's response. Lack of this balance was seen as causing health problems. For the same reason masturbation was criticized for men, at times even forbidden in principle, but tolerated for women so long as they did not use foreign objects.

As Chinese society matured during the classical period, elements of this initial approach persisted but additional constraints were added. Already in the Zhou period the influential *Book of Songs* condemned premarital sex for women, stating that it would later cause abandonment by husbands and thus lead to destruction, since preservation of the family should be women's chief goal. With Confucianism and its emphasis on orderly political and social behavior, sexual conduct also came under greater scrutiny. New fears of deviance developed. Accusations of incest for example were frequently used to discredit enemies in political life, particularly under the Han dynasty.

Opportunities for multiple wives or concubines continued, though, given financial considerations, only in the upper classes. Men remained eager to demonstrate their sexual prowess and, in some cases, the urgency of siring sons added to the impetus. Fairly strict rules established hierarchies between first wife and others, and according to the best Confucian principles, concubines were expected to be submissive and orderly, though many conflicts developed in fact. Elaborate protocol emerged around the emperor's sex life. Officials looked after the many concubines and kept records of how often each concubine visited the emperor, because the more visits the higher the status. (Sex with the first wife, or empress, was confined to the time in the month when the emperor's potency was presumably at its peak.) Outside the imperial domain, numbers of concubines were seen as a reflection of the wealth a man had achieved—needed for the concubines themselves, but also for childcare.

For men in all social classes, though primarily in the cities, prostitutes were available, and their use was seen as acceptable whether men were married or not. This was simply part of amusement or recreation, so long as men did not indulge in excess. Brothels, or "houses of singing girls," provided food, drink, and other entertainment, as well as sexual access.

Emphasis on the importance of regulating women's sexuality (prostitutes aside) increased with time, primarily, of course, for wives or those hoping to marry. Virginity was carefully protected by a girl's parents, because its loss could ruin any chances for marriage. For women, marriage normally occurred quite young, shortly after puberty. Men, as was typical in agricultural societies where economic establishment was vital before a family could be formed, usually married 10–15 years later, which meant they usually brought prior sexual experience as well as seniority to a marriage, which may in turn have helped them, at least in most circumstances, in regulating their wives—as greater experience added to male clout. Confucian thought heightened concern about the disorderly potential of sexuality, its threat to stable family life. Women's behavior needed particular attention, for fidelity was vital to assure that men could be certain that they had sired their children. Grave suspicions existed about women's capacity for disrupting the patriline.

Confucianism also encouraged new warnings to men as well—not in terms of strict fidelity, but because of the dangers of overindulgence. From the later Zhou onward, poems and also doctors' texts urged moderation for the sake of good health. Confucian family regulations urged that husbands and wives not touch each other outside the marriage bed. Men, of course, had options outside this strict etiquette, which women, at least officially, did not.

No particular concern was directed toward male homosexuality, and legend indeed held that some particularly creative emperors had indulged in homosexual behavior. One story told of an emperor cutting off his sleeve so his male lover could continue to sleep on it. Love affairs between men were seen as poetic, even romantic. "Sharing the peach" became a term referring to anal sex, based on a story of two men sharing the fruit as a symbol of their love. Partly because homosexual acts were apparently accepted as normal, we lack much indication of their actual incidence.

Chinese society also moved early on to create an important group of eunuchs—men who were castrated and who came to be seen as appropriate for certain kinds of special service. Initially, under the Zhou, the procedure was a punishment for certain convicted traitors—since the Chinese so vigorously emphasized male prowess and the importance of semen, the move could be seen as particularly degrading. The result was unexpected: by the time of the Han, a group of about 5,000 eunuchs existed, in and around the imperial court, with considerable privilege and power. They most obviously could serve as guardians of the imperial harem, because they would have neither reason nor basis for interfering with the emperor's wives and concubines. From this position in turn, many because confidential advisors to the emperors, because they were regarded as reliable and non-threatening. Eunuchs could and did amass great power on this basis. Emperors expected that all regions would contribute eunuchs, and parents often sold boys for this purpose, having them castrated and then brought to court—the results, despite the sexual constraint, could be far superior to a normal peasant existence.

Despite growing Confucian pressures, which in any event bore most heavily on the upper classes, sexuality continued to be a fairly open public topic, even under the later Han dynasty. Many sex handbooks were issued, maintaining the older emphasis on sexual expression in terms of yin and yang. Some were illustrated, apparently kept by bedsides for consultation (again, however, only a small minority would have direct access, given costs and the need for literacy). Some went into considerable detail, for example about the correct number and rhythm of strokes during intercourse. In addition, the Daoist religion provided some alternatives to Confucian emphases, seeing magical power in sexual union and focusing more on the physical and emotional needs of women than Confucianism did.

By the end of the classical period China had generated a fairly standard sexual regime, in terms of the norms of agricultural societies, but with some obvious twists. No particular disapproval attached to sexuality in general, though the cautions about moderation for the sake of good health and political order were not trivial. A fairly firm line separated respectable from unrespectable women, though occasionally a prostitute might be taken on as a concubine. Respectable women were highly regulated in terms of sexuality, while other women, though far lower in status, had different functions that were regarded as essentially natural. Men, though primarily upper-class and wealthy men, had far more outlets than women did, thanks to multiple partners and prostitutes. Interest in sexual pleasure was considerable and fairly open, sometimes with both genders targeted.

Concerns about limiting the numbers of children undoubtedly existed, but they were less prominent than one might expect. Partly this reflects the fact that most available sources emanate from the upper classes, who could afford many children and were eager for sons. Lower-class households surely limited sex at times, out of concern for pressures on the land, though Chinese knowledge about the precise mechanisms of reproduction remained a bit vague. It was true that pressures of overpopulation, in relation to available resources, already loomed periodically in classical China, and it was also true that infanticide was a common remedy for unwanted births.

China also did not generate an elaborate sexual art, in contrast to other classical societies. References in poetry and literature were common, and there were the regularly issued sex manuals. But early references to sex in relationship to gods and goddesses did not persist, as Chinese culture turned away from this kind of anthropomorphic polytheism. Confucian constraints on art might also have played a role—from early times, Chinese art emphasized controlled evocations, rather than earthy abundance. Possibly the availability of sexual outlets for men reduced the need for a vivid sexual culture in other respects. The relationship between artistic eroticism and other aspects of sexual behavior is complex, and the negative Chinese example is a first instance in which this intriguing topic can be explored.

Greece and Rome

Another major center of classical civilization sprang up in the Mediterranean—first focused on Greece, though with colonies fanning out in the Middle East and other parts of Southern Europe—then based increasingly on the expansion of Roman power. Classical Mediterranean civilization generated many precedents for later societies, in the Middle East, Eastern Europe, and Western Europe, though in the sexual sphere many characteristic patterns were substantially altered by subsequent religious developments. Within the classical period itself, from the initial rise of Greek city states around 800 BCE to the ultimate collapse of the Roman Empire 1300 years later, basic standards and expressions were widely shared, though it is best to look at Greece and Rome in sequence rather than as an absolutely unified whole.

Greek values and regulations worked hard to deal with the common agricultural desire to maintain appropriate controls over female sexuality. Marriages, of course, as in all agricultural societies, were based on economic arrangements—exchanges of property, in the upper classes, supervised by the parents—and not sexual attraction. This, and the assumption that the main purpose of marriage beyond economic activity was the production of children, strongly conditioned attitudes to marital sex and to the definition of female respectability. Mediterranean culture officially emphasized monogamy.

Great value was placed on female restraint and, before marriage, virginity. Some women served in religious activities on strength of their refraining from sex. Most girls were married quite young and, at least in respectable urban households, kept quite confined. Because of the valuation on virginity, Greek authors (mainly males) wrote widely about how anxious brides would and should be in anticipation of their first sexual experience. Greek culture held women in considerable disrespect, seeing them as by nature wanton and in need of external controls—for the ideal woman would emphasize considerable chastity and a devotion to motherhood. Respectable women were kept elaborately clothed and covered, in contrast to greater male opportunities—in athletic competition, for example—for substantial or total nudity. The greatest opportunity for women to venture into the public sphere—again, at a respectable level—involved participation in agricultural festivals, where it was assumed that women should experience periods of celibacy in order to conserve social energy for bountiful crops. The militaristic city state of Sparta offered some unusual variants on a standard pattern: males were taken from their families early and trained with other males, visiting wives (once marriage occurred) only infrequently and with emphasis on the importance of reproduction. Spartan women had a bit more freedom of public movement than did other Greeks, but only condition of a commitment to reproduction in the service of the state. Even in less fiercely organized Greek states, marriage was largely regarded in terms of its role in reproduction. Of course, women did not necessarily fully accept their assigned roles. Some women's groups may have explored sexual alternatives. By 500 BCE an industry to manufacture dildos, made from wood and padded leather to be used with olive oil as a lubricant, arose in the region of Miletus on the Greek mainland.

But there was little question about what men believed or hoped respectable women would accept in terms of sexual restraint and faithfulness. Greek attitudes to gender and sexuality came through clearly in intensely punitive attitudes toward adultery. Because wives owed husbands complete sexual fidelity, adultery was a massive offense, and an adulterous male could be put to death by the state or even legitimately killed by the offended husband. On the other hand, rape was punished less severely, since it was more an offense simply against a woman herself. This distinction had been evoked earlier in Mesopotamia and in Jewish law, but it now became still clearer. Legitimate sex was under the control of men and men's definitions.

Many Greeks displayed an interest in birth control complicated in some cases by ignorance about how precisely babies were conceived. In early centuries, as evidenced by Homeric epics, many believed that infants began from airborne particles, or animalculae, though later scientists saw conception in terms of a meeting of male and female seeds. Some Greeks made offerings to the gods to promote abortion of unwanted children, and some used a copper sulphate mixture as a contraceptive. On the other hand some evidence suggests a belief that female orgasm would help a woman get pregnant. As in many agricultural societies, Greeks widely used infanticide, or the killing or exposing of (particularly female) babies to help with population control, a clear sign of the tension between normal sexuality and family population goals.

Another standard feature of agricultural societies, fully consistent with the perceived gender differential, involved prostitution. Many female slaves were used as prostitutes, and for men, having enough money to spend on such women was something to brag about—though too much indulgence was a form of gluttony and seen as shameful. The philosopher Socrates called prostitutes an opportunity to "release compulsions of lust." Brothels varied widely, depending on the social class of urban patrons. A few elite prostitutes emerged, often praised for their beauty and artistic talent in contrast to the boredom of respectable wives.

Prominent Greek men also conducted affairs. The Athenian politician Pericles, in the fifth century, took a talented woman named Aspasia as his mistress, at least after divorcing his wife, and her role was openly recognized for 12 years or more, even as Pericles wielded great political power; she bore the statesman at least one child. Aspasia also owned and operated a brothel, and served as something of a symbol of the power available to elite Greek prostitutes. Several other Greek women rose to considerable heights, in Athens and elsewhere, on the strength of their roles as courtesans; a few, like Elpinice in the same period in Athens, were also openly promiscuous, in defiance of normal standards.

Masturbation was another outlet. Greek writers generally disapproved of female masturbation, though some plays mentioned the practice more neutrally. But the practice was regarded as a normal way for men to seek release when no other sex was available; some artists and philosophers even encouraged it as an act of self-sufficiency.

In general, Greeks seem to have regarded sexual activity as normal, but with strict regulation of most women aimed at focusing their participation in reproduction and fidelity. Men had far greater latitudes, serviced by special groups of women but by other approved outlets as well. Even male sex, however, could be influenced by a widespread concern about overindulgence: Greeks believed in the importance of moderation in all things, and there was some sense that orgasms could dull intellectual capacities at least temporarily; this could generate some praise for an ability to resist sexual desire. Men also seem to have worried considerably about impotence and about the sexual decline associated with ageing—for which wives might be blamed.

One final feature of the Greek sexual order, with significance at the time and long after, involved the use of castrated men, or eunuchs, for certain bureaucratic functions as well as to cut hair or to dress upper-class men. The development of eunuchs paralleled that in Zhou China, though the origins of the practice are less clear in Greece. Eunuchs in both societies came to be regarded as loyal and trustworthy, particularly of course for activities in which normal male sexuality might seem to get in the way. Again as in China, the situation suggested some strongly ambivalent attitudes about male sexual desire.

While elements of these patterns had some distinctive specifics, most bear out the common frameworks of sexuality in agricultural societies, with special privileges for more powerful men, assiduous attempts to regulate girls and wives and assure reproduction, but an accompanying concern about birth control, and wide tolerance for certain kinds of male release. The low interest in female sexual pleasure, compared to China, is clear, but hard to explain: of course the emphasis on monogamy was unusual as well for this period. Two features of the Greek approach to sexuality, both vigorously debated by historians in recent decades, offered a more distinctive flavor: considerable tolerance for, even encouragement of, male homosexuality, and a surprisingly erotic public and religious culture that contrasted in many ways with what seem to have been normal behaviors and standards.

Homosexuality

Greek art and literature frequently invoked homosexual desires and relationships, sometimes citing them as important in the good breeding of male citizens. More significant still was the widespread practice of apprenticing young, upper-class males to older men, sometimes through arrangements made by parents themselves. The resulting relationships were complicated, involving tutoring and sponsorship as well as sex. And there was no sense that the results were exclusive: the older men were normally married, and their activities with younger apprentices were simply another outlet; and the young men, presumably, would turn to marriage and heterosexual activities later on. Though approving discussions of homosexuality were widely available in public, the older mentors probably emerged primarily, if not exclusively, within an elite subculture. Certainly some prominent men were involved. The playwright Sophocles was widely known for his relationships; one story having him inducing a young wine-seller to sip from a cup he had just bought so that Sophocles could use the occasion to kiss and try to seduce him. Among Greek cities, Thebes seems to have been most tolerant of homosexuality, with some couples of the same age living together as if married.

Numerous writers praised homosexual acts: one urged homosexual outlets as good for military morale. The great god Zeus was notoriously depicted in his interest in beautiful young boys. Plato assumed that serious love was most likely to develop between an older and a younger man, not between man and woman, because it could involve a mixture of sex and compelling intellectual discourse. At the same time, Plato also reflected a concern about sexual pleasure as debased, a humiliation to be resisted, so his approval was at the least qualified; in later in life the philosopher attacked any sexual activity that was not reproductive (noting, incorrectly, that homosexuality did not exist in the animal world), though he admitted that some people seemed to want it. Aristotle worried about passive men—in general, men too clearly labeled as homosexuals, like male prostitutes, were looked down upon—but saw more occasional homosexuality as a good way to insure that women did not gain too much power.

Lesbianism was also discussed—it referred to the isle of Lesbos, where the female poet Sappho (c. 610–580 BCE) portrayed women expressing their mutual desire—but it is not clear that actual female sexual communities or liaisons were more than rarities. Sappho herself probably had sexual relationships with some women, though she also was married at some point and gave birth to at least one child.

Overall, at least among men, Greek openness and widespread assumption of a homosexual stage in the socialization of some young men, and of a corresponding partial outlet for some mature men, constituted a distinct part not just of the culture of sexuality, but of sexual behavior. The result could challenge later societies that looked back to Greece but that had to reprove or conceal this aspect of the classical precedent.

Sexual culture

The open, sometimes wanton, sexuality of Greek gods and goddesses form a fascinating contrast to the more complex, in most ways more repressive framework of real life. Goddesses as well as gods provided symbols of sexuality in their beauty—Greek art highlighted the importance of physical beauty—but also their lusts. While some divinities were restrained, praised for their chastity, ample alternatives were available in literature as well as art.

Thus the goddess Aphrodite (for Romans known as Venus) served simultaneously as representing love, beauty and sexual pleasure, lovely but sensuous, so potent in her sexuality that neither god nor mortal man could escape her power. The goddess had a host of affairs with gods and humans, despite her marriage to a single god; she would frequently be portrayed directly in the throes of sexual delight. She also stood for harmony and fertility, and could be worshipped independent of the sexual aura; but the fact that these qualities were ultimately combined in one of the most revered divinities constituted a fascinating mixture. A particular cult for Aphrodite featured a summer festival where, amid much wine, women imitated the cries of a woman mourning a lost lover.

The Greek pantheon also included Eros (in Roman culture, Cupid), the personification of sexual desire and the son of Aphrodite. Eros could paralyze humans with the power of love, often inflicted randomly or cruelly. But he could also symbolize the sexual attraction of a couple upon their marriage and was worshipped as a god of fertility.

Satyrs, though not gods, were another product of Greek mythology, devoted to wild desires for drink and sex. Often depicted with a large, permanently erect penis, satyrs stood both for a deplorable lack of self-control and for inexhaustible energy and sexual appetite. Depictions of satyrs often featured masturbation, sex with animals, and pursuit of innocent women. Female bacchae also displayed wild sexual interests. The scenes were designed to surprise, as against normal sexuality, while clearly representing excess, whether for reproof or titillation.

Greek literature could also portray human sexual desire. The whole story of the Trojan War was predicated on the abduction of Helen, a beautiful Greek princess, and the jealous passions unleashed as a result. Early Greek art—the designs on vases, for example—frequently represented love-making and group sex, mainly between men and courtesans rather than between husbands and wives. Homosexual erotic scenes also appeared.

All in all, Greek expression of sex, in approved and public art, was far racier than Greek sexuality itself. Since Americans today (as we will discuss) live in a public culture far more erotic than their more normal behavior on average, the question of what this all means is more than a historical exercise. Why do some societies indulge a fancy in sex, when reality is far more complex (in the Greek case, and probably also today to a lesser degree, particularly for women)?

And there are several answers, to be combined in some way for a full sense of significance. First, sexual stories and representations might excite but they could also warn. Aphrodite was loaded with desire, but she was also full of tricks and deceit, a possible red flag against what she stood for. Eros, particularly in early representations, was monstrous and frightening, not the cherub he later became; he was surrounded by imagery of disease, madness, and fire. Greeks might represent sex openly, but they also needed to express their real fear of its power and its frequent association with violence. The whole Trojan War story was one of the damage sexual passions could induce by driving men to rage and conflict. Other stories, like the play Oedipus, where a man unwittingly has sex with his own mother and is driven mad, clearly intended to highlight firm rules about regulating passion.

Sexual stories and designs could also express tensions around real-life rules. Greek myth was fascinated with virgins and the forces that could violate them, including outright rape.

Finally, of course, sexual representations could provide outright titillation or pleasure, another outlet (most obviously though not necessarily exclusively for men) in a society that could not indulge too much sexual activity lest women's respectability and the needs of birth control be violated. A number of Greek dramas (most of which have not directly survived) highlighted sexual innuendo, simulated sex acts, and nudity, with strong emphasis on women's as well as men's sexual desire. By the later centuries of Greek society, as again in the Roman Empire, growing urban luxury seems to have encouraged the use of what we would call pornography, deliberately to stimulate. An increasing practice of presenting partially nude female statues, mixing modesty and sexualization in a single figure, was one sign of this, and there were stories of young men visiting the art to masturbate, a clear indication of the statues erotic power. In a society also wary about too much sexual interest and loss of control, the emergence of this aspect of the public culture was an intriguing complexity. It might allow restraint in practice, by providing a harmless outlet, but it could also stimulate interest that real life might not fully satisfy.

There is no question that Greek culture was sexier than the normal conditions of life for most people, sexier as well than the most widely approved values. The correlation pointed in several directions, undoubtedly creating different impressions for different individuals. As with homosexuality, the result was a heritage that proved challenging for some later societies that might prefer to downplay this aspect of the record; but also stimulating, particularly for later art. It establishes an analytical complexity that would emerge in some other societies as well, where culture in some ways contrasted with, rather than directing enforcing, apparent practical standards.

Change and continuity in Rome

The development of Roman society maintained or copied a variety of Greek themes. Two shifts, however, were particularly noteworthy: a somewhat higher opinion of women, though still in a patriarchal framework, and a resultant interest in female as well as male sexual pleasure; and a widespread, though not uniform, disapproval of homosexuality, sometimes regarded as a symptom of Greek depravity, which stalwart Romans should not imitate.

Greek erotic culture had great echo in Rome, partly of course because basically the same set of gods and goddesses held sway, if under different names. Venus, like Aphrodite, was goddess of love—but in her case this included protection of virtuous marriage but also patronage of prostitutes and lascivious behavior. The Romans even added a god, Priapus, associated with sexuality and fertility, always portrayed with a (usually gigantic) erect penis. Artistic representations of Priapus were common, even in ordinary homes, and a set of poems under his name featured extreme obscenity and female lust. To be sure, elite Roman homes usually had more restrained representations that did homes from lower social status—the latter, for example, sometimes showing oral sex, anal sex, or sex with animals; and there was some increase in highly sexual art over time, as the Roman Empire became more prosperous and then entered the first phases of decline. Surviving art in Pompeii, the city buried by volcanic ash, show these differences and trends clearly (amusingly, some of the most vivid scenes, including representations of Priapus, would in the twentieth century be boxed in, opened only for tourists willing to pay an extra fee, not assumed as suitable for all visitors, as the Romans would have taken for granted). More clearly than in Greece, the presence of sexualized art in homes and public baths meant that the materials were available to women as well as men.

Roman literature featured considerable attention to sexuality. The love poems of Ovid, early in the Roman Empire, would long be regarded as pornographic in Christian Europe, though they continued to exercise fascination. The Romans also generated a large number of sex manuals, advising people on how to achieve maximum pleasure; most of these assumed the desirability of female as well as male enjoyment, with female orgasm seen as something men should strive for. Women were less regulated in public than had been true with the Greeks, another sign of a slightly different version of patriarchy that could relate to an interest in female sexual satisfaction. A few women managed to break free more fully, though they were decidedly exceptional: Clodia, for example, c. 95–c. 40 BCE, was a widow who notoriously took on many lovers, though she was publicly criticized for her licentious behavior.

As with the Greeks, Romans featured some special outlets for men. Male masturbation was regarded as wasteful but acceptable. Wealthy men frequently had lovers. The Emperor Augustus, who sponsored some strict family law, including efforts to limit husbands' sexual or physical abuse of wives, had his wife procure virgins for his pleasure. It was widely assumed that men would have sex outside marriage, whereas model wives married very young and devoted themselves (in principle) to motherhood and fidelity. Prostitution flourished, with various social and economic levels corresponding to male social rank. The government undertook some regulation, requiring prostitutes to register. Prostitution was seen as good by preventing men from interfering with other wives, thus inhibiting adultery (prostitution was not seen in this category) or as an outlet for sexual needs one could not satisfy with a respectable wife.

Roman religious practice also valued a small group of female virgins, the vestals, selected to serve as priestesses, six at any given time. If they violated virginity they were put to death. If faithful, however, they received a variety of special privileges, including financial independence from male supervision, normally granted only to men. A few other religious sects also emphasized a link between virginity and spiritual service, an interesting contrast to expectations and standards for the bulk of the Roman population.

Homosexuality existed in Rome: a number of emperors engaged in it. Most commonly, however, homosexuality suggested a master–slave relationship, a form of dominance, not the more complex life stage that had developed in Greece. Sex between older men and boys could be regarded as adultery, and dishonorable to both parties. The practice continued to some degree, though probably at a lower rate than had occurred amid the Greek upper classes, and certainly amid greater disapproval. The great emperor Hadrian, for example, though married, had a beautiful adolescent boy as his chief love. Accusing men of depraving young boys became a weapon in Roman politics to discredit an opponent—Cicero used the charge against Marc Anthony. Homoerotic literature existed, often copied from Greek, and Ovid's collection includes a lesbian love story. More representative was a third-century sex manual, by Philaemis, which described passive male homosexual behavior as totally obscene because of its violation of gender roles. Overall, with this important exception, Roman culture seemed to combine the same mixture of open expressiveness in art and literature, with careful patriarchal arrangements in practice, which had developed in Greece. Only the slightly greater attention to female sexuality shows the degree of variety possible within the classical Mediterranean tradition.

Persia

The Persian Empire developed early in the classical period, expanding over a huge territory including the Middle East and into Egypt. Knowledge of Persian sexuality, however, is, to date, somewhat limited, depending heavily on Greek sources. Persia and Greek settlements traded extensively and Greek military forces halted a Persian advance in the fifth century.

Perhaps with some similarities to China, the power of the Persian emperor had extensive sexual implications. Court politics filled with sexual intrigues. Greek observers, seeing the emperor surrounded by women—many of whom were doubtless concubines, with others simply entertainers—regarded the Persian court as decadent, too immersed in sexual intrigues, and simply too open to women's influence. The court also depended heavily on eunuchs, establishing this tradition in ways that would be widely accepted in later imperial regimes in the Middle East.

Persian emphasis on reproductive sex included firm rules against abortion, seen as murder. Some men were encouraged to marry slaves for breeding purposes.

Persia seems to have absorbed influences from a number of other cultures, including Egyptian precedents concerning sexuality, and also Indian ideas about the spirituality surrounding sex. Earlier Mesopotamian traditions were also important. The Greek traveler and geographer, Herodotus, writing in the fifth century, also claimed that Persians learned extensively from the Greeks, particularly with regard to homosexual relations between older and younger men in the elite classes.

India

India hosted the final great classical civilization, with its characteristic caste system and religious tradition—centered ultimately on Hinduism—spreading through the subcontinent. The Indian approach to sexuality, firmly within the norms of agricultural civilizations, emphasized a vigorous embrace of sexual enjoyment, often regarded as the best of all earthly pleasures, with religion and eroticism often intertwined, along with strong emphasis on the importance of reproduction. The link between sex and spirituality was vital, in what became the most important religious center of the classical world. Standards associated with reproduction led to some distinctive customs. As a particularly vivid form of social inequality, the caste system created growing differences in sexual habits.

Strong emphasis on sexuality showed in many ways. Early stories about gods and goddesses often involved sexual themes. There were important similarities here with the Greek pantheon, based on a common Indo-European religious heritage. Various incarnations of the gods had sexual liaisons. Krishna in many stories was the flute-playing lover of milkmaids, the most beautiful of whom was Radha. Shiva, god of fertility, was also a divine destroyer—the mixture of sex and violence was less prominent than in Greek mythology, but it did exist. Shiva's consort was a mother goddess, who took various forms; all major gods were paired with goddesses who provided the basic life force. Shiva took many brides, and had many divinities as children.

Not surprisingly, the sexuality associated with divinities spilled over into art, more graphically than was the case in Greece. Many representations of goddesses featured sexual attributes. Divine lovers like Krishna and Radha were directly portrayed. In the Gupta period, sculptors produced voluptuous mother-goddesses in pink stone, with almost lifelike fleshy qualities. Also in the Gupta period—the final centuries of the classical period in India, artists began to use painting to represent sexual scenes, in one case illustrating the *Kama Sutra* with detailed depictions of anatomy and sexual positions.

Indian writers generated a number of sex manuals, detailing positions and practices designed to maximize pleasure, as well as rituals associated with sexuality. The most important single textbook of love, Vatsyana's *Kama Sutra*, was probably written in the second century CE, but it had many antecedents. Ways to maximize pleasure for both men and women were carefully spelled out, with great attention to foreplay, at a level that would stand the test of time—translations of the *Kama Sutra* would become available as part of a growing interest in recreational sex in the twentieth century in the United States.

The strongly sexual public and religious culture spilled over into real life. Indians strongly emphasized parentally-arranged marriages, particularly in the upper castes, but they also stressed the importance of sexual pleasure within marriage and the man's responsibility to keep his wife happy, as well as himself. Mutuality was strongly emphasized. The enjoyment of love, or *kama*, definitely included sexual satisfaction, or *rati*. Custom dictated that newlyweds, who often had not met before the wedding, wait until the fourth night before attempting intercourse, in order to become properly acquainted; they should then remain secluded for another six days, hopefully time enough for a first conception. Women married young, at 12–16 (and sometimes marriages were concluded for outright children, though marital practice would wait until greater maturity); men were normally considerably older. Divorce was uncommon, except in the lower castes or in cases of insanity or impotence. Polygamy was widely allowed, but practiced more commonly in middle or lower castes. It was not emphasized as strongly as in China.

Sexual pleasure, though on a more gendered basis, also supported a varied range of prostitutes. Some Indian women were exchanged with other societies, with Egypt for example, often as entertainers but sometimes as concubines—one of the earliest examples of what we would today call the sex trade. In India itself, brothels, but also street prostitutes and private home visits, operated in most larger towns and cities, often supervised by the regional government and supplying tax revenues. An autumn Divali festival featured frequent visits to prostitutes. High-level prostitutes were accomplished and educated, enjoying considerable freedom, though the profession as a whole was regarded as greedy. Leaders kept prostitutes on salary in their palaces and sometimes on trips, and these women were seen as powerful, almost divine in their sexual force. On the other hand, prostitutes caught with ordinary married men might be punished, usually more than the offending man himself.

For sexual activity also involved regulation, in the interests of female virtue (for respectable women), family stability, and a reverence for reproduction and childbirth. Adultery was strongly disapproved; Indian stories sometimes told of women who deceived their husbands, but in practice this was vigorously condemned. Husbands as well as wives could be punished for adultery by annulment of a marriage. Virginity among women was also highly valued, and loss of virginity could make a single woman unmarriageable (in a society where marriage was regarded as essential, particularly for women). While many Indian families undoubtedly worried about having too many children, in principle family success was measured by numbers of children born as well as wealth; abortion was a major crime. Female beauty standards emphasized qualities appropriate for childbirth. Many rituals developed to encourage fertility. Pregnant women themselves were carefully coddled and monitored, and couples were not supposed to have sex until 90 days after childbirth so that the mother could recover and pay appropriate attention to the newborn.

Despite an erotic culture in other respects, Indian society looked down on homosexuality, as well as castration—a sign of the strong emphasis on the importance of reproduction. Eunuchs existed, but with far less significance than in China or the eastern Mediterranean/Middle East. The theme of homosexuality was far less prominent, even in literature, than in other classical cultures. Same-sex friendship and its romantic qualities and deep attachments gained attention, but without a sexual component. Some myths concerned cross-dressed women who married other women and then had a spiritual sex change; and myths also included miracle births from a male couple, with one partner assuming temporary female form to bear the child. But these stories had little connection with homosexuality in real life. Little male prostitution existed, again in contrast with several other societies at the time. In the final centuries BCE, some actual laws began to target non-vaginal sex, with fines much higher for men than for women, an unusually early example of state enforcement of this kind of sexual standard. Less unusually, strong taboos also applied to bestiality—explicitness here followed from larger Indian beliefs about the sacred qualities of certain animals and about defilement through animal contacts.

Religious culture also generated a final element, which managed to coexist with the vivid appreciation of sexual pleasure—which indeed perhaps helped to legitimate this pleasure. Hindus were expected to abstain from sex during various religious rites and festivals. Holy men might abstain from sex altogether, and young boys might take vows of celibacy as part of religious training. For the Brahmins, or priestly caste, initiation into maturity for boys occurred before puberty, as part of education and spiritual advancement, with much less connection to sexuality than was common in agricultural societies.

Conclusion

Standard features of sexuality in agricultural civilizations shine through all the varied classical civilizations. Connections between sexuality and reproduction were consistently emphasized. So, however, was the distinction between men and women in their access to sexual pleasure (though societies varied greatly in the degree of differentiation), and everywhere prostitution developed mainly to service men. This meant, as well, a pronounced, though often complex, distinction between respectable women, destined for marriage and with strict admonitions about virginity and fidelity, and the women involved with commercial sex, who were usually of low status but who might enjoy certain freedoms and prestige depending on talents and clientele. For men, distinctions applied as well, but particularly through the development of unusual sexual access for the wealthy and powerful.

Gender differences in the classical societies also included the fact that men married years after puberty, in contrast to most women, who married at a much younger age (as part of an emphasis on reproduction but also as a means of limiting female access to premarital sex). This age disparity helps explain (though only in part) how prostitution could flourish along with recommendations of family fidelity and, in some cases, hostility to adultery on the part of men as well as women. Gender distinctions in other words were complicated, and not just a matter of greater male access to pleasure.

Frequently, the attendant interest in birth control operated as well, though some societies seem to have placed more emphasis on this than others. Apparent differences here—the fact for example that we know more about Greek interests in contraceptive potions than we do about Indian—may largely reflect distinctions in available documentation, for the concern was widespread. But attention to abortion varied, from seeming nonchalance in parts of Greece to the vigorous disapproval in India.

The classical civilizations also illustrate, of course, the variations possible amid the common elements. Some societies paid much more attention to female pleasure than did others. Practices of monogamy or polygamy and the frequency of open concubinage differed considerably. Attitudes and apparent practices concerning homosexuality were a key variable, from open approval to efforts at prohibition. Approaches to the suitability of masturbation varied as well. The same applies to the role and frequency of eunuchs. A variety of approaches in these areas could seem compatible with the basic needs of an agricultural economy.

Variation also applies to the kind of culture that surrounded sex, and also the relationship between sex and religious experience. Sexual linkage with art varied from Indian openness and expressiveness to Chinese reticence. Sex manuals existed everywhere, a key use of writing, but they were more frequent and elaborate in China and India than in the Mediterranean. On the other hand, outright pornography—that is, somewhat furtive art or literature that defied normal standards, and seemed deliberately designed to titillate—was most pronounced in the Mediterranean. Variation applied as well to the extent that restraint from sex (aside from what was urged on respectable unmarried women) was regarded as valuable—Rome and particularly India developed values here that seem largely absent in China. It is not always possible to figure out why these cultural differentials developed but, once established in the classical period, they would remain culturally influential even later on.

Some tendency existed, finally, for increasing efforts at sexual constraint and regulation over time, during the classical period itself. As societies became better organized, they applied some of this organizational rigor to sex as well. Confucianism thus made inroads on the freer sexual culture of the early Zhou period in China; Indian attitudes toward homosexuality hardened; Romans officially at least disapproved of some practices common earlier in Greece. Most obviously in Confucianism, but possibly at least in imperial Rome, political order and propriety seemed to call for greater sexual order as well. Here was a theme that a more religious age, following the classical period, would definitely carry forward.

Further reading

On Greece and Rome, see A. Stewart, *Art, Desire and the Body in Ancient Greece* (Cambridge: Cambridge University Press, 1997); J. Davidson, *Courtesans and Fishcakes: The Consuming Passions of Classical Athens* (London: Fontana, 1998); M. Skinner, *Sexuality in Greek and Roman Culture* (Oxford: Blackwell, 2005); M. Nussbaum and J. Sihvola, *The Sleep of Reason: Erotic Experience and Sexual Ethics in Ancient Greece and Rome* (Chicago: University of Chicago Press, 2002); A. Varone, *Eroticism in Pompeii* (Los Angeles: Getty Museum, 2001); T. McGinn, *The Economy of Prostitution in the Roman World* (Ann Arbor: University of Michigan Press, 2004); R.L. Wildfang, *Rome's Vestal Virgins* (London: Routledge, 2006); J.R. Clarke, *Looking at Love-making: Constructions of Sexuality in Roman Art* (Berkeley: University of California Press, 1998); M. Johnson and T. Ryan, *Sexuality in Greek and Roman Society and Literature: A Sourcebook* (New York: Routledge, 2005); and B. Thornton, *Eros: The Myth of Ancient Greek Sexuality* (Boulder, CO: Westview, 1997).

For topics in India, see J. Anboyer, *Daily Life in Ancient India*, trans. S. Watson Taylor (New Delhi: Munshiram Manoharlal Publishers, 1994); A.L. Basham, *The Wonder that was India* (New Delhi: Rupa and Co., 1967); W. Doniger, *Splitting the Difference: Gender and Myth in Ancient Greece and India* (Chicago: University of Chicago Press, 1999); R.A. Jairazbhoy, *Foreign Influence in Ancient India* (London: Asia Publishing House, 1963); A. Jha, *Sexual Designs in Indian Culture* (New

Delhi: Vikas Publishing House, 1979); C. Benerji Sures, *Crime and Sex in Ancient India* (Calcutta: Naya Prokash, 1980); and R. Vanita and S. Kidwai, eds., *Same-sex Love in India: Readings from Literature and History* (New York: St. Martin's Press, 2000).

On China, see E.L. Shaughnessy, ed., *China: Empire and Civilization* (New York: Oxford University Press, 2000); C. Benn, *Daily Life in Traditional China* (Westport, CT: Greenwood Press, 2002); P.R. Goldin, *The Culture of Sex in Ancient China* (Honolulu: University of Hawaii Press, 2002); R.H. Gulik, *Sexual Life in Ancient China: A Preliminary Survey of Chinese Sex and Society from ca. 1500 BC till 1644 AD* (Boston, MA: Brill, 2003); V. Hansen, *The Open Empire: A History of China to 1600* (New York: W.W. Norton and Co., 2000); and M.E. Lewis, *The Early Chinese Empires: Qin and Han* (Cambridge, MA: Harvard University Press, 2007).

See also E. Abbot, *A History of Celibacy* (New York: Scribner, 2000); L. Allen, *The Persian Empire* (Chicago: University of Chicago Press, 2005); S. Caldwell, *Oh Terrifying Mother: Sexuality, Violence and the Worship of the Goddess Kali* (New York: Oxford University Press, 1999); L. Crompton, *Homosexuality and Civilization* (Cambridge, MA: Belknap Press, 2003); and L. McClure, ed., *Sexuality and Gender in the Classical World: Readings and Sources* (Oxford: Blackwell, 2002).

Chapter 4

The impact of religion on sexuality, to 1450

Religion and sexuality have often been closely related. We have seen that many early human societies equated sexual and religious experience. In many ways Hinduism also retained a positive relationship, with the highly sexualized representations of Hindu goddesses and much religious art in general. Daoism, in China, also established some linkage. On the other hand, Greeks and Romans used religious stories more ambivalently. On the one hand, the romps of gods and goddesses helped express a highly sexual imagination, though not always linked to any particular spirituality; on the other hand, many stories used gods' behaviors as warnings about the dangers of sexuality and its linkage to violence or excess. Chinese culture in general, with Daoism excepted, moved away from any particular connection between religion and sexuality. The variety was considerable.

With the fall of the great classical empires by the sixth century CE, and with increased missionary activity from several centers, several subsequent centuries of world history were heavily influenced by a new emphasis on religiosity and by massive conversions to one of the great world religions. Buddhism, though much older, began to spread more widely into China and East Asia, and into Southeast Asia. Christianity, previously moving widely through the Roman Empire, now began to reach northward, through Roman Catholicism in the West and Orthodox Christianity in the Byzantine Empire, and later Russia and other parts of Eastern Europe. Most dramatic of all was the emergence and rapid spread of Islam, from its base in the Middle East, widely across North Africa, and south into the sub-Sahara, into central and south Asia, and into Southeast Asia.

New levels of religious commitment hardly formed the only theme in world history between 600 and 1450. World trade increased, which could have its own impact on sexuality at least in growing port cities; new levels of consumer attainment, for example in urban China, could have consequences as well, with linkages between fashionable clothing and sexual appeal. A growing urban culture in China expanded the range of brothels and concubinage arrangements, though building on earlier precedent. It remains vital not to simplify the factors that helped shape sexual behavior in this dynamic period.

Religion, however, was the greatest new influence in world history overall, where sexuality was concerned. In contrast to many earlier religions, the new or expanding faiths often sought to downplay and regulate sexuality, rather than seeing it in any positive relationship with spirituality. New praise for celibacy, particularly in Christianity and Buddhism, was the most striking sign of this reorientation, but a variety of more specific regulatory efforts worked in a similar direction, highlighting the sense that sex was, or could be, a danger to proper human values.

Religion also added new vigor to the penalties associated with sexual violations. Instead of simply being bad for health or social propriety, sexual misbehavior could now be an offense before God, at least in Christianity and Islam, and a serious perversion of true human purpose even in Buddhism. The result courted divine punishment—hell and damnation for Christianity and Islam, deprivation of the chance to move toward union with the divine essence in Buddhism. As if this were not enough, the missionary religions helped prompt governments to add new secular penalties to violations of sexual regulations—including the death penalty in several instances. Sexual offenses became more serious business than ever before. Correspondingly, efforts to regulate and restrict any sexual overtones in public culture increased as well, another marked change from the classical centuries.

The spread of world religions generated clear changes in key aspects of sexuality. The spread also invites an explicit comparative effort, to discuss the differing sexual goals and approaches among the three largest faiths and between the religions and other cultural systems like that of China. Differences would prove crucial, at the time and since.

Beneath the comparative effort, however, three more fundamental challenges require analytical response. First, granting that the new religious framework placed sexuality in a less favorable light in some societies, with new penalties attached for certain behaviors: how much really changed? Did most people alter their sexual behavior significantly, and if so in what directions? How much, in other words, does a substantial cultural change—and religious conversion does qualify here—alter actual sexuality? The question is easier to ask than to answer, because some behaviors might persist but under greater concealment, yet the exploration is essential.

Second, as a related item: did religious change largely firm up the main features of sexuality in agricultural societies, around the apparent needs for regulation of women and the constraints of birth control, or were there really new directions, at least in intent? A more religious period in world history is undeniable, in the centuries after the fall of the classical empires; in terms of sexuality, was the result a fundamental set of innovations or more modest adjustments in course?

The third challenge really involves evaluation more than analysis. All societies generate some sexual rules or values to which other societies may object. Some contemporary readers may be shocked at some of the images and practices that the classical civilizations produced—concubinage is an obvious example of an arrangement clearly out of favor, at least officially, in the modern world, and other examples will easily come to mind. As the major religions spread, new barriers to sexual openness emerged that will strike other contemporary observers as repressive or cruel. There is no reason—and probably little possibility—for setting aside value judgments. However, they should temporarily be suspended so that the new religious systems can at least be understood and objectively compared (they did vary considerably). And of course—because contemporary opinion is deeply divided on sexual issues—some observers will breathe a sigh of relief in encountering the religious approach, just as others would prefer to linger in the racier classical world.

Buddhism

Buddhism was the oldest world religion, taking root first in India (where it greatly extended some of the more ascetic features of Hinduism), then losing ground there only to spread widely in Southeast Asia and East Asia. Chinese encounters with Buddhism occurred in the final centuries of the classical era, and Buddhism became a major cultural force there for several hundred years, then receding somewhat amid official disfavor but taking strong root in Korea and Japan. Southeast Asian Buddhism, including ultimately the conversion of Tibet, was a somewhat different variant, but quite successful in its own right.

Of all the major religions, whether missionary in outlook or more regionally con fined, Buddhism was in principle most hostile to earthly desire. Buddha's writings urged that the pains of mortal existence paled in comparison with the pursuit of worldly pleasures, which would distract a person from the true religious and contemplative pursuits that should inform this life and prepare for an ensuing higher plane of spiritual existence. Many Buddhist writers criticized sexual urgings specifically, sometimes linking them to the temptations of power in general—it was vital for a spiritual quest to separate from the passions and the senses. Desire was variously described as a dry meat bone, a pit of burning coal, a tree laden with fruit but too dangerous to climb. As the *Dazhidulum* states, "He who enjoys pleasures is never satiated; he who is deprived of them suffers greatly; When he does not possess them, he wants to possess them; When he possesses them, he is tormented." Not surprisingly, Buddhist religious orders almost uniformly banned sexual activity, on pain of expulsion from the order. This was not just a generalized prohibition; frequently, a variety of specific sex acts were listed, which may suggest that monks and nuns sometimes tested the limits.

While Buddhists sometimes praised female spirituality, there was also a frequent theme of women leading religious men into sexual temptation. Buddhist stories often featured the futility of earthly love: a monk falls in love with a courtesan, but she dies; the monk asks the king to auction her corpse, but no one buys. The moral: human beauty is impermanent, and the good monk never falls in love again. Another Chinese–Japanese Buddhist story featured a hermit who fell in love with a female temptress and is ridiculed, losing all his powers, when the two are seen in public. As in other cultures, sexual activity might be seen as a loss of male energy. Nirvana, the union with the spiritual essence, involved detachment from the body.

The ascetic impulses so deeply ingrained in Buddhism caused some problems when the religion moved into China, which may be one reason why early proponents glossed over the attacks on sexuality and desire. Chinese traditionalists felt particular concern about aspects of Buddhism that could lead people away from vital activities in this world, including political loyalties, but also family formation and procreation.

Buddhists, in turn, tried to compromise a bit with the Chinese approach. On the other hand, the Chinese also found some uses for Buddhist values: during the heyday of the religion in China, under the Tang dynasty, upper-class women whose sexual behavior was seen as improper were often sent to Buddhist nuns for counselling.

Hostility to sex was not, however, the whole story. Buddhism is also full of discussions of holy men who did have sex without contradicting their holiness. A seventh-century Korean story told of the monk Wonhyo, who frequently visited brothels but achieved salvation because he was open to his feelings of desire. Many Buddhist saints—the *bodhisattvas*—had sex but, because it expressed a love for humanity, were not defiled by it. One such, in the *Suramgama-sutra*, had sex with daughters of a demon in order to save them. Another story contrasts two monks, Prasannendriya and Agramati—the latter is devoted to purity but falls to hell because of false beliefs, whereas Prasannendriya commits immoral acts but gains salvation—bad behavior is not as dreadful as bad beliefs.

But the great Buddhist complexity involved a recurrent sense that desire and passion could help move a person toward spiritual transformation and that there was a type of love, possibly with a sexual element, that could so assist other people that it had to be regarded as holy. Thus it was compassion that led some saints to visit brothels or bars, without damage to their spirituality. Some *bodhisattvas* could directly liberate people through sexual acts, like the fifth-century nun who would move people to greater spirituality by kissing or embracing them. It was this kind of approach that led some actual monks, like the Japanese Zen leader Ikkya Sojun in the fifteenth century, to visit prostitutes; and Ikkya Sojun then recorded his experiences in a celebrated poetry collection.

This alternative approach, in turn, helps explain why Buddhism might also be linked with sexual appetite. Buddhist saints in Japan were often worshipped as gods of love and sources of fertility; in one case people even prayed to the dried genitals of a dead saint as part of a ritual seeking sexual vitality.

In the seventh century, one branch of Buddhism, which came to be known as Tantric Buddhism, took all this a step farther by developing an approach that seemed to turn the original sexual disdain on its head: sexual activities in this sect were seen as directly leading an individual toward union with the divine essence. Several writings talked of using sexual fluids as part of religious rituals. In one consecration, a Tantric master would have intercourse with his consort, and then anoint a disciple with the resulting mixture of fluids. Several sexual yogas were developed, described in Tantric writings, to help disciples advance spiritually, with a final consecration in which sexual union produced an ultimate awakening.

Many Buddhists regarded the Tantric writings as a high form of teaching. Some contended that they suggested a spiritual plane that superseded even normal monastic vows—monks and nuns could engage in these rituals, with carefully described sexual positions, without violating their pledge. Other Buddhists (and non-Buddhists) were deeply shocked, and insisted that the original ascetic principles must be observed. As Buddhism spread to Tibet, monks there tried to resolve the dilemma by representing sex symbolically, not through real public acts; private practices might still be carried out, but only in secret. But there were Tibetan figures who also openly celebrated sexuality.

Not surprisingly, both the ascetic and the sexual strands of Buddhism, and particularly in combination, gave rise to all sorts of critical or admiring comments about actual practices, particularly in the monasteries and convents. Buddhist monks and nuns were often portrayed as engaging in all sorts of wild behaviors; Chinese literature discussed nunneries rife with sex with outside men, lesbianism and general moral corruption. Some Buddhist temples may have been used as places where courtesans could safely go in public, because the Buddhist approach might pardon their transgressions.

As Buddhism spread in East Asia, it could at the same time be used to reinforce older rules, for example against adultery or easy divorce. Buddhist advice could help support the goal of female virginity before marriage.

But it is difficult, in fact, to determine what general impacts Buddhism had on sexuality. Obviously for a minority, destined for the monastery, the religion discouraged sexual activity; but for another minority, open to the Tantric approach, it provided important ritual outlets. Many ordinary people, sincere Buddhists, might well have concluded that the religion didn't in fact address sexuality particularly clearly, muting its impact on actual practice. Certainly, throughout Asia, the spread of Buddhism was compatible with continued folk interests in protection against male impotence, where both rituals and herbs might be used (bathing the male genitals in pistachio juice was a common approach in China) and with other earlier practices. The fact that Buddhism not only offered conflicting approaches, but also avoided most specific rules and regulations (except within bounded institutions like the monasteries) in favor of generalized stories and promptings toward contemplation, further reduced impact. Buddhist discussion of sexuality and even sexual positions was rich and varied, but a more detailed commentary on daily issues like birth control, abortion, or masturbation was largely absent.

A particular challenge exists concerning the relationship of Buddhism and homosexuality. Non-Buddhist popular opinion in places like China and Japan often accused Buddhist monks and nuns of engaging in rampant homosexuality—but as we have seen, a mixture of confusion and hostility often caused accusations of this sort without clear basis in fact. It is also important to remember that East Asia did not, traditionally, evince great concern about homosexuality. It is also true, however, that Buddhist statements did not specifically address homosexuality, even as they did comment on issues relating to heterosexual desire. At the least, it seems unlikely that Buddhism generated new strictures concerning this aspect of sexuality as the religion spread in Asia, thus implicitly confirming local, and often rather tolerant, customs.

Christianity

Like mainstream Buddhism, the basic approach to sexuality in the Christian tradition, as it developed in the centuries after the death of Jesus, differed strongly from the values of the classical civilizations. Christianity picked up and extended earlier minor strains—we have seen that ascetic denial of sex gained some value in earlier societies, for example with the Vestal Virgins in Rome. Other value systems including that of classical Greece had worried about the destructive possibilities of sex—its possible relationship to violence or immoderation.

But the Christian package, though using some earlier precedents, was new. It developed a fundamental suspicion of sexuality, almost at the core of beliefs about a tension between sexual activity and spirituality, which then expressed itself in a host of new efforts to reprove or regulate a variety of sexual practices. The approach was complicated by divisions within Christianity—the version that spread in the Western world, under Catholicism, was more suspicious than other Christian strains. It was also complicated, inevitably, by the clash with many fairly standard sexual expressions, and a variety of compromises, successes, and evasions resulted. In contrast to Buddhism, however, the Christian approach to sexuality did not develop a real dualism, in which anxiety about sexual desire in one strand would be countered by a link between sex and spirituality on the other. Degrees of suspicion about sexuality varied, with divisions in the religion as well as changes over time: but some suspicion, at the least, was a consistent component of the Christian worldview.

For most of the major Christian groups—Protestantism would, much later, come to differ—it was vital, at the outset, to establish that Jesus was born of a virgin, not as a result of normal sexual activity. As a part of the holy trinity, Jesus was regarded as divine, and in predominant Christian belief this divinity was not compatible with human copulation. So Mary was a virgin, with the baby Jesus implanted by divine intervention. This was of course a marked departure from other religions in the classical world that had not ventured such a complex statement about divine presence among mortals, and that had often been quite comfortable with the idea of sexual exploits among the gods and as sources of other gods.

The Christian approach built on the Jewish conception of divine power as far removed from the doings of ordinary humans. It would also pick up on Jewish emphasis on the importance of confining sex to marriage and to a focus on procreation. And it would build on other precedents, not only in Jewish law but also in Greek culture, that emphasized the moral weakness of women, the need for strong controls over members of a gender who, though they possessed immortal souls, were closer to animal behaviors than were men.

Christian hostility to expressive sexuality built steadily in the early centuries of the religion, in part perhaps in reaction to the sensuality so evident in the Roman upper classes. Pride in sexual restraint as a path to spirituality gained ground. Most early religious hermits—the prototypes of later monastic orders—renounced sex as part of their larger asceticism and rejection of things of this world. Some, like Saint Jerome, became famous for their massive and ultimately successful struggles against sexual temptation. Jerome lived a hermit life in Syria between 374 and 379 CE, and returned to Rome as an impassioned advocate for virginity, finding a ready audience among wealthy female Christian converts. Jerome urged that marriage was a distant second best, as a life choice, to virginity—virginity had been the human condition before the Fall in the Garden of Eden, whereas marriage drew the mind away from the contemplation of God. Jerome urged husbands and wives to become celibate and to raise their daughters to remain virgins. Marriage was preferable to outright fornication, but husbands must be warned against loving their wives too much; undue sex even within marriage was a spiritual mistake. Widows should not remarry, for doing so was only slightly better than prostitution.

These were extreme views in some respects, but it was true that the Western Church came increasingly to urge that a celibate life was spiritually preferable. Western monastic orders were uniformly vowed to celibacy, and over time priests were also required to remain celibate as a condition of their holy state. Marriage, in this state of things, was acceptable but inferior. Christian theologians like Augustine would add to the belief that sexual activity was only the result of human sin, not present in God's original creation. And Christian writers agreed that sex, as well as death, would be absent from the heavenly paradise to which Christians should aspire. To be sure, the Eastern Orthodox Church did not entirely agree, allowing priests to marry; this was a key difference between the two main branches of Christianity. Even in Orthodox Christianity, however, priests should be married before their ordination, and their sex lives once ordained were governed by elaborate rituals. And Orthodox monasteries urged celibacy outright. In the eleventh century, a group of women, probably prostitutes, approached the most famous monastic complex in Greece, trying to lure the monks away from their religious duties by disguising themselves as shepherds. The result was an edict not only confirming celibacy, but banning women from any proximity to the mountain on which the complex was located.

The existence of monasteries and convents, and in the West the priesthood, undoubtedly provided important refuge for people uncomfortable with sexual activity for whatever reason, though of course there were many other motives to join religious orders. At times, again particularly in Western Europe, individual monks and nuns developed apocalyptic religious visions or performed acts of extreme renunciation—including prolonged fasting—in ways that might have involved transferrals from sexual fantasies, though of course this point is open to dispute. On the other hand, some presumably celibate religious leaders could write persuasively about the validity and importance of sexual pleasure. The nun Hildegard of Bingen (twelfth-century Germany) wrote openly about the importance of pleasure in conceiving children—she argued that children conceived by passionate parents were more likely than others to be male, strong, and healthy, and her writings may contain the first Western description of a female orgasm, portrayed in terms of heat descending into the female genitals. Commitment to celibacy could have complex results.

The Christian approach had ambiguous implications for the use of eunuchs. On the one hand, Church leaders appreciated the sexual purity of a castrated man; on the other, they tended to look askance at the practice of castration. In the Byzantine Empire, hostility to eunuchs gradually changed, as some eunuchs became bishops and others served the emperor. In Western Catholicism, Church law in principle outlawed castration, and eunuchs were not widely used. On the other hand, in the later postclassical centuries castrated boys, or *castrati*, began to be widely celebrated for their singing ability, which extended into adulthood. This practice continued in Catholic regions into the eighteenth century, with peasant families in places like Spain often castrating some sons in hopes of placing them in a good job with a leading church choir.

More important results of the Christian impulse to place special value on chastity involved marriage itself. Expanding on the idea the marriage was a second-best spiritual state, both Catholic and Orthodox Churches not only urged restraint even in marital sex, but attempted to ban sexual activity outright during key religious periods of the year, most notably in Lent, the 40 days before Easter, but on other religious holidays as well, including Sundays. Within marriage, even on approved days, sex should be directed at procreation. Christian writings—despite mavericks like Hildegard—tended to stress the physical as well as spiritual dangers of sex: sex weakened the body (one common belief urged that a male orgasm was equivalent to losing 40 ounces of blood) and easily linked as well to the sin of gluttony. Careful diet was recommended as a means of reducing or controlling sexual desire. Some ideas circulated that only one sexual position, man on top, or what came to be known as the missionary position, was appropriate (presumably to maximize attention to procreation), and that even married couples should not remove their clothing for sex.

Following this general approach, almost all practices that might distract from procreative sex, or aim at pleasure alone, were newly and vigorously condemned. Church leaders devoted considerable attention to defining and attacking incest. Adultery, of course, was severely proscribed. Christian law (in both Eastern and Western Europe) gradually evolved to include punishments for male as well as female adulterers, though women continued to receive harsher treatment. In Western Europe a man convicted of adultery might lose his rights to his wife's dowry or any wedding gifts. But earlier Germanic law that had allowed a husband to kill an adulterous wife was gradually modified, and Christian leaders increasingly urged forgiveness, even by a wronged husband, so long as the wife completed extensive religious penance. Women, more than men, could be excommunicated from the Church for adulterous behavior.

Christian teaching strongly attacked both contraception and abortion. Abortion was murder, pure and simple, and in the Eastern Church even a natural miscarriage required a woman to do penance. Contraception, preventing births, was in principle an equal crime. Numerous Christian law codes, for example in England, stipulated the death penalty for abortion. Christian doctrines probably discouraged medical knowledge about abortion techniques, available for example in the Islamic world. On the other hand, Christian leaders debated the point at which a fetus acquired a soul—generally agreeing on about 18 weeks into a pregnancy; before that point, despite official disapproval, actual opposition to abortion was limited, and there were very few cases of actual prosecution for this crime.

Masturbation was another prime target in principle, again given the general concern about sex and the desire to focus it on procreation. The early Christian Church may have paid little attention to this issue, but it has been argued that high disease and mortality levels in the late classical and early post-classical period prompted new attention to the prevention of "wasting of seed." People were supposed to fast for 20 days if they were guilty of this sin, and punishment increased, to include flagellation, for masturbation committed in groups or by religious officials. Long penance was required of women who used instruments to please themselves sexually. Later, in the post-classical period, Christian theologians began linking male masturbation with witchcraft and the creation of demons; Thomas Aquinas termed the act a worse crime than rape, for it went against both nature and reason whereas rape was only against reason (only in the late nineteenth century did the Catholic Church officially reverse this view).

Rape itself did receive increased attention as a crime, though opinion differed as to whether it was a sexual crime or a property crime (damaging a daughter or wife who was property of father or husband). Certain types of rape, for example of a highly placed young woman, could receive severe punishments, including death. In fact, it was very hard for women to prove that they had not somehow consented, and in many Christian countries if pregnancy resulted from forcible sex it was no longer rape at all. At the same time, courts frequently ruled that a man had to marry a woman he raped (assuming both were unmarried at the time); this led to frequent rape accusations when the woman or more commonly both parties wanted to get married against parental resistance: the rape charge was a way around the parents. It is not clear, in an often-violent society, that women gained much actual protection against forced sex.

Christian Europe more generally produced a newly ambivalent view of women in relation to sexuality. On the one hand, virgins were valued; and a variety of male sexual actions could be regarded as sins—women were not the only offenders. Christianity probably reduced the inequality between women and men in sexual matters, compared to most of the classical societies. On the other hand, the idea that Eve was the first sinner (then drawing men into sin) and a more general belief that women were morally inferior to men helped justify greater penalties for women adulterers and the ambiguities surrounding rape. Gender differentials showed in beliefs concerning remarriage: widows were often discouraged from remarrying for several reasons but including distaste for female sexuality particularly if the woman already had children, whereas men who lost their wives were almost expected to remarry. They showed also in practices around divorce: Christian teaching urged against divorce and religious law made it difficult to obtain, but men (particularly in the upper classes) found more ways around these constraints than women could.

Christian ideas about sex affected three other major areas: prostitution, sexual culture and homosexuality. Christianity severely limited public representations of sex, particularly in art, which became overwhelming guided by religious themes. No civilization had so thoroughly reduced erotic cultural expression, as did Christian Europe, either before or during the classical period itself. Some sex manuals continued to be written and circulated, however, and as we have seen, individual Christian writers might comment in unexpected ways. Occasional pornographic writing also existed, describing practices condemned by the Church as emanating from the devil. More systematically, the revival of cities and urban culture in Western Europe helped generate some new openings by the thirteenth century. A series of French stories, called *fabliaux* or fables, strongly differed from the asexual kinds of romance being touted by the troubadours of the same time. The *fabliaux* depicted very earthy kinds of sex, taking delight in unfettered lust. Acrobatic sexual positions are described, probably partly as a source of humor. In one story a cowardly knight is embarrassed by having to kiss a woman's crotch, and in another ("the Knight who conjured voices") a woman's anus talks to her vagina to find out why the latter would not answer an invitation from a knight (the answer was, it was stuffed with cloth). This kind of pornographic writing would also influence more serious literary stuff, such as Chaucer's *Canterbury Tales*. References also to sexual symbols, such as the rose for the vagina, also increased with time, linking even the visual arts to sexual themes. It remains true, however, that the Christian orientation seriously, and distinctively, reduced sexual cultural outlets—and some historians have argued that this long drought helps explain why, by the sixteenth century, interest in sexual expression began to rise so rapidly in the same society, as a rebellion against earlier constraint.

Prostitution was a challenge to Christianity. On the one hand, it was clearly a sin. All kinds of women who indulged in sex for pleasure—including, at times, women who had sex before marriage—might be lumped under the heading prostitute in postclassical Europe. It was not new for a society to divide women between the respectable and the unrespectable, but Christianity tended to increase the vigor of these distinctions. More rarely, men who used prostitutes might also come in for comment: in the Byzantine Empire, a wife could divorce a man who consorted publicly with a prostitute. On the other hand, Christian forgiveness might also apply: important stories told of former prostitutes who renounced their evil ways and even attained sainthood. With time, the Church also became more open to the idea of prostitutes who abandoned their profession and sought to marry. Christian leaders also recognized not only that prostitution seemed inevitable, but that it might also provide a better way to deal with male lusts than other mechanisms. Even St. Augustine approved of prostitution on this basis, for it helped protect good women from the excesses of male desire.

In fact, prostitution flourished in Christian Europe, particularly as cities grew (and in the prosperous Byzantine Empire from the outset). Cities sometimes tried to outlaw prostitution, but more commonly they sought to regulate the practice and often to profit from it. By the late postclassical period, as sexual restrictions seemed to be easing in so many ways, some cities opened municipal brothels. Prostitutes might be required to wear special clothing or a marker—in Paris, a red knot on the shoulder was the badge. Streetwalkers conducted business in taverns, churchyards and bathhouses. Popular street names reflected concentrations, like Maiden Lane in London, or Rose Alley from the common phrase for sex with a prostitute, "to pluck a rose." Brothels often organized foreign women in cities, who had trouble getting other jobs; some prostitutes were forced by parents or husbands to earn extra money for the family. There was little protection for the profession; only in Sicily, exceptionally, did a law of 1231 condemn the rape of a prostitute. Birth control was widely practiced, mainly by using special herbs for contraception or abortion, for birth rates seem to have been low; some prostitutes probably also avoided vaginal sex in favor of other methods. Overall, Christianity, so important in other sexual areas, seems to have had relatively little impact on this aspect of urban sexuality, except perhaps in making the low social status of practitioners, their lack even of basic property rights, unusually clear.

Christian impact on homosexuality, on the other hand, was substantial. Here, the blanket of sin descended with potentially smothering results. We have seen that Roman commentary began to move away from approval of homosexuality, and to an

extent Christian ideas simply extended this. Jewish hostility to homosexuality as polluting, a sign of lack of restraint, also factored in. Historians have argued over whether
Christian opposition to homosexuality crested fairly early, or whether full condemnation awaited the eleventh or twelfth centuries, but, while the discussion is important,
there is obvious agreement on what ultimately happened. Certainly, urban regulation
of homosexuality, lax still under Rome, increased steadily under Christianity. By the
early sixth century evidence of homosexual activity virtually disappears—not of course
because the activity ceased, but because it had to go underground. Some inconsistency
remained. Pope Gregory III in the eighth century set penance for lesbian and male
homosexual acts (revealingly, twice as great for men, whose superior morality offered
less excuse; and more still for priests)—this suggested the sin, but also provided a way
to expiate. Spain was long known as more lax on homosexuality than other parts of
Europe, perhaps because of the Islamic heritage.

Condemnation of what contemporaries came to call sodomy did, however, increase
with time. While sodomy could refer to anal intercourse in general, Christian focus
rested primarily on male homosexuality. Homosexuals and homosexual acts were
linked to bestiality, to Jews, to Muslims, and to necrophiliacs. Accusing groups, including monks or priests, of homosexual behavior became a meaningful taunt.
Increasingly, not only Church rules but also State law set severe punishments for
homosexual activity. The plague of the fourteenth century, which massively reduced
population, led to an even more intense effort to focus sexuality on procreativity alone,
which helps explain the greater rigor toward homosexuality. By the thirteenth or fourteenth centuries, men convicted of homosexual behavior might be executed by burning, and a few cases did occur for an activity now regarded as the virtual equivalent of
heresy. One Church leader in 1400 called for the death penalty for lesbians as well, and
the Holy Roman Empire did incorporate this into its code in 1532. Some distinctions
were drawn between active and passive partners—in contrast to most cultures that
expressed concern about homosexual acts, where passivity was the troubling issue (as
in classical Greece), Christians tended to condemn the active more than the passive
partner. In law and in outlook, Christianity elevated homosexual behavior to a new
level of hostility. This was true in Orthodox as well as Catholic statements: Eastern
Church fathers early on equated homosexuality with the most serious acts of adultery,
and Byzantine law decreed a death penalty.

Sex in Christianity was a suspect act, justified only within marriage and for reproductive purposes. Even the rare praise of pleasure, as with Hildegard of Bingen, linked
this to procreation. Tensions about issues of gender, with women usually scorned for
potential irresponsibility but men sometimes held to higher standards, and the waver-
ing on prostitution constituted two exceptions to an otherwise impressively consistent
approach.

But how much, finally, did this all matter? Prostitution continued. We cannot assess
the impact of Christian thinking on the frequency of masturbation, but surely the connection was limited at best. Some adultery continued: brothels were sometimes not
only centers for prostitutes but havens for adulterous couples. We can speculate that
the wages of sin had some chilling effect, but it is not clear how much. Premarital sex

continued, with young men frequently engaging in sex before marriage; even more widely, engaged couples often had premarital sex, resulting in frequent births six or seven months after the wedding ceremony, with the Church turning a tolerant eye to the inevitable. Interest in contraception and abortion, both mainly through the use of particular plants, remained high, though as always effectiveness was often limited. Several texts provided information about herbal potions. Some plants, for example, had hormones that, taken after intercourse, could prevent implantation, while other plants, placed in the vagina, served as spermicides. Church leaders continued to criticize, but their urgings may have been widely ignored.

Even more vigorous targets partially withstood Christian onslaught. Homosexual behavior resurfaced with the rise of cities. By the eleventh century, while attacks increased, on the one hand, a sense also emerged that homosexual acts might be associated with artistic and intellectual creativity. We know less about the underground gay culture than we would like—a few centuries later, gay encounters in bathhouses and even secret banquets were part of the scene in places like London, but there is less sense of activity levels in the postclassical period. Many accounts suggest that sexual abuse remained common within ordinary families, including incest, particularly by fathers forcing themselves on daughters. Accusations about sexual activities in monasteries were sometimes exaggerated, but professions of celibacy were clearly not always taken literally. The emergence of a new, bawdy literature in the later postclassical centuries not only shows a new crack in religious repression; it also is sometimes taken as far more descriptive of what actually was going on than the Christian rules themselves.

And even Church and State practice shows the complex relationship between religious rules and sexual reality. For the most part, and with some exceptions in the last round of attacks on homosexuality, Church officials were eager to see specific sexual acts as sinful, rather than people as sinful. Homosexuals (at least until the end of the period), adulterers, prostitutes, and others could repent of their ways, do penance, and re-enter religious fellowship. The Church thus offered paths through which complex sexual behavior might be reconciled with Christian views—which helps explain why sexual interests continued to differ from the firmest prescriptions. Even the addition of government penalties need not be taken totally seriously. Most governments were reluctant to administer the toughest punishments on the books—at times, indeed, harsh penalties were so excessive that laws were essentially ignored. It was not hard for powerful men, for example, to escape rape charges, but even homosexuality convictions seem to have been rare—at least, of the sort that would encounter the death penalty. This was true, for example in the Byzantine Empire, and also in several Western cities that in principle imposed beheading, but in fact more commonly simply fined offenders. Penalties for abortion, though on the books, were only rarely applied, particularly of course because women themselves usually gathered the herbs that were used and kept their activities secret; outright surgeries were much less common. All of this additionally complicates assessment of the actual impact of the Christian teachings.

What is clear is that the Christian approach brought many innovations in principle, some of which have continuing impact in Christian or Christian-heritage cultures. The approach definitely altered artistic and other public expressions of sexuality, certainly in contrast to Rome, though new openings developed in the later post-classical centuries. Christian strictures also limited some traditional behaviors. Open use of concubines, for example, declined steadily, in contrast to Roman precedent and to other societies in the post-classical period itself; Christian leaders, both Catholic and Orthodox, made real progress in discouraging and punishing concubinage, though some priests, barred from marriage, engaged in the practice. Even more generally, while powerful men had sexual opportunities ordinary people lacked, the degree of difference in sexual access, based on wealth and status, was less than had been true in the classical civilizations or what remained true in Islam. Beyond this, Christianity undoubtedly impelled some behaviors to become more secretive and, probably, more fearful—as with homosexuality. And even when it is doubtful that new rules altered general behaviors, as with masturbation, they could create new guilts and hesitations that would have their own impact on sexual life. All of this operated, of course, within a recognizable agricultural context in which women's fidelity gained more attention than men's and in which sexuality was strongly linked with reproduction.

In the early twelfth century, the brilliant French theologian Peter Abelard, a priest, set out to seduce an attractive young student, Héloise, niece of a powerful bishop. A passionate affair ensued, with Héloise soon pregnant. Her uncle was willing to have the couple marry, but when he thought Abelard was backing out he sent thugs to the philosopher's apartment, who castrated him. Both Abelard and Héloise, deeply shamed, then accepted monastic life, while exchanging love letters that later turned more toward commentary on how Héloise's convent was functioning. The story shows how sex could overcome Christian scruples, a sign of the limitations of the religious approach. It also shows how religious standards could seem to legitimate a private punishment far different from what would seem suitable today. Christian sexuality, in the postclassical period, mixed biological impulses, some of the particular needs of agricultural society, and the vigor of a new set of cultural standards.

Islam

The emergence and rapid spread of Islam after 600 CE was one of the guiding developments of the post-classical period, with deep impacts on Africa, Europe and various parts of Asia. With foundations in Judaism and Christianity, which the Prophet Muhammad acknowledged as vital precursors of Islam, it was not surprising that there were many overlaps in beliefs and practices. Christianity and Islam had some violent encounters during the post-classical centuries, but there were also periods of considerable mutual tolerance, for example in Islamic Spain, shared trade, and shared influence, particularly as Christian leaders assimilated some of the commercial and philosophical advances in the Middle East. Islam and Christianity displayed far more similarities with each other than either did with Buddhism, reflecting Buddhism's quite different origins. In sexuality, however, there were some striking distinctions, reflecting intriguing divisions in beliefs: while Islam imposed some strict rules over aspects of sexual behavior, it did not reflect the basic suspicion of sexuality so striking in early Christianity.

Islam's impact on sexual behaviors was also conditioned by precedents and conditions in the Middle East; a far more urbanized and in measurable ways sophisticated society than Western Europe was during the postclassical centuries.

Islam developed no systematic stake in claiming that chastity created the highest spiritual state, or that sexuality was contrary to religious goals. In this, obviously, it differed from both Christianity and Buddhism. Islam generated no separate institutions in which extreme piety and sexual denial would be partners. It claimed no exemption from sexuality for religious leaders. It did not emphasize a sexless original creation which human sinfulness destroyed. The Islamic view of heaven, in marked contrast to the Christian counterpart and implicitly to the Buddhist idea of spiritual advancement, included sexual delights—this would be one of the rewards (admittedly, most clearly for men) of faithful religious observance. The Islamic paradise, in the popular view, promised unearthly potency for men, plus choice not only among a pool of virgins but also women spirits, called *houris*, with hair like silk, among whom men could have as many as they desired. Sex and reward for religious devotion here went hand in hand. And before paradise, here on earth, a sense could develop that since the love of men for God could not be fulfilled in this life, sensual love was an appropriate if obviously incomplete substitution.

Islam could, to be sure, generate systematic concerns about sexuality. In the ninth century, a separatist sect, Kharji, emerged with much more restrictive views than those prevalent in mainstream Islam, and with considerable support for the religious value of celibacy.

More important for most Muslims was the annual link between restraint and piety during the holy month of Ramadan, where no sexual activity was supposed to occur from dawn to dusk—accompanying the ban on food and drink. Here, Islam joined other major religions in seeing religious merit in control over appetite.

Aside from special points of religious obligation, however, Islam in the main combined a belief in the normalcy and desirability of sexual activity, with firm regulations designed to focus sex on marriage and to monitor the sexual behavior of women. Marriage was seen as a vital institution in controlling the sexual impulse, which, though valid, could get out of hand and lead into sin. The theologian al-Gahazli, writing in the eleventh century, saw one of the advantages of marriage in "the overcoming of carnal desire [to be protected from the devil]." Some Islamic writings urged men to limit their sexual activity with wives, focusing primarily on procreation. On the other hand, marriage was more generally viewed as a union of a chaste man and a chaste woman for whom sexual union was not an ordinary act, but an act of *sadaqa*, or worship, for each partner. Any form of sexual enjoyment was permissible except anal intercourse or sex during menstruation. Women were expected to shave their pubic hair as part of making themselves attractive. Husbands should perform sufficient foreplay that wives would be ready for pleasure, and should wait for wives' orgasm before enjoying their own. If a man is stimulated by seeing another woman he should hurry home and have sex with his wife to release, but also to control, his passion.

Islamic law was reasonably lax on the subject of abortion, and Middle Eastern doctors in the post-classical period gained increasing medical knowledge about successful procedures—ultimately influencing medical expertise in the West as well. Muhammad believed that only in the final phase of fetal development was a soul involved. All of this contributed to a tolerant approach toward contraception and abortion alike. Women could try to abort even without a husband's permission, provided that they had good reason for wanting the abortion. Contraception was even more openly endorsed, since the validity of sexual pleasure was clear. Laws recognized that problems with health or economic conditions might require protection against unwanted children. Muslims probably used a variety of contraceptive plants, and also employed *coitus interruptus*, for example in cases of intercourse with prostitutes or slaves. Islam regarded masturbation as a sin, though not as a major offense. In general on these issues the acceptance of sexuality reduced levels of religious concern or, through this, any effort to involve the state.

Islamic principles, building from the example of Muhammad itself, also allowed polygamy, though the careful requirement that men maintain the economic capacity to support more than one wife created clear social distinctions. Wealthy males, however, had approved opportunities for sexual activity with more than one spouse. It was assumed that a good wife would obey a husband's requests for sexual access. At the same time, religious writers, including al-Gahazli, emphasized women's right to sexual fulfillment.

Both men and women had rights to divorce, but the procedure was far easier for men. At least occasionally, Muslim men took wives fairly casually—this was true for example of the traveler Ibn Battuta, who occasionally married during his travels and then renounced the wife when he was ready to leave—and this could obviously have sexual implications. In Shiite Islam, a concept of *mut'a* or temporary marriage developed—a marriage of sexual pleasure—in which men and women got together with no intention either of reproduction or of forming a household. This was eventually prohibited by the Caliph Umar, but the practice lingered.

Islam offered complex views on homosexuality, but the overall approach included considerable tolerance. Homosexual relations among the elite were not uncommon, with the man taking the more passive role seen as essentially feminine. Cross-dressing was a popular form of entertainment in some circles. Male prostitutes, dressing like women, operated in the larger cities from the ninth to the eleventh centuries. Some revival of earlier Mediterranean traditions, with older men developing erotic relationships with younger men, was also reported, and some writers urged homosexual activity (along with heterosexual) for their sons as a means of gaining experience and avoiding boredom. In some cases even pederasty—that is, sexual relations with boys—was tolerated. Some visions of heaven included not only the *houris*, but also *ghilmaan*—boys "white as pearls," ready to serve the martyrs for the faith. Pubescent boys could be described as attractive and dangerous, as with women. On the other hand, some homosexual acts came under the heading of adultery and could be punished by law—though strict rules of evidence made it difficult to prove a case. Anal sex was a sin, and could call down God's wrath. Lesbian relations among women drew less comment, but there were widespread reports of lesbian contacts within the harems.

Islam strongly emphasized the importance of female virginity before marriage. A bride would be immediately repudiated if it were discovered she was not a virgin. Muslim girls were raised with marriage as a goal, and of course, in some contrast to Christianity, there was no sense that from a religious standpoint this was a second-best choice. In general, girls were given in marriage quite young, often at ages eight to nine; they were not expected to begin married life until after puberty, but the early age helped assure virginity prior to marriage. As Arab society evolved—this was not a general practice in Islam initially—respectable girls donned the veil at this age as well, as a symbol of modesty and chastity, a revival of traditions that had developed earlier in the Middle East. Stories praised women who resisted male sexual advances until an appropriate marriage could be arranged: thus a seventh-century tale from the Iraqi town of Wasit featured an emir who wooed a beautiful woman who refused him because he did not properly ask her family for her hand; when he tried to seize her, her brothers killed him. The moral of the story was that both the woman and her brothers had behaved in exemplary fashion in protecting her purity. A girl's chastity was vital to the honor of her whole family, and although not sanctioned by the *Quran* some families punished girls severely, even violently, if their chastity came into question.

Islamic law fiercely opposed adultery, and both parties, male and female, could be subject to harsh punishment. The *Quran* made it clear: "… the fornicatress and the fornicator—scourge each of them with a hundred stripes." Adultery might easily be likened to false belief or other crimes directly against religion. Many husbands felt authorized to take matters into their own hands and use violence against a suspected wife. At the same time, the law created a substantial burden of proof in principle—four witnesses were required, and if they could be not produced the accuser (usually though not always the wife) would be punished for slander. As in Christianity, Islamic authorities also urged couples to forgive each other if adultery occurred: ideally, the families of each spouse would intervene to encourage reconciliation, which was viewed as far preferable, personally and socially, to divorce. Islamic law also allowed, though it did not encourage, an adulteress to divorce her husband and marry her lover. The whole area of sex outside marriage thus involved some real complexity for Islam: the basic goals were firm, but various compromises, however unfortunate they might seem to the parties involved, might respond to actual sexual behavior.

The rise of Islam was compatible with a fairly open public culture concerning sexuality. Art, of course, was out of bounds—the religion forbade representations of humans or animals, and even cultures that violated this prohibition, as in Persia, certainly did not build in sexual content. In literature, however, there was wide and varied expressiveness. Considerable materials offered sexual instructions including how to maintain or increase potency for men or on the cosmetics women could use to enhance male arousal. Arab work on aphrodisiacs was routinely included in the sex manuals such as Ahmad bin Sulayman's *The Book of Age-Rejuvenescence in the Power of Concupiscence*, with particular attention to herbs that would increase penis size—a topic rarely mentioned in European handbooks in the same period. Love poetry abounded, some of it with sexual content. A scholar in 828 asked a Bedouin poet what love meant, and the answer was: "To look at each other constantly and to kiss each other repeatedly, this is already paradise." To which the scholar responded that for townsmen the definition was simpler: "You spread out her legs and go into her." Some writers urged love as an expression of soul, not body. In between, a book in 984 claimed that love had once been more spiritual, but "today" when a man loves a girl "he has nothing else in mind but how to lift her legs." The famous *1001 Nights* offered many sexual stories, including tales of women's infidelity: women were seen as interesting but dominated by passion, in principle unfaithful. Nefzawi's *The Perfumed Garden* was another work, describing sexual pleasures less edgily, that did not adhere to a strict Islamic agenda. Several poets also wrote favorably about homosexuality. A princess in the eleventh century, Wallada bint al-Mustaki, attacked Islamic conventions in celebrating her love affairs explicitly. Islam, in other words, opened the door to favorable evaluations of sexual activity and at the same time, during the bulk of the classical period, did not entirely dominate relevant cultural production. The result was a considerable outpouring of work.

In three areas, Islamic principles were clear enough, and clearly restrictive, but they had limited impact. The claims of the royal court, as Arab rulers gained in power and luxury, trumped religion when it came both to concubinage and to the use of eunuchs. The Quran allowed eunuchs—those without the "defining skill of men," to work in female quarters, but it forbade castration. The prohibition was widely ignored, as eunuchs were pressed to serve as guards in the royal harems and, as in China, gained further roles in the bureaucracy of the Arab Caliphate. By the eighth century, as Arab prosperity and political power expanded, caliphs began to create huge harems, with women in veils, often drawn from Southeastern Europe, Georgia, or Armenia. Other wealthy men kept large numbers of slaves as concubines, in addition to up to four wives; when slaves bore their master children, they were automatically freed on his death. Other communities in Islamic territories, such as Jews, also developed traditions of concubinage and polygamy (in contrast to their counterpart communities in Europe, where monogamy gained further ground).

Prostitution was technically banned by Islam, but it flourished in the larger cities, with prostitutes often walking the streets. While, again technically, slaves were not supposed to be used as prostitutes, they often were compelled to practice the trade. Some prostitutes, both slave and free, also served as entertainers, like the singer Ulayya, who performed at the caliph's court and wielded considerable influence with the ruler. As in Christian Europe, prostitutes gained some credit for helping good women by appeasing the male sex drive. As with concubinage, foreign women and women from minority religions figured prominently in urban prostitution.

Overall, Islam's impact on sexuality was clearly mixed. On the one hand, it operated in a region where urban culture was already developed, and resulting sexual practices were somewhat immune to new religious concerns. At the same time, widespread Islamic approval of sexuality in many forms doubtless informed and encouraged many among the faithful, particularly men, but women as well. Finally, however, a few areas of intense scrutiny, especially around the protection of virginity before marriage and the effort to prohibit adultery, could generate not only considerable concern, but active punishments. The overall combination obviously shared some features with other religions but established distinctive characteristics as well.

Conclusion: the complexities of a religious age

The spread of world religions, one of the central developments of this period in world history with impacts still active today, affected sexuality in various ways. New concerns about certain aspects of sexuality emerged, as with the Christian approach to homosexuality or Islamic attempts to inhibit adultery. Without question, characteristic sexual standards emerged in each religious region, adding to the identity of major societies. Approaches to sexuality fed a new set of comparative differentials dividing major parts of the world. In later periods (again including today), when the pace of global contacts increased, these different definitions could lead to tensions and even hostilities; they provided distinctive bases for later evolutions in sexual culture and sexual practice alike. During the postclassical period itself, contacts were not extensive enough for sexual differences to play a very explicit role in mutual perceptions. Islamic leaders, for example, looked down on West Europeans as uncouth and warlike, but they did not highlight sexuality in these impressions. Christians objected to Islam as a heretical religion, but again sexual issues were not at the forefront in these attitudes. The heritage of religious differences over sexuality would emerge much more strongly later on.

During the postclassical centuries themselves, the impact of world religions on sexuality was complicated by several factors. First, of course, was the differential geography of the religious surge. China's sexual history during the post-classical period, though touched by Buddhism and by Confucian concern about Buddhism as a possible distraction from family values, including reproductive sexuality, did not develop primarily under religious auspices. Older themes predominated, interacting with newer economic trends. Buddhism's vagueness and internal inconsistencies reduced its capacity to generate behavioral change, where sex was concerned, in any event. Growing commercial and urban expansion in much of the world of Asian Buddhism expanded opportunities for recreational sex. Prostitution flourished in places like China, despite the Buddhist influence. Marco Polo claimed that there were 20,000 prostitutes in one of the cities he visited. Under the Song (960–1268) and later dynasties, the government operated some brothels directly, for profit, competing with private enterprises. There is some evidence that rates of venereal disease increased in the period, which would follow from the expansion of urban opportunities for sexual activity. At the high end of the scale, talented courtesans developed relationships with powerful men, including emperors, intertwining sexual attractions with key developments in Chinese political history. Sexual manuals continued to proliferate, offering advice on maximizing pleasure for both men and women. Erotic novels also reflected a lack of prudery in post-classical China, such as Li Yu's *The Carnal Prayer Mat.* Homosexual relationships were widely tolerated, and some were described in considerable detail during the period. Confucian leaders did generate some new concern about women's sexual behavior, calling for greater seclusion in the interests of chastity, and toward the end of the period Chinese governments began sporadically to censor erotic literature. Overall, however, even taking some Buddhist influence into account, China's sexual history was not primarily shaped by otherworldly religious values, and a similar gap, between genuine religious impact and considerable continuity in sexuality, seems to describe other parts of Eastern Asia in the postclassical period, including Japan.

The spread of Islam to an unusually wide array of societies inevitably created variations in sexual impact. As Islam became a minority religion in India, it did encourage, though gradually, attempts to keep respectable women out of public view, even among Hindu families. For the most part, however, for the Hindu majority, sexual patterns built on earlier precedents, rather than the newer religious impulses. Prostitution flourished, even, for a group known as *devadasis*, in direct association with some Hindu temples. Hindu art continued to encourage a strong erotic element, and stories still depicted the great passions of the gods. Sexual manuals maintained the earlier tradition. Along with new editions of the *Kama Sutra*, novel works included the *Panca Sayaka* (*Five Arrows of the God of Love*) and the *Ananga Ranga*, a more accessible version of the *Kama Sutra*. On the whole, these works maintained the Indian tradition of urging the importance of mutual pleasure in marriage, and the responsibility of the man to satisfy his wife. Some scholars believe that there was slightly less attention to the female side of things in advice in this period, reflecting a lower status for women; for example, the *Ananga Ranga* does not mention the use of fingers to stimulate pleasure. But there was no wholesale change in tone. Indian rulers continued to practice polygamy and concubinage; here, the example of Middle Eastern rulers actually expanded the use of harems. But monogamy persisted for most social groups in India. Homosexuality remained stigmatized as leading to impotence, in a society that continued to value reproductive sex. Legal codes imposed fines, but punishments were in fact relatively light. Though scorned as a third gender, groups of cross-dressing men gained institutional recognition as the *hijra* (the word meant impotent), serving as bodyguards and entertainers and living in separate communities in interaction both with Hinduism and Islam.

In sub-Saharan Africa, where the spread of Islam was quite selective, another set of distinctive impacts emerged. In some regions, particularly in the northeast, Islamic belief gradually blended with earlier practices such as female circumcision, producing deep regional convictims, still operating today, that circumcision was in fact a religious obligation. In other regions, particularly in West Africa, sincere conversion to Islam did not bring quick acceptance of practices like the seclusion of women. Muslim travelers from the Middle East and North Africa were frequently shocked by the revealing costumes and public roles of women in Islamic families. The great fourteenth-century traveler, Ibn Battuta, while praising Africans for their knowledge of the *Quran*, noted explicitly (though also with some probable exaggeration): "Among the bad things which they do—their serving women, slave women and little daughters appear before people naked, exposing their private parts. ... On the night of the twenty-seventh of Ramadan, I saw about a hundred slave girls coming of [the sultan's] palace with goods, with them were two of his daughters, they had full breasts and no clothes on."

Clearly, the spread of world religions interacted with prior sexual patterns, producing far less uniformity in values and practices than might have been expected, given the fervor of official texts and regulations.

This regional variety must, of course, be combined with the many limitations in the impact religious innovations had on sexual behavior even in the heartlands, like Christian Europe or the Islamic Middle East. Religious leaders often urged change—this was particularly true for aspects of Buddhism and for Christianity. They frequently sought to tighten some standard regulations, concerning adultery and premarital sex, for example, where earlier societies had gained only partial success, by urging new specificity and a new range of punishments by both God and man. They undoubtedly encouraged some individuals to rethink behavior, particularly, of course, those minorities that sincerely vowed themselves to chastity. But the religious surge, also undoubtedly, had less impact in altering average behaviors than spiritual leaders hoped, even as they granted the weakness of the human clay. World religions shifted practical sexual standards less than the introduction of agriculture had done.

But the religious approach must not be written off. It did create opportunities for new types of public disapprovals or private guilts that had realities of their own and could affect behavior at least for some. Though in quite different ways, all three of the world religions, like Judaism before, held sex against a set of higher purposes to a much greater extent than had been true in the dominant cultural systems of the classical era. This could affect both public expressions and private evaluations, at the same and later on, as well. Particularly with Islam and Christianity, concerns were established that could use sexual prohibitions as a buffer against change or outside cultural threat, in ways that continue to surface in the contemporary world. The strong impulse in both Christianity and Islam—and very clearly not usually in Buddhism—to translate religious standards into not only spiritual but also state-sponsored secular punishments created measurably new approaches to types of sexual behavior regarded as illegitimate, going well beyond what most earlier societies had attempted; here too, strong echoes persist today. Finally, despite considerable common ground, the differences among the three major religions opened opportunities for mutual misunderstanding and disapproval once interregional contacts increased: it would become easier than before for observers from one society to pinpoint ways in which another society seemed to be violating divinely-ordained sexual codes, either in behavior or public culture or both—to claim not just differences, but sweeping immoralities. For better or worse, more powerful religions generated new complexities for the world's sexual history.

Most obviously, in the period itself as well as later on, the rise of distinct religions increased, or at least made more visible, the amazing variety of beliefs people can have about sexuality and about what should be recommended or even required in the sexual arena. Unquestionably also, religions inspired corresponding individual behaviors, often in the name of spiritual fulfillment, from lifelong abstention, on the one hand, to considerable indulgence, on the other. In both respects—professed principles and individual behaviors—religion could also add a passionate fervor to sexual advocacies—in favor of some practices, hostile to others—that would affect societal reactions for many centuries.

Further reading

On Buddhism, see S. Young, *Courtesans and Tantric Consorts: Sexualities in Buddhist Narrative, Iconography and Ritual* (New York: Routledge, 2004); B. Faure, *The Red Thread: Buddhist Approaches to Sexuality* (Princeton, NJ: Princeton University Press, 1998); C. Benn, *Daily Life in Traditional China* (Westport, CT: Greenwood Press, 2002); P.B. Ebrey, *Confucianism and Family Rituals in Imperial China* (Princeton, NJ: Princeton University Press, 1991); J.I. Cabezon, ed., *Buddhism, Sexuality and Gender* (New York: SUNY Press, 1992); K. Ch'en, *Buddhism in China: A Historical Survey* (Princeton, NJ: Princeton University Press, 1964); R.H. Gulik, *Sexual Life in Ancient China: A Preliminary Survey of Chinese Sex and Society from ca. 1500 BC till 1644 AD* (Boston, MA: Brill, 2003); N.R. Reat, *Buddhism: A History* (Fremont, CA: Jain Publishing Company, 1994); and H.B. Urban, *Tantra: Sex, Secrecy, Politics, and Power in the Study of Religion* (Berkeley: University of California Press, 2003).

For topics in Christianity, see J.M. Bennett, et al., ed., *Sisters and Workers in the Middle Ages* (Chicago: University of Chicago Press, 1989); J. Boswell, *Christianity, Social Tolerance, and Homosexuality* (Chicago: University of Chicago Press, 1980); P. Brown, *The Body and Society: Men, Women, and Sexual Renunciation in Early Christianity* (New York: Columbia University Press, 1998); E. Levin, *Sex and Society in the World of the Orthodox Slavs, 900–1700* (Ithaca: Cornell University Press, 1989); S.A. McKinion, ed., *Life and Practice in the Early Church: A Documentary Reader* (New York: New York University Press, 2001); E. Pagels, *Adam, Eve, and the Serpent* (New York: Random House, 1998); J. Richards, *Sex, Dissidence, and Damnation: Minority Groups in the Middle Ages* (New York: Routledge; 1990); and T. Shaw, *The Burden of the Flesh: Fasting and Sexuality in Early Christianity* (Minneapolis, MN: Fortress Press, 1998).

On Islam, refer to K. El-Rouayheb, *Before Homosexuality in the Arab-Islamic World* (Chicago: University of Chicago Press, 2005); Y.Y. Haddad and J.L. Esposity, eds., *Islam, Gender, and Social Change* (New York: Oxford University Press, 1998); G.R.G. Hanbly, ed., *Women in the Medieval Islamic World* (New York: St. Martin's Press, 1998); N.R. Keddie, *Women in the Middle East* (Princeton, NJ: Princeton University Press, 2007); G. Nashat, *Women in Iran from the Rise of Islam to 1800* (Urbana: University of Illinois Press, 2003); B. Rogerson, *The Heirs of Muhammed* (New York: Overlook Press, 2006); M. Ruthven, *Islam in the World*, 3rd ed. (New York: Oxford University Press, 2006); and W. Walther, *Women in Islam from Medieval to Modern Times* (Princeton, NJ: Markus Wiener Publishers, 1999).

Chapter 5

Sex in an age of trade and colonies

World history during the period 1450–1750 was marked particularly by an intensification of global trade, now including the Americas, and the development of new European colonial and maritime power. Many parts of Asia, headed by China, profited from production for global trade, as European merchants used silver produced in the Americas to pay for Chinese and Indian crafts and Southeast Asian spices increasingly popular back home. In many regions, growing consumer interests emerged. The inclusion of the Americas in the early modern global system brought provided new opportunities to exchange crops, diseases, and people. New foodstuffs, like corn and the potato, were adopted in Asia and Africa. European and African diseases caused massive epidemics in the Americas, where over 80 percent of the native population would die off within two centuries. This development in turn facilitated the imposition of European colonial regimes throughout many parts of the Americas, while a new slave trade from Africa affected Africa (through loss of population), Europe (through wealth gained from organizing the trade), and the Americas alike.

These diverse developments did not generate a decisive new stage in sexual belief or practice on a global scale. While new versions of Confucian thinking addressed sexual issues in China during the period, for example, actual patterns of Chinese sexuality built on older trends, now further promoted by the expansion of urban prosperity. Western Europeans began to introduce significant changes in family structure, known as the European-style family, with deep implications for sexuality in the region—but there were few obviously global implications in this development.

Overall, and again without claiming any kind of uniform pattern, the biggest changes and challenges in sexuality during the period involved the new encounters among peoples. European merchants and colonial officials began to formulate views about sexuality in other regions. European dominance and population change had a huge impact on sexual standards and behaviors in the Americas, with some long-term effects. New forms of slavery had obvious consequences in evaluations of sexuality and in actual sexual behaviors. Haltingly, and with varied implications, sex began to be intertwined with evaluations of diverse peoples and societies, even linked to emerging ideas about race. While some of the results were short term, as population disruptions began to ease, there were durable legacies as well for world history yet to come. Attention focuses particularly on developments in the new Atlantic world of the

Americas, Africa, and Europe, though European–Asian interactions played a role as well at least in showing how sexuality helped shape mutual perceptions and misperceptions.

Asian developments

The early modern period saw tremendous changes in Asia, particularly with the expansion of the manufacturing economy and the rise of several new empires; but the impacts on sexuality were relatively modest.

The expansion of bureaucracy and legal apparatus in China, particularly, under the Qing dynasty, produced additional discussion of sexual issues. Rape gained new attention, with careful rules about what kinds of evidence might be adduced, but also the penalties for false accusation. In fact, the difficulties of proving rape, plus the need for a woman making such accusations to admit publicly that she had lost her virtue, made it extremely difficult to press charges. It was often agreed that suicide was the best option for a raped woman, and the Qing government paid the funeral expenses in such instances and also provided a plaque attesting to a woman who chose death over dishonor. This kind of development, however, merely added new details to a situation long prevalent in China and in most agricultural societies, in which protections against rape, though discussed, were largely ineffective.

The advent of the Ottoman Empire in the Middle East and Southeastern Europe maintained many previous aspects of Islamic culture concerning sexuality. While the greatest works of Arab, Persian, and North African sexual literature, including erotic poetry but also mystical Islamic discussions of love, had been written in the late post-classical period, materials continued to circulate widely. The basic Islamic stances, urging the validity of sexual pleasure but imposing various prohibitions concerning certain behaviors, continued. Sexual enjoyment in marriage was actively recommended, though couples should cleanse themselves afterwards out of respect for Allah. Oral sex was not prohibited, but as in many cultures strongly oriented toward masculinity it was regarded as somewhat degrading; anal sex was in principle outlawed. Again, themes of this sort simply confirmed previous patterns. Punishments for adultery might become harsher—there are records of death by stoning, for what continued to be seen as a major offense; in general, however, the older approach of whippings followed by efforts at family reconciliation persisted. Women who accused husbands of infidelity but could not prove their charge were allowed to divorce, though prohibited from remarriage, again elaborating an earlier theme.

The power of the Ottoman sultan did expand the practice of concubinage, now bringing the harem directly to Constantinople. A major section of the royal palace, Topkapi, was built for the harem, and of course eunuchs were used in its administration.

The new Mughal Empire in India brought some change to South Asia. Early Mughal emperors, though tolerant in most respects, were, as Muslims, shocked by the open eroticism of some Indian art. Several major statues were defaced or destroyed. Islamic examples also encouraged the increasing seclusion and concealing dress of many respectable Hindu women. The Mughals also established an elaborate harem, with up to 5,000 women available for the emperor. A staff of doctors was on hand to oversee health conditions, including of course the sexual vitality of the ruler himself. Both Hindu and Muslin principles encouraged sexual pleasure within the family. Women often used elaborate perfumes and cosmetics to make themselves sexually attractive within the home. Despite limitations on women in public, some market places became centers for men and women to meet and to indulge in flirtations. Presumably Emperor Jehangir, who ultimately built the Taj Mahal to honor his love for Nur Jehan, met his delight in such a market. Hindu erotic art also continued to flourish, particularly in a new style of love poetry. The poet Upendra Bhanja (1670–1730) offered an ornate celebration of love-making. Songs in Bengali dealt with lovemaking outside of marriage. Praise for beautiful women abounded. Older stories about lovemaking between gods and mortals were also revived and elaborated, with new emphasis on the passionate union between a female believer, a mortal, and the god Krishna. Paintings as well as literature used these themes. All of this provided important embellishment and some novel nuance, but without fundamental change.

Japan experienced some innovations in public culture relating to sexuality in this period, related to general economic and urban expansion, but they were also contested. New theater forms, such as Kabuki, emerged in the sixteenth century. Many plays were organized by women, some of them former prostitutes seeking to leave the profession, and they often included many bawdy references as well as political satire. In 1629, the new Tokugawa shogunate banned female performers, and the genre turned to men, some of whom portrayed women. Dramatic displays of public affection continued to be popular on stage, including representations of "love-suicide." Even with this, however, there is little sense that basic sexual standards were shifting significantly in Japan.

The European style family

More basic innovations were taking shape in Europe, along some unexpected lines. It is not entirely clear why a new family pattern began to emerge in Western Europe by the sixteenth century, but the goal of protecting peasant property from the burdens of too many children played a crucial role. The European-style family, in other words, was a new response to the classical problem of population control in the agricultural environment.

In this distinctive pattern, Europeans began marrying later—at age 27 or so for men, and only a bit younger for women—thus having fewer childbearing years as a married couple. Furthermore, a substantial minority of the poorest people, up to 20 percent of the population, would never marry at all because they lacked access to landed property and depended, lifelong, on wage labor. Here was another key gesture toward population control in a rapidly changing economy and amid new social divisions. The results unquestionably helped stabilize European population for several decades, particularly in the seventeenth century.

The upper classes did not participate in this pattern, continued to feature a younger marriage age for women and larger families, and often displayed more varied sexual interests. Powerful royal courts, as monarchy gained ground, routinely included frequent royal mistresses and other arrangements, though without the elaborate apparatus of the emperors in Asia. Henry VIII, famously, in his desperate quest for a male heir, went through a number of wives in sequence, though this was an expression of procreation concerns more than lust.

But the big development was far distant from the doings of the nobility and royalty, in ordinary peasant and artisan households. Obviously, the European-style family contrasted with more common behaviors in Asia and Africa, where women were married early and higher percentages of the population did form families. The European pattern was, however, translated at least to the British colonies in the Americas, except for the fact that more abundant land permitted a slightly lower marriage age for women (around 23 on average) and a smaller unmarried minority.

Even in North America, and certainly in Europe, the movement toward this new framework had huge implications for sexuality. It could focus attention on sexual pleasure within marriage, as many commentators began to recommend; and certainly the need to have some children, once marriage occurred, was as vivid as ever. But for the unmarrieds or the not-yet-marrieds, real challenges loomed. What kinds of sexual outlets were available for young adults in the ten-plus years between puberty and marriage, or for the minority that never married? The question is particularly salient for the rural masses, where formal prostitution did not normally exist. Rates of illegitimacy went up slightly, to about 3 percent of all children born—not surprisingly, this was a higher level than prevailed in societies like the Middle East, where the marriage age for women was far younger. To a great extent, however, the European pattern seems to have been achieved by a substantial amount of sexual restraint and careful community monitoring of the sexual habits of young people. Courtship activities, for example, usually occurred in public groups at least until engagement was announced. Other arrangements aimed at preventing premarital sex. In colonial New England, for example, when suitors sometimes had to stay overnight in a visit to a fiancée, a bundling board was placed between the man and his betrothed (who were also supposed to remain fully clothed); so that though they might express affection they would not be able to engage in intercourse outright.

The system was not flawless. Illegitimacy was a crack in the control system, though a fairly small one. Pre-bridal pregnancies—pregnancies, that is, which were started by couples who began to have intercourse after engagement but before marriage once property availability allowed a date to be set, constituted a crack as well, but not a very serious one since marriage did normally ensue.

The strong emphasis on sexual restraint did not necessarily prevent continued sexual references and bawdiness in the popular culture. It was not built into a new level of condemnation of sex in general. Active interest in birth control persisted, along with the new family style. Religious condemnations of birth control and abortion actually increased, now from the Protestant as well as the Catholic side. During the witchcraft hysteria of the early seventeenth century, claims of evil magic might be directed against any effort to limit family size. In practice, abortions on the part of married women were usually tolerated if administered for the sake of health or the family economy. Beatings, tight-lacing, and herbal potions like ergot of rye or juniper were the most common methods employed. Herbs, either taken orally or used as tampons, were used for contraception as well, though belief in their effectiveness declined by the eighteenth century, which, as a result, placed new emphasis on sheer sexual restraint.

For though it hardly covered all sexual culture or practice, the new family pattern was serious business, particularly where young people were involved. Communities put a great deal of energy into close if informal sexual regulation. In some places, as in colonial New England, rules and punishments as well as informal shaming were brought into play. Enough prosecutions occurred for homosexuality or bestiality to alert us to the fact that not everyone played by the rules but that punishments were not an idle threat; in 1677, for example, a Massachusetts man was executed for having sex with a horse. On a milder note, in 1660, one Samuel Stearns of Cambridge was charged because he "had Sarah Boatson in his lap and did kiss her," though he was later released. Adulterers, as Nathaniel Hawthorne's famous (later) novel, *The Scarlet Letter*, suggested, might be branded with the scarlet letter A, and placed in the stocks for public ridicule—another sign of active community oversight for sexuality. The European-style family and its North American extension helped generate new kinds of concerns about sexual restraint and birth control that would find additional expression, though in a changing sexual context, in the nineteenth century.

The European system was, of course, quite consistent with Christian morality, which so praised sexual restraint and a focus on reproduction within marriage, though religion does not seem to have caused the system. Certainly, some versions of Protestantism, particularly the Calvinist strain, vigorously supported community campaigns against any kind of sexual activity outside the family. The European system did set Westerners apart in sexual behaviors from much of the rest of the world—and the results of this particular dependence on repression may well have colored European reactions to the more open sexuality and the more sexually-responsive marriage patterns of other societies. This was the main way, in this period, that the European and North American systems connected particularly with global developments, for no other society at this point moved in the Western-style family direction. However, given growing European global presence, this additional stimulus toward condemnation of other cultural styles, whether in shock or with envious licentiousness or both, was no small matter.

The Atlantic world

The biggest news for sexuality during the early modern period involved the new biological exchanges resulting from the inclusion of the Americas in global trade. The new diseases that decimated American populations created obvious opportunities for small numbers of Europeans, mostly men, to gain positions of great power in the New World. Their mastery of guns and horses anchored their military superiority. Their ability to bring in millions of African slaves, to fill out a labor force otherwise squeezed by the results of disease, added another vital component. Sexual imposition was a vital part of this whole process of change, expressing the Europeans' power position but cementing it as well.

The use of sexual force by an invading group was hardly novel in the early modern period. Nor was a belief that the conquered population was somehow sexually inferior and therefore legitimately open to exploitation. The scale of the sexual surge in the Americas was, however, unusually massive. Furthermore, the distinctive features of Christian sexual morality, now enhanced by the further constraints imposed by the European family system, may have generated unusually great opportunities both to condemn local sexual practices and to see the local population in terms of otherwise-forbidden sexual bounty.

The early modern sexual surge associated with European colonialism was not a global development, but an Atlantic one. As we have seen, Asia, though participating strongly in the global economy and in accepting American foods, was not deeply affected.

Even Africa, profoundly impacted by the slave trade, did not see a massive change in sexual patterns. The main new force, resulting from the slave trade, was an altered gender balance in West Africa, combined with overall population loss. Over 65 percent of the slaves seized were male, which created a growing surplus of women in many regions. The response was an increase in polygamy, mainly for economic reasons. Men took multiple wives to create a family labor force that could continue to operate successfully. Indeed, some women formed families themselves, using other, subordinate women as the labor force without any clear sexual implications. But polygamy, not new in the region in any event, was the main result, and with population loss the pressure on wives to conceive a larger number of children was considerable. Some men also complained that, given the excess of women, women became harder to control, and efforts to use sexuality and some outright force to keep women in line may have increased. Domestic slaves within West Africa were often women, used mainly for household functions; and they were regarded as appropriate sexual targets. Finally, in coastal enclaves, European men often took African women as "wives" or mistresses, with little stigma attached, even when the men had wives in Europe, for the women themselves or for the children born of such unions.

Latin America

European explorers and conquerors quickly concluded that Native Americans were sexually loose and immoral. Some of them bemoaned this fact and urged remediation. Others delighted in what seemed to be an obvious opportunity. Some did both.

The differences seemed stark. From Columbus onward, comments proliferated about the revealing costumes and near nudity of the natives, though some Indian groups constituted exceptions, and Europeans were capable of writing about their modest dress. Columbus himself captured a number of Indian (Caribe) women whom he took as his slaves. He gave one to his friend Michele de Cuneo, who later wrote: "I captured a very beautiful Caribe woman ... when I had taken her to my cabin she was naked, as was their custom. I was filled with my desire to take my pleasure with her. She was unwilling, and so treated me with her nails that I wished I had never begun ... I then took a piece of rope and whipped her soundly ... she seemed to have been brought up in a school for harlots."

More than styles of dress were involved. Many Native American groups tolerated or even encouraged sexual activity before marriage, and this was widely perceived, and exaggerated, as part of a larger licentiousness. Thus the French Jesuit Paul Le Jeune wrote in 1639, "There is a most evil custom among the savages. Those who seek a girl or a woman in marriage go to her to make love at night." Europeans also wrote about Indian brothels, though these almost certainly did not exist—but the sense of Indian deviance and the desire to use sexual criticism to justify European actions were not constrained by accuracy.

Europeans also quickly picked up on the common Indian custom of identifying certain groups who would take on the traits of the opposite gender, sometimes engaging in homosexual or more often bisexual activity. A Spaniard in Florida, in the sixteenth century, "saw one man married to another" and described this as "a devilish thing." Others wrote that sodomy—the term for homosexuality as well as anal sex, both soundly forbidden in Europe, was common—"freely permitted," as one put it. French explorers gave the term *berdaches* to these groups, and added their own condemnations.

The ease of defeating Indians in war, plus the recognition of special practices like the so-called *berdaches*, easily created a European sense that Indian men were effeminate, legitimately put aside in any sexual competition. Native women, however, were easily and widely eroticized. European artists in the early modern period not uncommonly portrayed the Americas in terms of female nudity. Explorers like Americus Vespucci wrote more specially about how lusty the native women were, how sexually open, telling one story of women using venomous insects to bite their lovers' penises so that they would grow, with the men later becoming ill and impotent once their service was over. A Portuguese explorer more simply commented that he had inspected the "privy parts" of native women but "even when we examined them very closely they did not grow embarrassed."

Finally, there was the simple fact that, particularly in the Caribbean and in Latin America, relatively few European women crossed over, creating a huge gender imbalance within this small but dominant population. Single women were not in principle allowed to go at all to the Spanish domains. Even if a husband sought to take his wife, he required special royal permission. Gradually, of course, a female population of European origin did accumulate, but it took time, and during the crucial formative decades European male conquerors were there largely alone—except for the indigenous masses.

These several factors generated a complex sequence of results, to some extent throughout the Americas, but particularly in Latin America and the Caribbean. First, Christian missionary groups and other leaders sought to change native ways, toward greater sexual restraint as Europeans would define the term. Missions tried to induce Indian to dress more fully, and gradually they did gain results. They tried to break up extended households, for example among Mayan Indians, in favor of simpler, nuclear families—the extended arrangements were, among other things, seen as sources of adultery or sexual abuse. Mayan customs that had permitted a period of bride service, in which a woman continued to live with her parents but had sex with the husband—

an arrangement that allowed a couple to call things off if they proved incompatible—were attacked as scandalous, as Europeans tried, again with gradual success, to impose once-and-for-all marriages. The result, in some households, was an increase in domestic violence, when there seemed no way out of an incompatible relationship. Attacks on presumed native homosexuality also began early, and here too made steady inroads on a highly traditional practice for particular groups.

The main emphasis, in this aspect of European–native interactions, was on sexual control over women. European influence encouraged growing male dominance within the family, even through violence if necessary. Opportunities for a woman to leave her husband, traditionally fairly liberal, were now severely restricted by colonial law. Girls, also, had to be watched. A Christian Indian girl might be punished simply for being in a cabin with a man. Emphasis on sin and punishment could have measurable consequences. One Indian girl wept because she had allowed a man to touch her hand, "being greatly afraid that it would prevent her from being a Virgin."

Native American habits did not suddenly or completely yield to the new standards of sexual control. Older patterns persisted and considerable confusion could develop as well. Gradually, however, there was impact.

The second main result of the new interaction was simply the often forcible imposition of European male desire on native women. Of course there were many variations on a theme. Indian leaders sometimes offered women to the conquerors as a gift. Some women developed sincere attachment to a European, whether they married or not. Some, more calculating, were willing to engage in sex in hopes of some attendant gain. But there was a great deal of outright rape as well, particularly in the early decades of contact. Not surprisingly, many Indian groups were deeply shocked by these behaviors (which would make later European moralism seem all the more strange and irrelevant), and native communities were often deeply disrupted as well.

The Englishman John Lawson wrote that, "The English traders are seldom without an Indian female for his Bedfellow, alleging these Reasons as sufficient. ... First ... that it preserves their Friendship with the Heathens ... and ... this Correspondence makes them learn the Indian Tongue much the sooner." One Spanish conqueror allegedly fathered 30 children by various indigenous women in just seven years.

Many Europeans recorded their sexual conquests as a matter of great pride, as a sense of virile right began to form part of an American definition of masculinity. The Spanish conqueror Cortes, in Mexico, who quickly took a native mistress with whom he had at least one child, became known as *el shingon*—the fucker—with *huevos d'oro*, or "golden balls." A French Jesuit lamented that the Frenchmen who developed sexual relations with Indian women "all became libertines"—doubtless an exaggeration based on racial prejudice, but an accurate indication that, in some cases, European men did come to regard native women as fair game. The result, among other things, was a rapid increase of mixed-blood children, or *mestizos*, who would come to make up the bulk of the population in many Latin American countries as the pure native stock succumbed to disease. Another result was that, while brothels ultimately developed in some of the larger Latin American cities by the eighteenth century, they contained mainly single women of European origin who could not get other jobs. Native women were seen as sexually available, again by force if necessary, so that the idea of their selling sex for money simply made no sense.

Of course there were efforts to resist, particularly as colonial society became more organized. Individual women, like the unwilling partner of Columbus' friend, might fight back—a Spaniard in Florida tried to rape a woman who squeezed his testicles so hard that he gave up in pain. Some outright warfare resulted, at least in part from resentment at European sexual depravations. Guillermo Como wrote that, "Bad feelings arose and broke out into warfare because of the licentious conduct of our men toward the Indian women, for each Spaniard had five women to minister to his pleasure." Other indigenous communities simply tried to hide their women whenever they heard the Spanish were coming. By the eighteenth century, some native or *mestizo* women also tried to have recourse to law. In Mexico, Catarina Maria brought an indigenous man to court on the charge of rape, asking either for money or marriage; she lost because the court could not be sure she was a virgin before the encounter. As always, the accuser's own reputation suffered in the process. Married women had greater success in going to the courts in rape cases, but the resultant penalties for rapists were not great, and most women did not find the process worth the trouble; few cases were brought, compared to the larger number of efforts by single women.

European missionaries and religious leaders themselves tried to intervene, again particularly by the eighteenth century. One whole army garrison in Mexico was excommunicated because of frequent rapes.

Most important, the problem of sexual violence meant that many families themselves tried to take matters in their own hands, sometimes by attacking an offender directly but most often by trying to regulate the public behavior of their daughters with great care. Protection of honor became a great concern. In Mexico, again, a man named Mariano Guadalupe was whipped because he refused to cover the honor of a cousin he had raped by marrying her. A man who wanted to marry her raped Leonarda Antonia, an indigenous woman, but when she hesitated her own sister whipped her to induce her quickly to marry the rapist.

The overall results of this long period of sexual adjustment in Latin America, and among indigenous populations more generally, were several. First, as we have seen, local habits changed, sometimes entirely in favor of official European standards, sometimes amid greater mixture and confusion. Even when European definitions of respectability did not seem relevant, the need to protect family honor and maintain the marriageability of daughters might compel new restrictions.

Second, a durable pattern emerged in which large numbers of Latin Americans had sex outside of marriage, resulting in an unusually high rate of illegitimacy into the present day. No matter what the Europeans seemed to preach, their actual behavior did not encourage a sense that marriage mattered very much, even for people who were sincerely religious in other respects. As conditions settled, much of the illegitimacy resulted from stable couples who simply did not bother with a ceremony—it was not a consistent sign of sexual promiscuity or violence. It did, however, constitute a distinctive pattern, different from behaviors prevalent in Europe at least until very recently.

The same pattern created a durable divide within Latin American society, in which leaders and upper classes more generally urged a pattern of European-style respectability, with sex confined to marriage and wives and daughters carefully shielded, which contrasted with popular norms (and with the actual behavior of many upper-class men themselves). Recurrently, upper-class movements or reformist governments would try to campaign against real or imagined popular sexual immorality.

Finally, in various social groups, a culture of sexual virility became a key part of the definition of masculinity—a basic element in Latin America's fabled *machismo*. Stories of sexual adventures, bragging about one's prowess figured strongly in Latin American male culture, even when routine behaviors were more sedate. Conquest—linking sex to the colonial experience—became a male badge, without much attention in principle to mutuality or even pleasure.

Atlantic slavery

Many of the same developments occurred amid slave populations brought to the Americas from Africa, as emerged in European–indigenous interactions—except that slaves had, if anything, even less remedy. Sexual exploitation of slaves had been a common part of slave systems in many societies. The American system painted these relationships with a larger brush.

Many American owners assumed that sexual access to slave women was a natural prerogative of ownership. Slave women might participate willingly, hoping for better conditions or even freedom; but there was a great deal of outright force as well. Some urban slave women in colonial North America were forced into prostitution to make money for their masters. A number of colonial American and Caribbean planters kept careful records of the sexual encounters with slaves as a matter of pride, hoping to sleep with as many as possible. Some English immigrants to Jamaica (where there were very few European women) claimed to have been motivated less by the money they could make as planters than by opportunities for sex. In 1709, the Virginia planter William Byrd, known for his prolific sexual relations with servants and slaves (presumably including some males), wrote unapologetically, "I sent for the wench to clean my room and when she came I kissed her and felt her." Rape of slave women, sometimes in the sight of their fathers or husbands, could not only express white power but also serve as a means of control through humiliation. Not a few planter-fathers oversaw the sexual initiation of their sons by arranging for a slave woman.

African women in this situation were frequently described as sensual and wanton—as with Native Americans, these descriptions could be used to justify male desire. Black women thus might be depicted as "hot constitution'd," and as people who "refused to confine themselves to a single connexion to the other sex ... and made no scruple to prostitute themselves to the Europeans for a very slender profit." In colonial North America, given the respectability surrounding white women, black women could easily become objects of sexual fantasy.

The system of slavery also created a complex set of fears and images about black men. On the one hand, black men were regarded as weak and emasculated simply by dint of being slaves, particularly when they could not defend their women. On the other hand, the anxieties and guilts in this form of slave owning created images about the sexual power of African men, including stories about the size of their sexual organs, that fostered vigorous efforts to defend the purity of white women against largely imagined assault. During the early modern period and well beyond, punishments for any suspected sexual approach to a white woman were extremely severe. White women themselves, usually quite aware that their planter-husbands often had sexual relations with slaves but powerless to prevent, had their own reasons for developing unfavorable images of black sexuality.

Impacts on the slave community itself were predictably complex. Fear, here, was sure and justified. An escaped slave, Bethany Veney, wrote: "My dear white lady, in your pleasant home made joyous by the tender love of husband and children all your own, you can never understand the slave mother's emotions as she clasps her newborn children … and when that child is a girl … from her own experience she sees its almost certain doom is to minister to the unbridled lust of the slave owner." Sexual depredations by white owners obviously created a growing number of illegitimate offspring. They also created tensions within some slave families, with some black men using violence or sexual assault to demonstrate their masculinity and attempt to impose some control over female sexuality. Some slave men themselves gave sexual aggression by white men as the most frequent reason they beat their wives.

Conclusion

The Atlantic world of sexuality in the early modern period, created amid violence and cultural stereotyping, had some impact in Europe itself. European images of the New World were various, but they could include fantasies about sexual freedom (in contrast to conditions back home) or condemnations over the immorality of savages, in ways that could condition larger colonial policies, at this point and later on. Increasing European dependence on maritime trade obviously boosted the importance of navies; port centers developed in many parts of Europe accompanied by prostitutes and free-and-easy sexual exchanges very different from standards prevailing elsewhere. On ships, new concerns arose about the possibility of homosexuality. The eighteenth-century British navy developed careful regulations against what it called "buggery," and there were some severe penalties.

Europe's access to the New World also coincided with a rapid increase in venereal disease, literally from the 1490s onward. At one point it was believed that syphilis itself was an American disease, brought back by Columbus' fleet. This now seems less likely. Rather, maritime activity and a new round of wars, initially by French and Spanish armies invading Italy, provided conditions in which venereal disease spread. The result certainly roused concern about what was long known as the "French pox." Doctors, particularly in France (where there was predictable dislike of the catch phrase), began to do new research on the transmission of the disease, and the term "venereal disease" was introduced in the sixteenth century. New condoms were developed in the late sixteenth century, initially not as contraception but as protections against disease. Initially linen sheaths were used, and the use of animal bladders expanded as well. Gradually, awareness of birth control implications would emerge, though major linkages awaited the nineteenth century.

Europe's dynamism, even in a period of considerable sexual restraint overall, thus had varied consequences on the home side of the Atlantic.

The most important results of the Atlantic interactions in the early modern period focused, however, on popular sexual behaviors in many American groups and on attitudes formed about sexuality based on highly differential power relationships. These were centuries, to be sure, before the concept of race was fully articulated. Nevertheless, beliefs about sexual behaviors and sexual appetites, and imagined lusts and fears that attached to these, would have a long lifespan and would help define racial thinking when it further emerged. Most obviously, those in power, particularly white men, often developed assumptions about the sexual availability of women in other groups. Indigenous and slave populations themselves could generate complex self-images in reaction, particularly where masculinity was involved. And at least for a time, the link between sex and violence emerged as rarely before in human history.

Further reading

On Latin America see G.D. Jones, *The Conquest of the Last Maya Kingdom* (Stanford, CT: Stanford University Press, 1998); M.D. Smith, ed., *Sex and Sexuality in Early America* (New York: New York University Press, 1998); J.L. Kessell, *Spain in the Southwest: A Narrative History of Colonial New Mexico, Arizona, Texas, and California* (Norman: University of Oklahoma Press, 2002); M. Restall, *Maya Conquistador* (Boston, MA: Beacon, 1998) and *Seven Myths of the Spanish Conquest* (New York: Oxford University Press, 2003); G. Sayre, "Native American sexuality in the eyes of the beholders, 1535–1710," in M.D. Smith, ed., *Sex and Sexuality in Early America* (New York: New York University Press, 1998); R. Thompson, *Sex in Middlesex* (Amherst: University of Massachusetts Press, 1986); and M. Wood, *Conquistadors* (Berkeley: University of California Press, 2000).

On Africa, refer to T. Burnard, "The sexual life of an 18th-century Jamaican slave overseer," in M.D. Smith, ed., *Sex and Sexuality in Early America* (New York: New York University Press, 1998); W.H. Dunaway, *The African-American Family in Slavery and Emancipation* (New York: Cambridge University Press, 2003); R. Goldbeer, "William Byrd's 'flourish': The sexual cosmos of a southern planter," in M.D. Smith, ed., *Sex and Sexuality in Early America* (New York: New York University Press, 1998); J.E. Inikari and S.L. Engerman, eds., *The Atlantic Slave Trade: Effects on Economics, Societies and Peoples in Africa, the Americas and Europe* (Durham, NC: Duke University Press, 1992); P.E. Lovejoy, ed., *Identity in the Shadow of Slavery* (New York: Continuum, 2000); K. Mann, *Slavery and the Birth of an African City* (Bloomington: Indiana University Press, 2000); N. Zacak, "Sex, sexuality, and social control in the eighteenth-century Leeward Islands," in M.D. Smith, ed., *Sex and Sexuality in Early America* (New York: NYU, 1998); and I. Berlin, *Many Thousands Gone: The First Two Centuries of Slavery in North America* (Cambridge, MA: Belknap Press, 1998).

For other developments, see L. Stone, *The Family, Sex, and Marriage in England, 1500–1800* (New York: Penguin, 1990); M. Hartman, *The Household and the Making of History: A Subversive*

View of the Western Past (Cambridge: Cambridge University Press, 2004); M. Perrot, ed., *A History of Women in the West, Volume III: Renaissance and the Enlightenment Paradoxes* (Massachusetts: Harvard University Press, 1993); and M. Perrot, ed., *A History of Private Life, Volume III: Passions of the Renaissance* (Massachusetts: Harvard University Press, 1989).

Part II

Sex in the modern world, 1750–1950

Some of the most fascinating changes in the history of human sexuality began to take shape in the eighteenth and nineteenth centuries. It was in this period, for example, that dramatic new artificial birth control devices were introduced (which is not the same thing, of course, as claiming they were uniformly available, or desired), including the condom and the diaphragm. In the long run, these devices would increase the opportunity to separate sex from procreation and emphasize sex for pleasure alone—though the evolution here proved extremely complicated. It was also in this period that doctors began to claim a new role in sexual matters, urging that their advice was crucial to sexual morality and sexual health—this was one of the reasons that some of the new birth control devices passed under their control. It was also in this period that a significant new pornographic industry blossomed, using new combinations of print and image and often playing, however perversely, on global themes. In yet another indication of dramatic change, Japan toward the end of the period adopted its first-ever laws against homosexuality, while in Western society definitions of homosexuality changed decisively. There was a lot going on.

A pattern of basic, if disputed, change began in Western Europe and North America, involving both new sexual behaviors and new—though very complex and divided—attitudes to sexuality. Western change inevitably affected other parts of the world, simply because Western power was growing thanks to the society's leadership in industrialization and a new, vigorous round of imperialist expansion. Various societies had to figure out what Western sexual values were all about and how to react to them, or, if possible, ignore them. By the twentieth century even major revolutions, like Russia's in 1917, raised questions about sexuality, another sign that the subject was generating fundamental questions for various parts of the world.

It was also in this modern period that new levels of contact among the various regions of the world, combined with firmly rooted beliefs in the superiority of some sexual cultures and cultural standards over others, began to create serious issues around different sexual traditions that had taken shape in earlier periods. Hints of this obviously had occurred during the early modern centuries, when Europeans judged and condemned Native American sexual habits. But now the implications of contact were more widespread. Westerners were free to judge virtually every other society in light of their own (admittedly complex) values, and by the same token other societies had to begin to decide how to react to Western slurs. The result was a series of changes in public cultures and in legislation designed to fend off global accusations of sexual laxity or to protect regional traditions against outside contagion. The process continues to this day, but it was launched in the previous period.

This section looks at a 200-year span of time, from the first clear emergence of new sexual behaviors in the West to a point at which reactions to change had taken on reasonably clear shape, again in various places, but a point that also was about to witness significant additional innovations—like the widely-heralded "sexual revolution" of the 1960s. This is not a standard periodization in the history of sexuality, or in world history, but it captures key issues in the movement of sexuality away from purely traditional patterns, in many, though not all, parts of the world, and the efforts of traditionalists to hold the line. It also captures the first results of the new confrontations among different sexual traditions. These were two centuries of tremendous dispute, in the West and elsewhere, as new behaviors were matched by conservative reactions (some of them surprisingly successful) and in which extreme statements of pleasure seeking and disapproval both abounded. Every action, whether in new behaviors or in new uses of sexuality in public culture, stimulated counter-action. The one constant, even amid efforts to defend traditional values, was that sex gained growing amounts of public attention, becoming a topic rather than a set of hallowed assumptions. Even social conservatives who wished that sex could be banished from public discourse had trouble staying away from the subject.

We begin with the changes in the West, which seem to have set off the process of reexamination and debate, and then the diverse kinds of reaction around the world, ending with a status report as of around 1950.

Lots of specific subjects figure into the discussion, but there is, at least potentially, a unifying thread. The two chapters in this section explore the relationship between the advent of modern processes like industrialization, or mass consumerism, or new levels of global contact, on the one hand, and sexual behaviors and attitudes, on the other. It asks whether some distinctive relationship exists between these broader changes and sexuality in what is sometimes summed up as "modernization." Not surprisingly, in fact, books have been written about the modernization of sex itself. The term is dangerous, because it ignores the massive modern disputes and the great variations between one society and the next. But modern trends have unleashed new questions about sexuality, in many places, and new challenges to established arrangements. In turn, changes in sexuality and sexual assumptions, and shocked reactions to these changes, have had their own serious influence on world history. Materials in this section open the analysis of the complex relationship between sexuality and modern times.

Chapter 6

Western society, 1750–1950

A first sexual revolution and the Victorian response

At least three forces prompted fundamental changes in sexual behavior and outlook in Western society by the eighteenth century. The economy began to shift toward greater commercialization and more manufacturing, even before the industrial revolution. This disrupted established value systems and gave some young people new levels of freedom and earning power. Ultimately these developments would coalesce in an outright industrial revolution, which would have its own effects on sexual behavior and would add factory life and urbanization to the factors shaping the experience of many people. Cultural changes emerged as well, some prompted by the implications of Protestantism, others encouraged by the eighteenth-century Enlightenment. Basic cultural transformations were not initially aimed at sexuality, but they could have implications at least concerning attitudes toward sex, and in some cases they altered behavior outright. Finally, as the third basic factor, improved nutrition (for many groups; not all) and urbanization generated actual changes in the physical context for sex, particularly in terms of the age of puberty.

Symptoms of cultural change came first. Protestant attacks on Catholicism, beginning in the sixteenth century, had, among other things, urged that chastity did not put people on a higher level of spirituality than did married life. Martin Luther, the pioneer Reformation leader and a former monk, himself pointedly married (a former nun), as Protestants generally condemned the traditional Catholic emphasis on the importance of priestly celibacy and monastic orders. None of this had immediate implications for sexuality, but by the seventeenth century Protestant writers in various places, including Britain, were beginning to emphasize the pleasures of married life, including sexual satisfaction for partners as well as overall compatibility and affection. This was not a revolutionary expression of sexuality, and opposition to sex before or outside of marriage remained very firm as part of maintaining the European-style family system. Protestant thunder on improper sexuality could easily eclipse the quiet reemphasis on marriage and on relationships within marriage. This was the context in which, in 1684, a surprisingly candid sex manual, called *Aristotle's Masterpiece*, appeared in England. This book was widely circulated and translated (a version was printed in the American colonies in 1766), with sales into the 1930s. The book, claiming scientific inspiration, provided information on how best to obtain sexual pleasure, with a definite assumption that both partners should be able to pursue this goal. Soft lighting, sexy clothing, and thoughts about seductive music were among the recommendations. The book offered no contraceptive advice however, urging that the basic purpose of sex was to have children. Nevertheless, despite some traditional elements, something was clearly going on in Western culture.

The impact of economic and social change was more direct and in many ways more measurable, though it moved in the same direction in terms of increasing the valuation of sexual expression. The big change involved the spread of manufacturing and a more commercial economy, even before major technological innovations like the steam engine. Hundreds of thousands of rural workers, both men and women, but all disproportionately young, began by the eighteenth century, to make thread or cloth or simple metal products in their homes, for sale on the market. Some of this was part-time work, some full-time. It had the result of reducing total dependence on agriculture and of putting money wages, however modest, in the pockets of many workers who previously had been dependent on the agricultural household. They could now contemplate behaviors of which parents and community leaders might not fully approve. As they dealt with traveling merchants, to sell their goods, they also learned a bit about urban habits and styles, another potential source of change even in advance of outright urbanization. By the eighteenth century also, population growth began to increase the number of people who could not really hope to inherit much land (population levels rose a full 100 percent in Britain and Prussia between 1750 and 1800, for example). This confirmed the importance of manufacturing jobs, and also began to drive some workers to the cities outright. It also served as another source of relaxing parental controls: if one's father could offer no assurances of an inheritance, there was less reason to accept his full authority—a major threat to the control over youth that had been part of the European family system.

Joining economic changes to new cultural values was a measurable growth in popular consumerism by the eighteenth century, again throughout the Western world. Many ordinary people began to purchase new kinds of household items and furniture. They also showed a growing interest in more fashionable and colorful clothing. This interest in appearance had probably been triggered by new contacts with Asian cloth, thanks to Europe's growing role in world trade. Colorful Indian printed cottons gained particular popularity. By the eighteenth century, these types of cloth began to be made at home, and became far more widely available. The passion for stylish clothing drove a lively second-hand market, for people desperate for consumption but unable to afford first market price, and thefts of clothing rose as well. Not every aspect of the new consumerism related to sexuality, but the growing interest in attractive clothing and appearance surely reflected the kind of cultural change in which sexual contact and expression would become more important as well.

A final factor in the new sexual equation resulted from a gradual but measurable drop in the average age of puberty, which had traditionally been rather high in Western Europe (and particularly the more northern regions). Improvements in nutrition, including protein consumptions, and greater contact with strangers (the result of commercial exchanges and ultimately urbanization), combined to produce this result. By the later eighteenth century, puberty for girls began to drop down from 17 or 18 years of age, and boys had a similar experience. Indeed, it became harder to recruit boys' choirs, as voices began to change at an earlier age. The trend may have been disrupted by the first decades of industrialization, when urban poverty challenged nutritional levels particularly for women, but then it would resume after 1850, leading for several decades to a three-month drop in average onset in every succeeding generation. Obviously, younger ages at puberty automatically raised issues and possibilities for youth sex. They also, and inevitably, produced opportunities for confusion between adults—accustomed to assumptions about one normal age—and the actual experience of their children. One result, emerging in the nineteenth century, was a new focus on adolescence as a time of sexual confusion and danger.

New cultural approval of sexuality, at least in certain contexts, and rapid social and economic change that disrupted established expectations and lines of authority, along with physical changes in sexual maturation that challenged generational relations, all combined to set the stage for truly dramatic shifts in the ways some ordinary people began to display sexual interests. The notion that a first modern sexual revolution followed from these wider transformations is not far-fetched, and historians' discovery of the evidence of this revolution led to dramatic revisions in the understanding of the past, and how the past relates to contemporary life—though it generated fierce debates as well.

*   *   *

The most dramatic development, again starting in the Western world and gradually including the American colonies and then the new United States, from the late eighteenth century onward, involves a startling surge of illegitimate births, and what this surge suggests about relationships between sex and marriage and, probably, about young people and sexuality more generally. This is the change that has drawn the greatest attention and requires the most extensive historical evaluation. But there were concurrent developments added in as well, including quieter changes even in marital sexual behavior and the rise of sexual themes in backroom popular culture. It is the overall package that ultimately requires analysis.

Young people, sex, and marriage

Before the late eighteenth century, the number of babies born outside marriage—that is, the percentage of illegitimate births—had hovered around 2 to 3 percent in Western society. There had been a small increase in some places, like Britain, in the later sixteenth century, only to see levels drop back again in the following decades; and there was some regional variety. It is also true, of course, that the records on this sort of thing before the nineteenth century are not entirely reliable: some illegitimate births may have gone unreported, even in close-knit village communities; some unwanted babies may have been secretly killed. Still, there is general agreement that from the second half of the eighteenth century until after 1850, from central and western Germany through Western Europe, but also in American colonies like Massachusetts, the percentage of illegitimate births rose three or four times over traditional levels, reaching an average of 6 percent by 1850, but in some particular regions rising to 10 percent of all births or even a bit more. More and more young people were having sex before marriage and then, for whatever set of reasons, not getting married. Most, though not all, historians go beyond this statement to conclude more simply that more young people were having sex, period—which of course is where the idea of a first modern sexual revolution comes from. Illegitimacy figures in these evaluations form only part of the story, for, inevitably, given chance, infertility, or primitive precautions (common in some peasant regions) like shouting "watch out" right before male orgasm and thus encouraging *coitus interruptus*, far more premarital sex occurred than the statistics convey. Of course, it is vital to remember that most children were still born within marriage, and that in many rural regions courting couples had often engaged in sex before the actual marriage ceremony—the behavior that resulted in pre-bridal pregnancies—so not everything was turned upside down. But the idea of a substantial change in the sexual habits of many young people, toward more frequent and possibly earlier sexual expression, has a great deal of evidence behind it.

This probable transformation related fairly clearly to the social and economic disruptions of the period. It was most common among elements of the lower classes who were participating in the growing system of domestic manufacturing, who were unsure of any access to landed property, or who headed to the cities outright. Urban workers and craftsmen were also heavily involved. The change would be confirmed and extended by the early nineteenth century in many of the factory cities. It thus expressed new opportunities—to dress more stylishly and to defy parental controls—but also new tensions—the lack of security that resulted from the growing inability to count on landed inheritance in many peasant or farm families. Not all lower-class young people were involved in this new mixture of greater latitude and new social tensions—but enough were drawn in to create a real upheaval in popular behavior.

The change in the records is clear. The cultural and social context is clear. What is less clear is what it all means in terms of human motivations and consequences. Was this first modern sexual revolution a sign of a new youth culture that included a commitment to sexual expression, a joyous rebellion against traditional sexual repression, or was it a troubled reaction to new difficulties in ordinary life—particularly onerous for young women?

Some young people seem genuinely to have given freer rein not only to sexual appetites, but to a larger emotional involvement we might call love. In 1787, a journeyman cabinetmaker in France seduced the daughter of his employer. He did not have the economic resources to get married, and he fled to avoid jail time—not a new set of circumstances. What was arguably new was the attachment he continued to display to the young woman. He wrote ardent letters claiming that he was "unable to forget" the girl: "Everyday I think of you and hope you do the same for me. Tell me how you feel, if you want to make me happy. I remain your close companion." More broadly, observers began to note a growing number of young people who formed attachments based on physical and emotional attraction, often including sex, rather than accepting traditional arrangements that would have included parental approvals and some kind of property settlement, or dowry. Of course, given economic disruptions, dowries were not always easy to come by in any event, but the possibility that some young people were putting romantic feelings and lustful yearnings ahead of economic advantage is very strong—and it is obviously consistent with the fact of increased illegitimacy.

There are other intriguing asides. Some young people seemed to think that the authorities condoned new sexual behaviors. In fact, some changes in law concerning the treatment of illegitimate children, and the interests of governments in promoting population growth, might have given that impression. A young Bavarian woman was asked why she kept having illegitimate children, and her response was simply, and apparently quite happily, "It's okay to have babies, the king has okayed it." For some young people, the idea of sexual pleasure became more widely known, and the opportunities to pursue it more widely available, than in the past. This is the optimistic side of the sexual revolution.

But the downside was stark. For some young men, expressions of sexual appetite became demonstrations of prowess designed to compensate for new economic and status insecurities and boring, demanding jobs. A boy in a German factory, around 1850, watches as young male adults capture a woman in the factory yard, cheering while one of their number simulates sexual intercourse while the woman spits at him. In mixed-sex factories, where workers often dressed scantily because of the heat, opportunities for abusive sex undoubtedly increased, and with them another setting for the increase in illegitimacy.

Amid economic disruption, with traditional, property-based marriage more difficult to arrange, many men surely took advantage of young women who hoped that sex would lead to a durable relationship. They had sex, and then, when the consequences became apparent, ran off, possibly to another city in a highly mobile early industrial climate. They certainly sought sexual pleasure, but hardly a larger intimacy or any kind of mutuality. And the women involved, even when not directly coerced, might have felt they had little choice, through some combination of a hope that sex might produce marriage (or at least stability) and a realization that, for a single woman, economic opportunities were not bright. For some working-class women, unable to offer property to help cement a marriage arrangement, sex might seem the only alternative available—and it did not always work. This was the setting, of course, in many early industrial cities, in which outright prostitution increased. Female workers in a French factory town, paid far less than their male counterparts, talked about selling their bodies as the "fifth quarter" of their working day. There was sexual revolution here too, but a revolution of quiet desperation, not a joyous reach for new freedom of expression.

Not surprisingly, historians have thrown a fair amount of dirt at each other amid these deeply conflicting interpretations of sexual change. Contemporary issues, including feminist outrage at abuses of women, inevitably mix with historical analysis. It seems likely, in fact, that both sides are partly right. New contexts and expectations generated new or more open sexual interests among some lower-class young people, some young women included. For probably a larger number, however, change generated new opportunities for abuse—including a new male sense that sexual expression was an essential compensation for accepting the dirty work of manufacturing jobs and growing economic insecurity—and new limitations on women's ability to appeal to community controls for protection. And one point was quite clear: as the sexual revolution generated new numbers of illegitimate children, often, though not always, abandoned by their fathers, it created durable burdens for their single mothers, often subject to shame as well as poverty, and frequent hardships for the children themselves.

Certainly contemporary observers, quite aware of changes in broad outline, characteristically expressed shocked disapproval (along with frequent exaggeration), even when the abusive aspects of change were not apparent to them. A Bavarian official around 1800 claimed that, "both sexes are so inclined to debauchery that you scarcely find a girl of twenty who's not already a mother." Virgins, another official claimed, were not only rare, but were looked down upon. "Every time single boys and girls go out dancing or to some other public entertainment, they end up in bed." Change was clearly distressing in these accounts, but it was also unmistakably visible—adding to the evidence of the birth records themselves. Whether for good or ill, new types of sexual standards were emerging among many young people in key segments of the lower classes.

The conception cycle

At the same time, again beginning in the later eighteenth century, another striking statistical transformation was underway—involving the distribution of births during the year. In most rural societies in the northern hemisphere, a disproportionate number of births traditionally took place in February and March, which means that a disproportionate number of conceptions occurred in May and June, an expression of the creative juices of the spring season. Up to 40 percent of all conceptions might cluster in those two months. Aside from seasonal influences, the biggest reason for this odd imbalance seems to rest with the need for women's work in a rural household. Having women's work unavailable, even if briefly, in late winter was least damaging to the household—it would not affect their gardening; it did not conflict with planting or harvesting. So, presumably, many peasant families made a deliberate effort to concentrate their procreative sex. But this also means, given the lack of effective birth control devices, that they probably also limited their sexual activity in other months (there was also a small spike in births in September, possibly reflecting some relaxation of caution during the holiday season). Of course, some births occurred at other times, and, of course, there were some birth control efforts or use of plants that could encourage abortion, so there's no implication that no sex occurred outside the spring; but there was a disproportionate focus. Revealingly, this seasonal conception cycle was much less pronounced in cities, where needs for women's work were also less seasonal.

What now began to occur in rural areas was a similar, if gradual, evening out of the conception cycle, reducing this difference between countryside and city. Even today there are still modest concentrations of births, reflecting some seasonality, but distributions are fairly even. This quiet but massive transformation of the conception cycle actually constitutes a dramatic change, certainly in birth records, but probably also in sexuality as well. The immediate cause seems fairly clear: with more non-agricultural work available, including manufacturing that could be done in the home, the need to focus on seasonal factors gradually diminished. From the standpoint of sexuality, the key point was that sexual activity could occur more regularly through the year. Another set of constraints on sexual expression and, possibly, pleasure was loosened—this time not just for the young and certainly not just for the unmarried, but for adults as well. All of this constitutes the second facet of the first modern sexual revolution.

Sexual ideas: pornography and free love

The third branch of the sexual revolution was more purely cultural, though it embraced behaviors at least for a small group—this time more at the upper than the lower end of the social scale. Explicitly pornographic materials were hardly an innovation in the European eighteenth century. Sexual symbolism had been used in European art even in the Middle Ages, building, for example, on the visual connection between the rose and the vagina. The Renaissance, and the printing press, encouraged more overtly pornographic writing, detailing various sexual acts and perversions including flagellation, from the fifteenth century onward.

What happened in the eighteenth century was an acceleration in the production of pornographic literature, probably an intensification of the graphic contents, and certainly an expansion of audience. Specific new themes, like frequent references to male sexual apparatus as "machine-like," also may have suggested a sexualization of wider developments such as technological change. During the eighteenth-century Enlightenment, a number of pornographic authors, and also their booksellers, associated pornography with broader attacks on the political and religious establishment. For a brief period, pornography and reform showed real affinity. This was not a link that would entirely survive, but it suggested, in yet another way, the association of changes in sexuality with some of the wider developments in Western life.

In 1749 John Cleland wrote *Fanny Hill*, under the title *Memoirs of a Woman of Pleasure*, hoping that a large array of erotic scenes would lure a wide audience and allow him to pay his bills (he was in jail for his debts). The book began with an abortive rape scene, which presumably stimulated the heroine, a rural girl who had made her way to London, to seek a life of sexual pleasure. Voyeurism—watching the sex acts of others in a brothel—and masturbation are only the beginning for Fanny, who also later indulges in flagellation, enjoying the sexual stimulation of whips that drew blood, as well as a variety of lovers of various social ranks. Another rape incident and a homosexual scene also crop up. The book drew wide attack and it was ultimately banned (until the later twentieth century), but it was a sign of a widening sexual culture in which explicit stimulation helped draw a substantial readership.

Eager authors by this point were being aided by improvements in printing, which lowered book costs, and by the expansion of literacy. By the later eighteenth century, at least in places like Britain and France, a wide variety of individuals might seize upon pornographic readings. While some copies were particularly destined for the upper classes, and particularly upper-class males, given their prices of production, in other instances shopkeepers and servant girls were identified as avid, if secretive, consumers.

At least occasionally, and not surprisingly, pornography also linked with real life. A French nobleman, the Marquis de Sade, born in 1740, filled his adult years with links to prostitutes, the use of violence in sex (the word sadism was derived from his name), and acts of sodomy, along with periodic orgies in which he seemed to engage in a variety of activities in sequence. Frequently arrested, de Sade used jail time to write novels and plays about efforts to extend the limits of perversion, while also engaging in a variety of sexual activities with his jailers. There is no reason to claim that de Sade was unique in his indulgence of appetite—surely, individuals of this sort have cropped up in many times and places—but he was distinctive in attracting so much attention and in trying to encourage wider public participation.

It is impossible to say how influential this varied surge of pornography was. Many people were unaware of it; many others merely read it for interest and stimulation without regarding it as a guide to life. There were cases, however, as with de Sade, in which groups began to form more widely and openly to pursue certain kinds of sexual gratification, such as sexually-linked flagellation. More generally, the rise of popular pornography unquestionably formed part of the new level of interest in defining and seeking sexual pleasure—even if, in some cases, only on paper.

Distant from pornography, and building more explicitly on the idea that a sexual transformation was a vital part of social reform, a number of writers (both male and female) began by the early nineteenth century to write about the need to cast aside some of the traditional assumptions around sexual behavior. Notably, they began to question the idea of marriage and, with this, the notion that it is normal or desirable for an adult to have only a single sexual partner. Some reformers focused particularly on gender inequalities, arguing that marriage too often, in fact, let men indulge in sexual affairs while their wives were tied to monogamy; both genders, according to this argument, should have freer play. Considerable comment focused on sexual jealousy (and particularly male jealousy), arguing that in an ideal world this possessive emotion should be overcome so that people could seek the maximum possible sexual pleasure. Thus Max Lazarus, in the United States, blasted any idea of an "exclusive property" in a loved one.

Some advocates of change tried to translate their ideals into actual community life, part of the larger utopian movement that crested in the middle decades of the nineteenth century with particular traction in the United States. Many utopian communities focused on other social reforms, either not interested in sexual change or hopeful indeed that sexuality could be played down altogether through attention to other types of social improvement. But a few communities centered on the issue of greater sexual freedom. The Oneida (New York) community, most notably, under John Humphrey Noyes, urged men and women alike to cast aside "private feelings" in favor of larger community sexual access and frequent exchanges of partners. Most of these communities encountered massive public hostility, though there were a few exceptions; and many, including Oneida, found that possessiveness reasserted itself toward a reinvigoration of something like marriage, as actual participants disputed the leaders' advice. But the ideals of free love persisted. A few couples, apart from failed communities, advocated periodic sexual experiences with others: the mid-nineteenth century reformer Moses Hull, for example, told his wife that he had enjoyed other partners and ultimately persuaded her that free love made better people of all involved.

Issues of social class

The clearest evidence of wide changes in sexual behavior, in this first modern sexual revolutionary period, comes from the lower classes. Pornography, however, makes it evident that new sexual interests could also emanate from other social groups.

The class structure of the emerging early industrial society that was forming in the West, along with more open sexual appetites, also created a variety of situations in which class advantage could be pressed for purposes of gratification. This was not a new theme in human history, but its outcroppings became more common and sometimes more disruptive.

Several scenarios were involved. Use of prostitutes by middle- and upper-class men constituted the first, not a brand new circumstance but one that became far more widespread than before. The fact was the economic opportunities for women did not keep pace with demand in the early stages of the industrial revolution. Population pressure on the land was combined with the competition of factory products for goods women had traditionally produced by hand, such as thread. Many women moved to the cities in hope of work, but were disappointed. Some of course may also have been stimulated by aspects of the sex trade—it is important not to oversimplify prostitutes or their motives; but economic pressures were paramount. The result was a growing group of urban women with sex for sale. Many working-class men—particularly single migrants or immigrants—took advantage of these opportunities. But many middle-class adults also participated, often combining these activities with public defenses of respectability and even, in some instances, participating in campaigns to regulate and redeem prostitutes themselves. A significant clientele also developed among secondary school boys and university students. Brothels in Paris, for example, were particularly bustling during school holidays, by the middle of the nineteenth century.

Servanthood and factory employment provided other settings. While there is no way to measure frequency, some factory owners and foremen abused their right to hire and fire women to claim sexual favors. Probably more common still was the sexual exploitation of female servants. During the nineteenth century, working as a household servant, usually living in, became the most common single job for urban women. In this domestic atmosphere, and given the subordination of the position, husbands and older sons of the employing family not infrequently took advantage of the situation. Seduction of servants, some of whom were simply forced, others of whom may briefly have dreamed of marriage and upward mobility, was a not-infrequent consequence, and a substantial minority of servants was disgraced as a result—sometimes contributing to the illegitimacy rates in the process. This could be, among other things, a source of ultimate prostitution, when the young women found no alternate means of livelihood. Patterns of this sort were not brand new, but the situations in which they occurred became more common, with the rise of urban employment for working-class women and amid some cultural encouragements to new expressions of sexuality by men. Stories of fathers treating their sons to a brothel visit for a first sexual experience on a birthday, or looking the other way at a dalliance with a servant, were not just the stuff of fiction by the middle of the nineteenth century.

The first sexual revolution and social reactions

The century after 1750 was filled with significant if varied changes in sexual behavior and some aspects of the public culture. Sexual activity increased for many young people. Expectations of sexual access rose for some men, of various social classes, and the idea of sexual pleasure expanded even for some women. At the same time, important imbalances existed between the two genders and among social classes, and opportunities for abuse and coercion undoubtedly increased as well. The capacity of parents and communities to regulate sexual activity markedly declined overall, amid rapid social change and relocation.

Some historians have assumed a direct link between these changes and later developments that would expand sexual expectations still further—a link for example between this youth revolution and the more widely heralded sexual revolution of the 1960s. In truth, a connection does exist. By the later nineteenth century it was clear that some of the new expectations and behaviors that had developed previously were settling into established practice and public culture alike, though with some adaptations and modifications; this absorption in turn would set the stage for further changes later on. Some of the problems vividly raised by the first sexual revolution would also persist, including complicated questions about gender relationships and equity in modern sexuality.

But the future implications of the first modern sexual revolution were massively complicated by a huge social reaction designed both to defend more traditional standards and to create new constraints aimed at meeting problems widely seen in the sexual revolution itself. The result was a new movement, often called Victorianism after the long reign of the British Queen, which defined a new-old blend of sexual morality with immense power over culture, law, and behavior alike. The height of this Victorian movement centered on the middle decades of the nineteenth century—even as aspects of the sexual revolution were proceeding. But its impact continued well beyond this, and strong traces operate in Western society (and perhaps particularly the United States) even today.

The bases for Victorianism

New efforts to constrain sexuality rested on several related problems. First, most obviously, was simply the shock at the widening gap between traditional values, including Christian standards, and many of the innovations in popular behavior and public culture. As we have seen, many observers were truly appalled at what they thought they saw in popular behavior. Many feared as well the danger of contagion into their own families: it was bad enough that the lower classes were siring illegitimate children; the possibility that a bastard might sully the respectability of an upstanding business or professional family was too awful to contemplate. Small wonder that stories and pictures, by the later nineteenth century, frequently featured the dishonor brought on families by a daughter who found herself pregnant out of wedlock, and the need to cast such a miscreant out of the household.

But tradition and respectability, by themselves, were not the only point. The second basis of Victorianism was the implicit, sometimes explicit, recognition that merely repeating traditional formulas was not likely to work, in an increasingly urban environment in which not only community authority but, in many cases, religious leadership was being rejected or ignored. New tactics and arguments were essential. Here was an opening, as well, for new assertions of relevance by types of experts not previously heavily engaged in sexual issues. Most importantly, doctors and medical spokesmen began to offer assistance to beleaguered traditionalists, urging that many sexual practices had results in health as well as morality and that the authority of doctors in this area might count as much as or more than that of priests. Many doctors, seeking new status and income, clearly sought to benefit from claiming a new role in matters sexual. The result was a crucial innovation in the types of consequences now publicly discussed in sexual matters and the kinds of sexual practices now brought up for review. And the "medicalization" of sex would easily outlast Victorianism itself.

Third, a wide variety of social groups began to realize that they had a birth control problem different from that faced by purely agricultural societies, and that regulation of sexuality was a vital response in this area as well. Here, the focus was on the lower classes to an extent, but much more urgently one's own group, indeed one's own immediate family. The problem was, in other words, both social and personal. While death rates for young children remained very high, the late eighteenth century did see a modest drop, which meant that more families had a larger number of surviving children than they had expected—a key factor in the rapid Western population growth rate overall. New interest in sexuality could actually spur the birth rate directly—certainly the rising level of illegitimacy added to population. There was reason, in other words, to worry about whether population was outstripping social and personal resources. Prominent and pessimistic economists like Thomas Malthus urged a resounding yes to the problem at the social level, arguing that the lower classes trended constantly to over-breed, thus exacerbating poverty by depressing wages. Individual parents—like an Alsatian businessman late in the eighteenth century who found he had 12 children on his hands, each one needing schooling, a dowry, or a business to run—might feel a new level of strain within the family.

But population pressure was only part of the problem. For the growing middle classes and soon other groups as well, children were beginning to cost money rather than adding to the family labor force. The middle class was eagerly persuaded of the importance of providing education to their offspring—at least primary level, and maybe a bit more. And there wasn't a lot of useful work for children to do in middle-class jobs in any event. Furthermore, the class felt a traditional obligation to offer some kind of dowry to daughters and to help sons establish themselves in business or a profession. They simply could not see children as a resource, and quickly realized that they had to plan new levels of investment simply to meet modern expectations. This meant, in turn, that many families not only wanted to avoid birth rate increase, but actually wanted to cut back, below traditional levels. Many middle-class and property-owning families in France and also in key American cities like Philadelphia began to reduce birth rates as early as the 1790s, and other groups would soon follow.

This in turn brought the focus back to sexuality. The only sure way, before the 1840s, to reduce birth rates was to reduce sexual activity. Of course there were some traditional devices that might be used, and of course there was *coitus interruptus*, and doubtless both strategies gained new attention; but both were unreliable, and some of the magical beliefs around traditional methods were declining in any event. For many groups urgently feeling the need to reduce the number of children, at this point and for many decades, heightened levels of sexual abstinence, at key phases of life not only before but also during marriage, constituted a vital response to an agonizing problem. The pinch hit the middle classes first—the classes that were beginning to take responsibility for setting moral standards for society more generally—though ultimately it would spread more widely. A large component of the Victorian sexual ethic derived from a deeply personal need to promote values that would assist in controlling sexual activity among one's own children and in one's own life.

Victorianism, as a result, sought to address both sexual issues for society at large, and sexual issues that would be encountered by young people growing up in the middle classes themselves—the "respectable" classes as they were now often termed. In turn, Victorianism was a new, and not simply traditional, sexual code because it responded both to new behaviors and to new types of problems.

The nature of Victorian sexual morality

No single authority ever defined Victorianism, and, in fact, there were many variants. There were, however, some common impulses. Familiar components included a deep belief that sexual activity should be confined to marriage and that young people's impulses needed to be controlled—with particular attention to young men. Even within marriage, sexual pleasure must be moderated by appropriate standards of restraint. Marital fidelity was vital. Decorum must also surround the public culture, so that sexuality would not be irresponsibly encouraged or vulgarities find the light of day.

From this conventional framework, however, innovations were at least as striking, responding to the new issues that Victorianism sought to address. Health issues associated with sexual activity gained unprecedented attention. To be sure, earlier European folk wisdom had considered male orgasms as taxing, possibly the equivalent of loss of blood. Now, however, excessive sexual activity—in some renderings, having intercourse more than once a week—might cause problems ranging from premature death to insanity. By the later nineteenth century, warnings about venereal disease also increased, along with dramatic accounts of how dangerously over stimulating it was to sleep with someone other than one's spouse. (Some French doctors around 1900 even ingeniously argued that marriage was vital to health because it led to sexual boredom and thus protected from heart attacks.)

Within this framework in turn, massive concern poured into warnings against masturbation. Long regarded as a sin, this now became a source of huge risks, including, but not confined to, a later life of sexual perversion, mental difficulties, premature ageing, sterility, blindness, acne—this was a long list. Quite obviously, new interest in finding ways to warn young people, particularly boys, against sexuality translated into usually sincere beliefs that fondling one's genitals was a gateway to perdition. Various devices were offered to prevent masturbation or provide evidence that it had occurred, and at an extreme some young men were sent to asylums for treatment because of apparently obsessive masturbation. Though concern about girls' behavior was less intense, there were warnings and treatment in this category as well: in the United States, several dozen cliterodectomies were performed against "habitual" masturbators. Childhood, in the Victorian view, should be kept free from sexual references of any sort, and children who could not measure up to these standards of innocence were correspondingly singled out.

Gender and sexuality gained new definitions in Victorianism. In contrast to traditional beliefs that women were more likely to sin, now the tables were turned. Men were held to be more naturally, sometimes dangerously, sexually aggressive, with women the innately-programmed civilizing agents to keep them in check. Victorian moralists argued that women had little or no sexual desire—certainly far less than men. It therefore should be easy for them, and certainly should be their responsibility, to hold male appetite in check, rejecting sex before marriage and moderating the amount of sex even in the marital bed. Wives certainly should be willing to engage in some sex, for procreation and to make sure husbands did not stray. One extreme Victorian recommended that to fulfill these functions, a respectable wife should simply "close her eyes and think of England"—because, of course, she would have no real pleasure as her husband had his way. At another extreme, piano legs should be covered and oranges should not be sucked in public, lest women be led astray by sexual connotations. Victorians were also eager to condemn women who did seem sexually aggressive, for they violated not only morality but femininity; whereas male offenders could be more easily excused given their larger levels of desire. All of this gave some women a powerful moral role, within the family and in society at large; but it often came at real cost to what today would be regarded as normal sexual functioning and led to some new forms of psychological suffering.

The Victorian state won a new role in defending public culture, partly of course replacing churches whose overall power was declining but also partly because of perceived new threats from pornography and other sources. By the early nineteenth century, many governments, on both sides of the Atlantic, became newly-vigilant in banning art and literature regarded as lewd. Even novels like *Madame Bovary*, which treated adultery, came under fire. The notion that cultural products might affect behavior and that respectability was on shaky ground, profoundly influenced government action for well over a century.

A particular target—and there was real irony here—involved birth control devices. Interest in birth control devices began clearly to increase by the 1820s, particularly on the part of married couples (women particularly) who wanted new limits on family size without depending entirely on abstinence. New devices began to be available, particularly an early form of the diaphragm for women (known in the nineteenth century as a check pessary). Then, in the 1840s with the vulcanization of rubber, much more effective and much cheaper rubber devices became possible, including a new form of the condom. But Victorian moralists and officials pulled back in fright, arguing that encouraging new devices would also encourage sexuality, which, even aside from population growth, was a Bad Thing. So governments worked quickly to discourage any widespread publicity or sale for manufactured birth control items. In the United States a zealous postmaster, Anthony Comstock, sponsored legislation in the 1870s to ban sending devices or their advertisements (as well as any other stimulating materials) through the mails.

Victorianism also attacked abortion, which had not previously been a matter for particular government concern. Again the argument rested on the need to discourage sexuality by holding out unwanted pregnancy as a penalty, without means of escape. This, at the time, rather than arguments about the life of the fetus, justified a wide legal attack on abortion. Most American states passed new legislation from the 1830s onward, pushed by Protestant clergy, and many European governments banned the practice as well, often jailing the people who performed abortions (sometimes doctors, more often midwives). Actions of this sort were strongly supported by most medical personnel, who bought into the argument about the dangerous effects of unchecked sexuality and who also resented what they tried to portray as fringe groups, like midwives, who historically had participated in performing abortion procedures.

Victorianism rested, finally, on a new and vivid kind of class division over sexual standards. Poor people, often including immigrants and racial minorities, were now widely condemned for loose morals, including, of course, their propensity to have large numbers of children. Traditional relationships were being overturned, as the middle class led the way in birth control and the lower classes lagged—hence the overpopulation charge. But evidence of premarital sex and other reproved activities was also hauled out, and often exaggerated, as part of a dramatic divide between respectable people—mainly though not exclusively middle class—and the masses. Middle-class scorn also poured on unreconstructed aristocrats who did not follow a strict sexual code and additionally on a new category of artists known as bohemian, assumed to be sexually licentious.

Victorianism was a very real force in Western society by the mid-nineteenth century. It defined a host of moralistic publications that promoted the new vision of female restraint and the health dangers of excessive sex. It obviously supported a major wave of legislation. It led to new food products, particularly in the United States: several Victorian experts claimed that pure and bland foods would help hold sexual behavior in check, and so introduced healthy items like Graham crackers (named for Sylvester Graham) and corn flakes as part of the Victorian crusade. It massively affected childrearing, as parents anxiously supervised children and tried to control any impulse toward masturbatory touching. Victorianism helped sponsor a new definition of love, in which a courting couple was encouraged to develop a high level of romantic intensity made pure by the avoidance of any physical expression. Torrents of letters from engaged partners testified to the extent to which middle-class young people tried to separate emotional attraction from sex—and the extent to which deep guilt surrounded any lapse. Guilt, indeed, was a Victorian watchword, and many people were affected for their entire lives by Victorian feelings about the danger of erotic impulses or even the moral uncleanliness their own sexual organs. From guilt, at least in extreme situations, also often came fear: France by the 1860s recorded cases in which young women believed that sitting in a train seat previously occupied by a man might lead to pregnancy or venereal disease. From France as well, a divorce suit filed by a wife because her husband displayed a good bit of sexual zeal and subjected her to "unnatural caresses"; and a larger number of instances, from many countries, in which men simply did not expect their respectable wives to be particularly interested in sex and who adapted accordingly.

Adjusting to Victorianism

Real as the Victorian ethic was, and deep as its impact could be, sexual reality in the Victorian decades remained complex—partly, of course, because the effects of the first modern sexual revolution could not entirely be undone. Illegitimacy rates did decline after about 1870, partly because of the power of Victorian strictures but also because working-class families began more effectively to insist on marriage if premarital intercourse resulted in pregnancy. But Victorianism did not describe sexuality as fully as historians once assumed.

A key reason for this is the fact that Victorian moral and medical authorities did not present an entirely united front. They all agreed, for example, that women's sexual desire differed from that of men, but only an extreme faction contended that women could not, and (in marriage) should not, seek some sexual pleasure. Advice was publicly available, in other words, that could help women understand that some sexual interest was natural, that respectability did not require them to hold back entirely once they were married. This helps explain why available evidence suggests that a substantial number of middle-class women, in places like the United States, reported that they knew about orgasm and enjoyed it with some regularity in their marital relations, at least by the later nineteenth century (though it is relevant to note that women who came to sexual maturity in the 1870s were noticeably more likely to report this than women whose maturation was two decades earlier, suggesting that the force of Victorianism declined a bit with time).

Victorianism had even less applicability to middle-class men than it did to women, though we must not rush to assume that all, or even most, men defied its strictures frequently. The incidence of male guilt about sexual impulses undoubtedly rose. Unquestionably, however, and partly encouraged by Victorian gender ideas themselves, many men indulged in double-standard sexuality, insisting that their wives play by the rules while themselves occasionally visiting prostitutes, sometimes (where funds permitted) maintaining a mistress. A French husband expressed a common sentiment (though more openly than would have been true in some other countries): "I make love with my wife when I want a child. The rest of the time I make love with my mistresses. Wives are to produce heirs. For pleasure men seek other women." Boys, similarly, were far less likely to observe the rules about premarital sex than girls were, in part, of course, because they would not bear the burden and shame of pregnancy. These results could affect even later adulthood, when men, more sexually experienced than their wives and less burdened with Victorian emphasis on restraint, found their brides unresponsive. An important side-effect of double-standard sexual behavior by the later nineteenth century was a rising rate of venereal disease, particularly syphilis, among some men in various social classes. This added fuel, of course, to medical warnings about improper sex and to efforts to improve health inspections of prostitutes.

Men and women alike in the middle classes also adjusted to Victorianism by surprisingly intense same-sex friendships during early adulthood. This, of course, could be perfectly compatible with the Victorian ethic, but it has also raised some intriguing questions. Precisely because elaborate contacts between young men and women were discouraged—even educational facilities were often separate by the time of secondary school if not before—deep emotions were often poured into friendships with others of the same sex. Needs here were at least as great for men as for women, if only because the male marriage age was several years later (because of the necessity of establishing the economic basis for a respectable standard of family living). Many young women loved one or more friends, and the same applied to men; and in both cases, physical expressions and verbal references to these expressions were part of the package. Thus one American girl, Mary Hallock Foote, wrote her friend: "Imagine yourself kissed a dozen times my darling. Perhaps it is well for us that we are far apart. You might find my thanks so expressed rather overwhelming." Young men could use similar language, referring to themselves as "fervent lovers" in relation to friends. And the contacts were not matters of words alone. Young men commonly slept with each other, for example in shared hotel rooms, and this allowed expressions of love quite directly: "Our hearts were full of that true friendship which could not find utterance by words, we laid our heads upon each other's bosom and wept, it may be unmanly to weep, but care not, the spirit was touched."

Not surprisingly, historians have spent some time trying to figure out if relationships of this sort were what we would call today overtly homosexual or lesbian, or whether physicality fell short of sex. There is no way to be sure, for this was a very different emotional culture from that recommended today. The best guess is sometimes yes, often no. What is clear is that same-sex friendships helped fill gaps before heterosexual courtship was possible, making Victorian constraints on intercourse before marriage more endurable. For men, revealingly, most of the intense friendships ended with marriage. Women however maintained their intensity, which of course might help compensate for a somewhat less-than-ardent version of Victorian matrimony and in some cases for the pain (whether openly acknowledged or not) of double-standard behavior by husbands.

For the Western middle class, in sum, a few individuals openly defied Victorian sexual standards. A handful of vigorously promiscuous women ultimately wrote of their triumphs, and beneath the public glare there were probably others. Far more common was a combination of common-sense modifications of severe Victorianism, as in the possibility of mutual sexual interest and satisfaction in marriage, but also some particular compensations, admittedly with more options for men than for women, that would make other aspects of Victorianism endurable. We cannot know, of course, how widely some Victorian rules were breached, for example with regard to masturbation.

Victorianism did not even absolutely dominate public culture. A pornography industry persisted, though it tended to shift away from the open hedonism of a *Fanny Hill* toward more explorations of sex and violence or more discussions of exotic settings, often with an apparently scientific veneer through interests in the doings of more primitive peoples. During the middle decades of the century, a good bit of pornography increased in cost, aiming more explicitly at upper-class men, and men's clubs, than had been the case previously. But materials were available for others. A new genre of police reports and pulp fiction often featured accounts of lurid crimes, some with a clear sexual element. Schoolboys could also circulate copies of old standbys like *Aristotle's Handbook*, sometimes revised to include more masturbatory content.

For the lower classes, the objects of such concern and scorn in respectable Victorian eyes, Victorianism had even less relevance to actual beliefs and behaviors. To be sure, some worker families—sometimes guided by a wife who had absorbed respectability standards during a stint as a domestic servant in a middle-class household—aspired to sexual propriety as a means of demonstrating self-worth and also helping to limit the birth rate as a time when schooling was gaining ground and the costs of having children were clearly rising. Some agreed with middle-class advice that sexual restraint was vital for family prosperity and, possibly, upward mobility. Many labor leaders, in the later nineteenth century and beyond, also advocated sexual restraints as part of their interest in helping workers focus on what they saw as more important goals, like trade union activism.

Many workers, however, ignored key aspects of Victorianism, and a few defied it directly. Sex before marriage remained common. Young male workers frequently talked about sex, sometimes stimulated by pornography or even teasing by older women in the factories. In one German factory, city male workers at age 13 sometimes smeared sap on their faces and pubic areas in hopes of looking more manly—pretending, obviously, to have pubescent hair before the real thing arrived. Many workers, disaffected from religion, formed relationships that never ended in marriage. More common, as the rawest novelty of industrial life wore off, was a pattern of sexual pursuit and premarital activity—sometimes with one young woman, sometimes with several—that would end, however, under family pressure, when a girl got pregnant. Thus a British worker slept with his girlfriend for 23 months before, though still in "no hurry" to marry, he could no longer honorably delay. As another noted, "If I hadn't got my 'bride' pregnant, I probably wouldn't have married for a long time."

Working-class sex, particularly before marriage, was also affected by growing awareness of the use of condoms. A new factory worker from rural Germany in the 1870s is teased because he had never heard of these devices, which his friends, interestingly, called "Parisian articles."

Many younger workers also enjoyed the burgeoning popular entertainments offered by the music hall (called vaudeville in the United States), where bawdy references and sexual allusions, by female as well as male performers, were common by the 1870s. This was not the Victorian world.

Working-class sexuality was increasingly constrained, however, not by a literal Victorianism but by the urgent demands of birth control, from the mid-nineteenth century well into the twentieth. Amid low wages and recurrent unemployment, and with school attendance now enforced, in Western countries, at least through the primary grades, it was disastrous to have too many children, and the class's birth rate began to drop rapidly, though remaining slightly above middle-class levels. Working-class immigrants to the United States fairly quickly learned the same lesson, adjusting birth rates with sometimes surprising speed. The necessity was clear: the question was by what means it could be met. Condoms might assist youth sexuality, but they were too unreliable or simply too expensive to meet the needs of adult married couples. The only recourse involved increasingly frequent periods of abstinence, clearly limiting sexual expression in marriage for many workers after the second or third child was born. To be sure, workers did make use of abortions, despite their illegality—this was true of some unmarried women, but many wives as well. In Berlin by the 1890s it was estimated that at least a quarter of all pregnancies in the growing working class ended in abortion. The procedure was risky, and it could take its own toll on later sexuality, but its use further illustrated the gap between working-class sexual culture and Victorian preachments. Working-class sex was hardly unrestrained, and indeed it became increasingly confined particularly after courtship and the first years of marriage, but it did not directly resonate to several key Victorian values.

And, of course, middle-class observers continued to pounce on signs of the gap, maintaining a campaign against working-class non-respectability. School children who displayed too much interest in sex were frequently hauled up for discipline, and some girls—mainly though not exclusively from the working class—were designated outright deviants. Arrests for sexual misbehavior were the most commonly punished forms of delinquency for girls. Worker use of brothels was also widely noted, and often exaggerated (with convenient downplaying of middle-class use). Chinese immigrants to the United States, with few women accompanying them, drew a wide reputation for sexual immorality because of patronage of prostitutes. Large worker families, as among many first-generation immigrant groups in the United States, were taken as another sign of lack of sexual restraint.

Debate over sexuality, however veiled in the interests of propriety, was a basic feature of nineteenth-century life in the Western world. It helped divide social classes. It inspired key aspects of childrearing in the middle classes. It played a key role in defining gender, establishing severe constraints on respectable women but challenging standards also for men, often called upon simultaneously to show restraint within their own class but to demonstrate sexual prowess in other ways. It stimulated vigorous efforts to regulate public culture in the interests of decency, significantly impeding awareness of new birth control options in the process. The debate clearly informed the growing feminist movement of the later nineteenth century. While some feminists worried about overemphasis on female purity and objected to characterizations of lack of sexual desire, on the whole the movement's leaders utilized the purity argument to help further other goals, such as demanding the vote; and they spent more time attacking male double-standard behavior than in urging new sexual freedom for women. Feminists did pay attention to conditions of prostitutes, often pressing for health inspections against venereal disease. Many also supported additional efforts at birth control, as a means of freeing women up for other activities; but here they often reinforced aspects of Victorianism by touting the need for sexual restraint. Victorianism, in other words, was not a static force, proving capable of picking up some new allies as time went on. Overall, the Victorian reaction hardly triumphed in full in the Western world, but it successfully complicated the momentum and implications of the sexual revolution that had preceded it and that continued to display some force.

Beyond Victorianism

The clash between Victorianism and the pressures for sexual transformation eased a bit in the decades around 1900 and into the twentieth century, though it did not disappear and, indeed, picked up some powerful and unexpected new baggage. Adjustments and modifications became more important, however, and if the results were hardly revolutionary they did restore momentum to aspects of sexual change. Now, of course, the targets for a new breed of explicit or unwitting reformers included not only sheer traditionalism, but the Victorian overlay as well.

In 1918 a British scientist named Marie Stopes issued a book called *Married Love*, essentially dedicated to the idea that sexual pleasure was a vital aspect of marriage and that it must include full recognition of women's desire and capacity. Stopes opened the first edition with a personal plea: "In my first marriage I paid such a terrible price for sex-ignorance that I feel that how I gained it at such cost should be placed at the service of humanity." The book was a quiet bombshell, drawing criticism from Protestant and Catholic religious leaders but winning a massive popular following, not just in Britain but throughout the English-speaking world (while a first American edition was not permitted until 1931, Stopes' articles and commentary gained attention earlier). Literally thousands of women began writing to Stopes every year, thanking her for her message but seeking more specific advice about how to define and achieve sexual pleasure. Stopes also became a leading advocate for more availability of birth control devices, another step on her work to free sexuality, and particularly female sexuality, from the trammels of Victorianism.

Stopes' work, and its reception, testified to the hold of older traditions. Despite modifications of Victorianism, massive numbers of women remained sexually ignorant, with men, equally ignorant, unaware of the possibility of mutuality in a respectable marriage. Yet Stopes' work is also a sign that Victorianism had hardly triumphed in full and that its hold was beginning to relax somewhat. Open sexual advice was now possible, and widely sought. An interest in more rewarding sexual lives, not entirely throttled by Victorianism, was clearly growing.

Attacks on Victorianism became increasingly widespread. Sigmund Freud and other practitioners of the rising profession of psychiatry deplored unnecessary sexual repression, particularly in childhood socialization. Freud made it clear that sexuality was immensely complicated psychologically, and at the same time he repeated some Victorian ideas, for example about women's lower level of desire. On the whole, however, his work and that of others in the field helped reduce Victorian emphasis on regulating masturbation and other expressions of children's sexuality.

Marriage reformers, on both sides of the Atlantic, began to urge greater equality in marriage, including sexual reciprocity, while attacking sexual possessiveness. A growing campaign to limit jealousy included changes in law: in most American states by the 1930s it was no longer possible to claim jealousy as a reason to attack an adulterous spouse or her lover (this kind of defense had never been available to women). In fact, the frequency of adultery began, in all probability, to increase, particularly as more middle-class women began to spend more time outside the household. And a study of an "average" Midwestern American city (Muncie, Indiana) suggested that public shock at revelations of adultery had clearly declined by the 1930s compared to just a decade earlier. Adultery was hardly either common or approved practice, but it, too, was subject to change.

Premarital sex began to increase in the middle classes, again without yet becoming the norm. In the United States the practice of dating began between 1910 and 1920, removing courtship from the home and the watchful eyes of parents. Respectable dating still involved assumptions that outright sexual activity would not occur and that young men would obey the restraining orders of their conscientious dates. But dating did encourage more serious emotional entanglements amid high school and college students. It began to generate a complex and progressive series of physical acts, from initial handholding to ultimate "necking" or "petting," often in the back seats of cars. It clearly promoted increasing opportunities for "going all the way," though men undoubtedly boasted that they had achieved this more often than was in fact the case, while respectable girls learned how important it was to lie when they had crossed the line. Working-class dating often even more frankly assumed that sexual favors would reward a young man's shelling out the money for dinner or a movie.

Public culture shifted. Dress styles became more informal, with skirts shorter than had been the case with Victorianism. Early beauty pageants, by the 1920s, revealed even more of the female body, in bathing suits—though far less than would be true later on. Not only sexual advice literature but also general marriage manuals began to discuss sexual practices and pleasures more openly. A new generation of pornography, beginning in the later nineteenth century, featured far more illustrations—including inexpensive postcards—and far greater availability. Serious literature and drama began to include more sexual themes: a popular play in Paris before 1910 urged the desirability of premarital intercourse as part of preparing a happy adulthood.

A crucial development, becoming commonplace in Western (and Latin American) cities in the later nineteenth century, involved the establishment of "red light" districts, in which prostitutes, striptease shows and other sexually provocative activities were implicitly tolerated by authorities. Red light districts constituted a recognition by post-Victorian leaders that full respectability could simply not be achieved. Better to allow one part of town to monopolize the lures of degeneracy than to risk contagion in the city as a whole. Urban reformers might hope, of course, that the new districts would draw mainly workers and immigrants. In fact, however, a growing number of middle-class young people were lured into the districts as well, seeking racier entertainment fare through "slumming." Growing interest in working-class recreational forms like music hall both reflected and encouraged a growing movement of middle-class cultural interests away from Victorian staples and toward a wider engagement with sexual themes.

The most decisive blow to Victorianism came, however, through the growing campaigns to make modern birth control devices more widely available and acceptable— one of the key planks in Marie Stopes' program of sexual liberalization. In many countries, reformers emerged to advocate more extensive birth control, in the interests of greater sexual freedom, and also in hopes of reducing the dangerous incidence of recourse to abortion (which, remaining illegal, often put women at serious risks of maiming or infection). Some practitioners were local doctors and midwives who simply tried to make more information available by establishing neighborhood clinics. Others were national spokespeople. In the United States, Margaret Sanger emerged as a leading force in urging modification of the laws that restricted publicizing and selling birth control devices. Often attacked by conservatives, Sanger nevertheless advanced the cause steadily, while offering compromises, most notably with the medical profession, which now became responsible for prescribing devices such as diaphragms. In turn, medical organizations increasingly turned away from earlier opposition, arguing that safe and healthy sex was a more important goal than maximum restraint.

In fact, growing numbers of married couples, and doubtless some unmarried adepts as well, did turn to the use of birth control, particularly, in the middle classes, in the form of female-regulated preventives such as diaphragms and spermicides. Great resistance remained, now spearheaded by the Catholic Church, and in the United States a few jurisdictions still technically outlawed the use of anything other than restraint. But the movement was steady, in decades in which the birth rate continued its massive decline. Quietly but decisively, at least within marriage, and at least within the middle classes, the acceptance of recreational sex, and its importance to marital happiness, became an established fact by the 1920s and 1930s. And this was, in turn, the fundamental transformation that adjusted sexual behavior to the conditions of industrial as opposed to agricultural society.

Victorianism hardly rolled over and died. Many people continued to believe fully in Victorian strictures. Far more harbored strong remnants: for example, while exemplary punishments of masturbation ended, many parents continued to try to keep it in check as they monitored their adolescent children. Gender assumptions persisted, though in modified form. The belief that women's sexual desire was lower than that of

men—though not, now, non-existent—continued to influence both advice and practice—as in the assumption that "good" girls would keep boys in check on a date, even
in the newly-enticing automobile back seat. The idea of doctors as regulators of sexual
standards actually gained ground, though the content of their advice loosened up.
Massive class divides remained. Reliable birth control was now far more available to
middle-class than to working-class families, as the latter tended to shy away from doctors and from the expense involved, still relying extensively on abstention. Middle-
class sexual practice, somewhat ironically given the Victorian past, at this point clearly
became more venturesome, the pursuit of pleasure (and sometimes, at least, mutual
pleasure) more vigorous than was true of most working-class couples. Restraints on
public culture persisted. After a brief fling with more open sexual themes, Hollywood,
the world capital of the new film industry by the 1920s, adopted clear and restrictive
rules, including depiction of couples, including married couples, in carefully separate
twin beds in appropriately concealing night dress. National differences did increase,
with French censorship, for example, noticeably lighter than that of Britain or the
United States. But, at least in the latter countries, a host of books by would-be pioneers,
like D. H. Lawrence's *Lady Chatterley's Lover*, continued to be banned, save for the well-
heeled tourists who simply bought them in Paris.

Resurgent Victorianism could also crop up, more fully, in unlikely places. A key
aspect of the Nazi movement in Germany was its protest against modern fashion and
sexual license, attacking the decadent films and nightclubs of the 1920s while urging
that pure Aryan women step up to the responsibility of having more children. A number of Nazi leaders were themselves sexually dissolute, but the public face of the movement revived Victorian strictures in a number of ways.

More important still (though also a part of Nazism) was a new entrant to the list of
sexual regulations, even as (and perhaps partly because) Victorianism was easing in
other respects. Homosexuality gained new definition and new attention, generating
widespread hostility and anxiety.

Same-sex attraction had not roused great public interest in the nineteenth century.
Homosexual acts were still regarded as sinful, and were still illegal, but there was little
sense of a major problem—compared to the other aspects of sexuality that were gaining so much attention. European doctors began to do research on homosexuality from
the 1850s onward, however, which gradually brought a new sense that the condition
was somehow endemic to certain individuals and (in the judgment of most experts)
pathological. The term "homosexuality" itself was introduced, initially in Germany, in
1869, reflecting the new expert interest. Increasingly, scientists argued that homosexuality was a character trait developed as a result of some failure in childhood upbringing. Instead of focusing on acts of sexuality between members of the same sex—the
traditional view, however reproving—the idea that some individuals were (deplorably)
homosexual by nature gained ground, encouraged by the psychological studies of
Freud and others. All of this occurred in a climate of growing concern about masculinity in a world filled with machines, office work, and (increasingly) female school teachers—all of which could be seen as emasculating. Gradually, expert ideas were
translated into wider public consciousness. A number of trials, including a famous

action against British author Oscar Wilde, helped publicize new concern about homosexuality along with the idea that it was a condition, rather than an occasional behavior.

The results were threefold. First, people interested in homosexual acts (particularly male, but also female) increasingly felt that they had an identity, albeit one that was under attack. Literary movements and a few products implicitly directed toward homosexuals, such as certain kinds of body-building magazines, began to emerge in the 1920s. This would yield greater importance later on. Second, homosexuality was increasingly insulted, sometimes literally attacked in expressions regarded as acceptable public culture. Third, quite clearly by the 1920s, many parents began to worry increasingly that their children might become homosexuals, and many young people themselves developed similar anxieties. This was a subject of some anguished self-doubt among college students in the 1920s, for example. Intense same-sex friendships, of the nineteenth-century sort, quickly dropped away, particularly among men. The result helped the trend of focusing new interest on heterosexual expressions, including dating, but it ironically added a new concern in the area of sexuality overall at a time when, in general, greater permissiveness seemed to be gaining ground, however modestly.

*   *   *

Two powerful types of change emerged in the Western world in the two centuries after 1750, clashing with each other, but, to some extent, feeding off each other as well. The most important, ultimately, was a new interest in sexual pleasure in various stages of life, including marriage, and, by the later nineteenth century, an increasing utilization of new devices that limited the chance of pregnancy and encouraged sexuality for recreational purposes. This was a complex trend, even by itself, with variations by region, social class, and gender. Along with this, however, came the new level of concern about various aspects of sexuality and a new set of experts, in and around the medical profession, who took it upon themselves to establish standards; a variety of novel legislation correspondingly sought to support sexual repression. Both of these trends were significant. Both remained active, even innovative, well after 1950. Both, finally, strongly influenced the relationship of Western societies to other parts of the world in an age of growing imperialism and new types of global connections. Western sexual complexities did not define the global history of sex in the two centuries after 1750. Important regional variations and responses persisted. But interaction with Western signals played a vital role, just as sexuality proved unexpectedly important in new aspects of global encounters.

Further reading

Classic debates about the sexual revolution of the eighteenth century include E. Shorter, *Making of the Modern Family* (New York: Basic Books, 1975) and L. Tilly, *Women, Work and Family* (New York: Routledge, 1989). On the modernization notion, see P. Robinson, *The Modernization of Sex* (New York: HarperCollins, 1977). See also R. Godbeer, *Sexual Revolution in Early America*

(Baltimore, MD: Johns Hopkins University Press, 2002). On the rise of consumerism and its relationship to emotional and sexual change, C. Campbell, *The Romantic Ethic and the Spirit of Modern Consumerism* (London: WritersPrintShop, 2005). On prostitution, see A. Corbin, *Women for Hire: Prostitution and Sexuality in France after 1850* (Cambridge, MA: Harvard University Press, 1990) and J. Ringdal, *Love for Sale: A World History of Prostitution* (New York: Drove, 2002).

Important surveys include J. D'Emilio and Estelle Friedman, *Intimate Matters: A History of Sexuality in America*, rev. ed. (Chicago: University of Chicago Press, 1998); K. Crawford, *European Sexualities, 1400–1800* (New York: Cambridge University Press, 2007); A. Burguiere et al., *A History of the Family, Volume II: The Impact of Modernity* (Cambridge, MA: Harvard University Press, 1996); and C. Lyons, *Sex among the Rabble: An Intimate History of Gender and Power in the Age of Revolution, Philadelphia, 1730–1830* (North Carolina: University of North Carolina Press, 2006). P. Gay, *Pleasure Wars: The Bourgeois Experience: Victoria to Freud* (New York: W.W. Norton and Company, 1993) combines fascinating data with a Freudian approach.

On jealousy and changes relating to sexuality, see P.N. Stearns, *Jealousy: Evolution of an Emotion in American History* (New York: New York University Press, 1989). On homosexuality, F. Tamagne, *History of Homosexuality in Europe* (New York: Arno, 2004); L. Faderman, *Surpassing the Love of Men: Romantic Friendship and Love Between Women from the Renaissance to the Present* (New York: Harper Paperbacks, 1998); J. Weeks, *Sexuality and its Discontents: Meanings, Myths and Modern Sexualities* (London: Routledge, 1990); and G. Chauncey, *Gay New York: Gender, Urban Culture, and the Making of the Gay Male World, 1890–1940* (New York: Basic Books, 1994). On pornography, refer to L.Z. Sigel, *Governing Pleasures: Pornography and Social Change in England, 1815–1914* (Newark, NJ: Rutgers University Press, 2002); and J. Peakman, *Lewd Books: The Development of Pornography in Eighteenth-Century England* (London: Palgrave, 2003). On birth control, see J. Brodie, *Contraception and Abortion in Nineteenth-Century America* (Ithaca, NY: Cornell, 1994); L. Gordon, *The Moral Property of Women; A History of Birth Control Politics in America*, rev. ed. (Urbana: University of Illinois Press, 2002); A. Tone, *Devices and Desires: A History of Contraceptives in America* (New York: Hill and Wang, 2001); and A. McLaren, *A History of Contraception: From Antiquity to the Present Day* (Oxford: Blackwell, 1990). On censorship, see N. Beisel, *Imperiled Innocents: Anthony Comstock and Family Reproduction in America* (Princeton, NJ: Princeton University Press, 1997).

Chapter 7

Global trends and variations in the age of imperialism

Between 1750 and 1950, almost all regions of the world were drawn into increasing economic and political relationships. By the later nineteenth century, no major society could remain isolated. Global economic dislocations were widespread, as European factory output cut into traditional manual production, displacing tens of thousands of workers (disproportionately female) in places like India and Latin America. While no full industrial revolution occurred outside the Western world before the 1890s, pilot factories and railroads emerged in several places; and by 1900, Russia and Japan were moving rapidly toward an outright industrialization process. Production for export to the world market disrupted peasant agriculture even more widely. Along with economic change came the new military and political power of Europe and the United States. New Western-dominated empires spread in Africa, Southeast Asia, and the Pacific, with inroads into China and fringes of the Middle East as well. Latin America, technically independent after 1820, saw continued Western intervention and influence.

Economic change and imperialism inevitably had significant impact on sexual behaviors and values. Most obviously, European judgments about other societies, sometimes at least partially enforced through imperial rules and commentary, affected the context for sexual behaviors and local self-perceptions. More subtly, economic dislocations could have some of the same effects on other societies as was occurring in Europe, and by the twentieth century the example of European urban culture could supplement these effects as well. It is vital to realize that substantial regional differences persisted, based on previous cultural standards and very different relationships to the emerging world economy; comparison remains essential. Nevertheless, some genuine global trends can be identified.

The impact of Western evaluations of sexual practices in other societies is the easiest theme to identify, and of course this continued and intensified patterns that had already begun to emerge amid European colonialism in the early modern period. The differences, now, were the increased power and reach of the Western presence and the fact that European public standards were themselves changing, and in many ways becoming less tolerant. At the same time, however, European contacts and the sheer pace of commercial growth and new migration could push in other directions, promoting change but hardly in keeping with what now passed for European respectability.

*   *   *

From the 1870s into the early twentieth century, a massive global campaign against "white slavery" took shape. A variety of reformers, mostly feminist leaders, worked to mobilize public opinion against the forcible seizure of women for prostitution. An International Federation of Friends of Young Women was founded in 1877 by 32 women from seven Western countries. British leaders helped develop the initial pressure, but Americans and many others became heavily involved. The idea was that a growing number of innocent young women were being captured in Western countries for sale by international agents to brothels and harems in other parts of the world. International Jewish organizations played a prominent role in this human rights movement, in part to protect immigrant women at a time of massive Jewish migration—immigrants were seen as particularly vulnerable to seizure—and in part to counter charges of Jewish involvement in procurement. A series of national congresses in the 1890s generated a Women's Purity Federation in 1900, as well as an ensuing Paris conference in 1902. An international agreement followed, with an international bureau established to monitor compliance, with strong participation by French officials.

The white slavery crusade, one of the largest global movements of the nineteenth century after abolitionism, had many intriguing components. It reflected growing concern, particularly by women's leaders, about prostitution itself; if the domestic version could not be fully attacked (this all developed during the same period as the establishment of red light districts) then a foreign enemy could be fought. It expressed understandable indignation about an awful kind of crime against vulnerable women, but it also channeled a great deal of Victorian moral prudery that was uneasy about outright sexual pleasure seeking. Historians of the subject virtually unanimously agree that the actual number of white slavery seizures was far lower than the campaigners, apparently sincerely, claimed. Outrage at unacceptable sexuality prompted gross exaggeration. And so, of course, did obvious racism and xenophobia. The whole white slavery scare was based on moral revulsion at foreigners gaining sexual access to pure Western womanhood. Reformers openly scorned women from India and other places for their (so it was claimed) loose sexual morals. They further argued that white men, or at least Anglo-Saxon men, would never patronize white slave brothels—it was debased foreigners who were at fault, an unsavory assortment of Mediterraneans, Jews, and Chinese.

The white slavery crusade clearly reveals the extent to which Victorian sexual standards could take on global meaning, particularly through insulting judgments about sexual habits in other societies. Reformers argued that Western opinion and government support were essential because countries in other civilizations would otherwise take no action. A British leader thus referred to "the absence of any local public opinion on the moral question." Claims of debased sexuality in Asia and Africa constituted a key expression of the growing insistence on the superiority of Western society, and its responsibility for policing the world.

The same movement showed, however, how much Western moral sentiment, however inaccurate, could count in the imperialist age. By 1904, a number of governments in Latin America and elsewhere were introducing new laws against prostitution and the immigration of single females, to demonstrate, through novel sexual regulations, that they could be as civilized as anyone else. Leading reformers, like Alfredo Palacios, who sponsored legislation to provide women protection from pimps, specifically noted how embarrassed, even shamed he and the rest of the Argentine middle class was by the European perception that Buenos Aires had become "the worst of all centers of the immoral commerce in women." European beliefs persisted anyway, with claims even in the 1920s that, "the hotbed of the abominable trade is Argentina," but this merely triggered more regulatory efforts to deflect the charges. A League of Nations visit to Argentina in 1924 prompted a new round of reform seeking to limit prostitution of any sort. Only after World War II, following two major laws and a massive public relations effort, was this global sexual deficit finally put to rest.

*   *   *

As Victorianism was forming, in the later eighteenth and early nineteenth centuries, a fascination with real or imagined sexual habits in the Middle East began to take shape. Growing belief in the corruption of the government of the Ottoman Empire included frequent and fanciful descriptions of the sexual depravity common in the sultan's harem. Here was a double boon at the time: first, a hated foreign government could be attacked in a new way, and, second, the result, while officially deploring sexual degeneracy, actually allowed public discussions of sexual excesses that otherwise should be hidden from a respectable European audience. Not only promiscuity, but also deviant sexual positions and same-sex dalliance could be evoked or at least hinted at as part of the attempt to show how the Ottoman government should no longer count as a responsible international agent. Middle Eastern, as well as "native" African and Asian women, could also be evoked for purposes of implicit or explicit pornography. Explicitly, the surge of more popular pornography in the later nineteenth century included vivid postcards showing presumably Islamic women entirely nude except for a facial veil, as well as the inevitable putative harem scenes. Implicitly, new popular magazines, like *National Geographic*, featured (and arguably gained audiences by) recurrent images of bare-breasted native women in New Guinea or West Africa. Billed as scientific or anthropological, the results could easily provide titillation back home, and another realization of how different, and sexually questionable, most other people in the world were when measured by the standards Victorians were trying to assert in their own societies.

Western opinion formed from other sources as well, beyond pornography and popularized science. Missionaries were one: a growing wave of Christian missions fanned out in the nineteenth century, for the first time including Protestants as well as Catholics. The result, not surprisingly, was a widely-reported sense of dismay and shock at the gap between the sexual standards of populations the Europeans hoped to convert, and what was currently regarded as morally essential. But missionaries did not provide the only new voices. As European imperialism matured, colonial officials in places like India and Africa were increasingly joined by their families. The result was a small, usually rather isolated community of European women in a foreign context. Some of these women, by the later nineteenth century, reached out actively to encourage new levels of education or other reforms among the populations around them. But others, more fearful, were content to repeat their impressions that the strangeness they saw in the "natives" must include sexual impropriety, and also to voice their concerns that the sexual license of local women was a direct threat to their relationships to their husbands and to other European men. With Victorian assumptions in mind, along with demeaning beliefs about Asian or African sexual immorality, it became easy to argue that "something must be done" to keep the lusts and lures of native women in check, because even European men could so easily be led astray. Here, if only in letters sent home, was another source of European critique of the sexual habits of other people.

A key question about global trends in sexuality in the decades after 1850, if not a bit earlier, involves trying to find out how various societies reacted to Western commentary—how much they ignored it, how much they rejected, how much they tried to introduce new standards or regulations to try to deflect Victorian perceptions.

A second set of trends is more subtle than the confrontation of Victorianism-plus-racial assumptions and real or imagined sexuality outside the West. The changes in many local economies, thanks to new attention to export production and some early factories, could well have some of the same effects that similar developments had in Europe from the eighteenth century onward—simply a bit later. In several instances—for example, late nineteenth-century Russia—a decline in community power to regulate and monitor sexuality, coupled with new earnings and a new interest in sexual expression, led to significant change. By the early twentieth century, change might also be encouraged by direct contacts with Western examples. Middle-class Africans, educated for a year or two in French or British schools, could bring back new knowledge of student habits and urban contacts that would help shape their sexual and consumer patterns back home. There were forces pushing for changes in sexual outlook and behavior beyond the need to come to terms with European criticisms. This added to the complexity of sexual patterns at a global scale, and certainly helps explain continued variety among different regions and social groups. The consistent strand, of course, was a growing pressure to rethink some aspects of established sexuality in favor of some acceptance of change.

As a result of these various themes, the nineteenth century witnessed both efforts at reform of various traditional practices, designed to bring societies more in line with official European morality, and increased openness and promiscuity, as evidenced by a clear expansion of prostitution, a probable increase in sexual violence against women, and definitely unprecedented levels of venereal disease (syphilis and gonorrhea), affecting virtually every part of the world.

By the early twentieth century, various leaders in many regions were trying to reconcile the contradictory trends. Not only European colonialists, but also regional doctors and early feminist leaders hoped to stem the tide of sexual license, at least as it was beginning to affect health as well as respectability through the rise of sexually-transmitted diseases. Communists and some nationalists tried other ways of promoting sexual restraint. But it proved difficult to put the genie back in the bottle. Even the Victorian West would be affected by the new global trends, as the exotic imagery of turn-of-the-century pornography suggested.

Again, the theme of change and contradiction should not be overdone. Regional traditions and reactions persisted. Rural inhabitants—still the vast majority—might be little affected either by reform attempts or the new promiscuity, maintaining customary patterns in most aspects of sexuality. But Western influences—which ironically could point both to heightened sexual restraint and to new license—and the sheer force of rapid commercial expansion and urban growth, did create some genuinely global themes and tensions. Arguably, at least by the later nineteenth and early twentieth centuries, sex became one of the first personal behaviors to be reshaped by the first round of globalization.

Imperialist settings

The force of European opinion bore particularly directly on colonies old and new—in the Pacific, in India, and in Africa most obviously. In places like Hawaii, Western missionaries by the 1830s were working hard to change what they saw and immoral customs, insisting on more concealing dress for women and trying to discourage premarital sex in favor of monogamy. Local traditions did not yield entirely, but there was gradual change.

In Africa and India, the Western imperial approach had a number of common ingredients: the local populations could be excused (as earlier in Latin America) for not being sure what the Western message was, given obvious contrasts between moral preachments and the actual behaviors of Western men.

Two points dominated the Western imagery, and while approaches to India and Africa were not identical, the themes applied to both colonial settings. First, local sexuality was described as immoral and wanton—usually in criticism, sometimes with a certain degree of envy. Westerners regarded African women and men alike as unduly sensual and unrestrained, a sexual danger to themselves and others. Second, however, indigenous men were seen as effeminate, not measuring up to Western standards of virility. The themes combined were less contradictory than might be imagined, for effeminacy could be compatible with visions of excessive and depraved sexuality as opposed to Victorian norms of manly restraint.

The sensuality theme came through clearly, again both in blame and in praise. The emphasis emerged early in comment on India. Alexander Hamilton, a Scotsman in the eighteenth century, dismissed Indian men as "the living Priapus," constantly lusting after sex. A naval officer in the same century described Indians as being "grossly and ridiculously [sexually] imposed upon by their Priests and Brahmins." Even Indian prostitutes were described as distinctive, seeming to enjoy sex in contrast to respectable European norms: "... they are sumptuously dressed, they wear the most costly jewels in profusion, they are well educated and sing sweetly ... they generally decorate their hair with clusters of clematis. ..." Indian women who shaved their genitals seemed particularly fascinating: "until you glance at their hard, full and enchanting breasts, handsome beyond compare, you fancy you have got hold of some unfledged girl. ..." The same point could be made differently: a Mrs. Colin Mackenzie wrote in 1857: "You may imagine the degraded condition of the people here, when I tell you we constantly pass women in the open street bare down to the hips…. They do not seem to have the least sense of decency." Hindu art, depicting various sexual positions, including oral sex, roused great interest. Specific practices, like Islamic polygamy and the child marriages of many Hindu girls, prompted obvious shock. A common criticism also assumed rampant homosexuality, ignoring the fact that Hinduism had normally looked down on the practice—when the overall vision assumed no restraint, genuine differences and imagined behaviors mingled almost seamlessly.

Terms applied to Africans were often quite similar, though an additional belief about sexual relations with animals displayed both wonderment at the natural environment in Africa and ridiculous ignorance about actual behaviors. One European noted what he claimed were Africans' "hot temperament, their fickle and licentious personalities." Another blamed the hot climate: "They can only restrain themselves with great difficulty, and once launched on debauchery, they maintain the most execrable voluptuousness. Hence the intimate relations between men and beasts that still give birth to monsters in Africa"—this a comment by a Frenchman, Jean Bodin. Even Voltaire, normally a humane skeptic, believed that African women participated in bestiality: "It is not improbable that (at times) the monkeys have subjugated girls." African sexual organs were described as inordinately large and animal-like; there were even claims that African women lacked hymens, which was said to account for their inordinate sexuality. But African beauty won praise as well, at least by the nineteenth century: women in Zanzibar were described as elegant and sensual, full of sexual tricks: "Nobody will be surprised that these magnificent beauties are very vain. They can make eyes at the passer-by in competition with any woman in the world." Again, specific practices drew comment, like the harems of African kings, which seemed repulsive by European standards, or the practice of female circumcision in some regions. And native dress, which frequently involved bare breasts for women, was widely remarked as a sign of sexual immorality.

African men seemed both effeminate and oversexed. Their robes looked feminine, but at the same time they were accused of lack of self-control, frequent orgies, and lusting after white women. Both African and Indian men were seen as weakened by too much sex, too young—a reason given for their lack of military success (though disparities in weaponry constituted the obvious relevant factor) and for widespread claims about laziness. The first British governor of Uganda thus blamed a perceived population decline on "the exhaustion of men and women by premature debauchery."

Comments on high levels of sexuality reflected in part a projection of European sexual fantasies onto local women, as against the restraints that Victorianism urged back home. But more than fantasizing might be involved: actual European men frequently acted out their beliefs about the sexual availability of local women, in patterns that recalled earlier behaviors in Latin America, though at a lower rate overall. British officers often took on multiple concubines in India, sometimes even admitting as much to their wives back home but claiming that the climate aroused their appetites to an controllable extent (Lord Wellesley wrote his wife that: "this climate excites one sexually most terribly," though in his case it is not clear what, if anything, he did about it). Sir David Ochterlony of Nepal reputedly had a harem of 13 Indian women. Edward

Sellon, an army cadet, wrote in 1834 that: "I now commenced a regular course of fucking with native women." Use of local prostitutes was common among British military personnel, prompting warnings about the financial and physical consequences of this kind of "irregular indulgence." Rape undoubtedly occurred as well, though it was not widely mentioned. In 1849 an army private wrote, "A man of the 3rd company of my regiment ... went into a room and took a young girl from her mother's side, and perpetrated the offence, for which he had to answer before God, who heard that poor girl's cries and petitions." For their part, not surprisingly, many Indian women complained not simply about European violence, but about the aggressive approach even to consensual sex—arguing that by Indian standards it was impossible really to make love with these men.

Broadly similar patterns emerged in Africa. Again, there is no way to calculate rates of rape and forced sex, though both undoubtedly occurred, particularly, of course, among European masters of slave women or local domestics. Marriages formed as well, whether officially or de facto, as many European men went single or unaccompanied to Africa. An eighteenth-century observer, worried about a growing interracial population, which might be less docile than the "natives," claimed that: "the [European] planters, without being aware of it, dug their graves with their penises." Many whites, of course, regarded these unions as only temporary, ending when they left the continent, so the pattern was borderline between marital sex and promiscuity.

European sexual intrusion did not affect the bulk of the population either in India or in Africa—this was not the same case as in Latin America earlier, for the overall demographic disruption through disease was far less great. Beliefs in wanton local sexuality, however, combined with undoubted European indulgence, furthered efforts to introduce greater constraint. Many leaders worried greatly about the effect of local habits on European morality. There were also quite practical problems with the spread of venereal disease—the incidence of syphilis in India began mounting steeply in the 1840s, as promiscuity increased and prostitution expanded due to rising poverty among Indian women. Both British and Indians were infected, with one-eighth to one-third of the ranks of British military garrisons involved each year during the second half of the nineteenth century.

Finally, the arrival of growing numbers of European women, as wives of colonial administrators or, more rarely, as teachers and missionaries, increased the temptation to condemn local wantonness as a means of trying to keep European men under greater control, as well as expressing back-home morality. One result was a growing prejudice against the children of mixed unions, in both India and Africa. Biracial children were widely seen as undermining the British family.

European moral concerns and the common view of the debauchery of local traditions combined to lead to some concrete efforts at change. Much of the critique of native ways remained, to be sure, at the rhetorical level. Many European administrators were reluctant in fact to interfere with established habits, lest this rouse unnecessary resistance to colonial rule—there were other goals, including political stability and economic profit, which took pride of place. Thus it was not until after 1950 that British or French governments tried to interfere with female circumcision in the relevant parts of

Africa under their control. Religion could induce hesitation also: many observers believed that only conversion to Christianity could redeem "native" sexuality, that lesser measures might well be futile. In India, the most concrete legal measure introduced in the nineteenth century affecting traditional sexual patterns, enacted only after long discussion, involved raising the age at which girls could marry, for child marriage and premature sexuality had long seemed shocking. A law in 1860 set 10 at the minimum age, and then the Age of Consent Act of 1891 raised this to 12—the latter law came following the widely-publicized death of a 9-year-old Bengali girl after her 35-year-old husband forced her to have sex.

In Africa, laws introduced in the later nineteenth century, for example in Nigeria, permitted women to divorce more easily than custom had allowed, and some observers claimed that the resulting independence not only allowed an end to unhappy marriages but also an increase in adultery. European pressure here too resulted in some reconsideration of promising girls in marriage at a young age. African attitudes on these subjects might change—it was a local who wrote as follows to a European railway commissioner in the early twentieth century: "Sir, a girl name Animatu, daughter of the Olowu [a ruler], has come to me to complain that the Olowu wishes to force her into marriage with one Jinadu, when she wishes to marry a young man called Peidu son of Agura. Also that he put her in irons for six days, and that she succeeded in escaping this morning. I hope you will help her in the matter if this story is true. She should not be forced to marry anyone."

In both India and Africa, evidence of increases in extramarital sex, as well as outright prostitution, increased with time. There were several reasons, and European intrusion was not the main factor overall. As noted, many women faced greater poverty, as local industries encountered new and overwhelming factory competition, and female domestic manufacturers were disproportionately affected. Many women came to see prostitution not simply as a remedy against disaster, but as more profitable than marriage itself. The growth of cities and internal migration, sometimes facilitated by expanding railroads, also created new opportunities for sale of sex. It became easier for women to run away from home. More important, particularly in Africa, economic changes often pulled men into cities or mining centers, while many women stayed back in rural areas—an obvious invitation to commercial sex in the cities because of disparities in gender ratios. Some historians have also speculated that European dominance and rhetoric encouraged certain local men to seek new kinds of sexual assertion against women, to demonstrate their masculinity in a direct way. When women were also seen as becoming increasingly independent, a common theme in Africa, this too could generate new efforts to assert sexual control.

By the twentieth century, there was also the fact of changing European standards, as Victorianism declined and more Europeans began openly to admit the pleasures of sexuality. African or Indian men who went to European schools for a period might learn that sexual experimentation was actually fashionable. A Nigerian novel, *No Longer at Ease*, thus describes a young man in Lagos, Nigeria, in the 1920s, who had received a Western-style education including a year in Britain and who greatly enjoyed the apparatus of the urban consumer world—including frequent sexual conquests among young women in his group. His attachment to this life was so great that he ignored customary family obligations, failing to go back to his home village when his mother died: sex, as part of a larger, Western-influenced urban life style, clearly won out. There were a variety of reasons, in other words, that sexual license seemed to spread. Sometimes the results could lead to court cases: a Nigerian merchant, who had provided a dowry for a future wife, sued his fiancée for being a prostitute, whereas in fact she was simply not the virgin he had assumed. In response, the woman argued that: "When I agreed to be your wife did not my father tell you that I had had connections with a man?"—but to the more traditionalist merchant, she simply seemed hopelessly wild, and not proper marriage material at all.

Many of these changes helped prompt a further surge of control efforts by the early twentieth century. Tribal authorities in Ghana in the 1920s began arresting more unmarried women on suspicion of prostitution, mainly they claimed as a means of limiting sexually transmitted diseases. These chiefs talked freely about the moral chaos of the modern day, in contrast to a purer past. One Ghanian leader in the 1930s issued an edict requiring all unmarried girls to acquire husbands in response to concerns about prostitution and disease. Nationalists, as well as traditionalists, though offering a very different set of goals, often had similar impulses when it came to sexuality. Many Indian leaders praised the purity of traditional Hindu women, against the corruptions that had come with European interference and the example of more public freedoms set by Western women. Older stories of female virtue were revived. An early nationalist blasted British arguments that Hindu women were morally lax in contrast to their English counterparts: "Let me tell our English friend this is a total travesty of truth." Some nationalists might even praise traditions particularly criticized by Europeans, because of a commitment to local custom and a desire to keep women in check in a dangerous age. Thus Jomo Kenyatta, later first president of independent Kenya, openly condoned female circumcision as a valuable custom that should not be surrendered to outside attack. Quite widely and understandably, though over-simply, many leaders showed nostalgia for the "good old days" when marriages could be arranged without complaint and relations between men and modest women were unproblematic. While specific colonial measures to regulate sexual relations were criticized as unwarranted interference by many nationalists, by the twentieth century it was the association of Western influence with increased promiscuity that was becoming the dominant theme, with traditional restraint, particularly on the part of women and the men responsible for wives and daughters, the obvious response.

Key issues in the imperialist setting remained unresolved by the 1950s, even as the colonies began gaining outright independence. Nationalist leaders inevitably hesitated before endorsing attacks on what by Western standards involved sexually-related abuse, whether the topic was child marriage or harsh penalties for adultery. Actual sexual changes had less to do with reform efforts than with urbanism and economic disruption, supplemented at least in a minor way by European sexual exploitation of native women and by the local desire to assert sexual masculinity. Here, local leaders shared concerns about the damaging effects of disease and the moral dangers of more open prostitution, and they sometimes worried about adverse, throwback foreign judgments about uncivilized sexuality as well.

Potential reflux impact on Europe is worth consideration as well. Most Europeans had no direct contact with the imperial sexual world, and there is no widespread sense that returning soldiers or administrators directly used their imperial experience to push for a reconsideration of Western prudery. Yet imagined worlds of Asian or African sensuality did show up at least in pornography. And the whole discussion of colonial sexual standards and problems was far more candid, with sexual patterns far more explicitly detailed, than was allowed in the domestic version of Victorian culture. Here too was an opening for changes in rhetoric and possibly in behavior as well, with foreign pleasures contrasted with European repression.

China and the Middle East

Major sexual developments in other parts of Asia and North Africa resembled imperial conditions in many ways, even for great empires, like that of the Ottomans, which remained technically independent. The impact of European views was a bit softer, because there was no direct colonial control or responsibility, but the growing economic and military power of the West created broadly similar opportunities for sexual commentary. Many Western observers loudly lamented the effeminacy of Chinese men, seen as too indulgent in sexual pursuits though also unkind to women. Chinese women came in for less criticism, partly because (aside from prostitutes and the concubines wealthier Westerners could arrange for) they were mostly walled off from Western men. Western women commented on excessive docility, and worked to reform such practices as foot binding. They also, as usual, criticized any relationships between white men and Chinese women—a missionary, Mrs. Betterton, wrote: "I have no patience with that idea, their wives are a sort of lap dog." At the same time, changes and deteriorations in local economic conditions created their own pressures for change. In nineteenth-century China, for example, a growing minority of men never married, while women's marriage age rose—symptoms of new problems in getting established economically. Marriage ages remained far lower than those of the West, at 21 for men and 17 for women by the 1890s, but there was a longer period between puberty and marriage than had been the case before. Along with urban growth and internal migration, changes of this sort would affect sexuality quite independent of any more direct Western influence.

Efforts to maintain tradition showed in many ways. Again in China, arranged marriages, particularly in the upper classes, remained standard. So did the goal, where wealth permitted, of multiple concubines—though by the twentieth century new standards, partly imported from the West, raised growing objections to this practice, now widely condemned as backward, and it would disappear conclusively in the throes of communist victory in the 1950s. Infanticide remained a leading form of birth control, vital in a society beset with new economic and political uncertainties. Rates here were high, with growing focus on female infanticide to such an extent that, in some regions, gender ratios became badly distorted. Obviously, a key goal was both to limit surviving children and to give great preference to male heirs, a pattern that was only new in its increasing extent.

Separate from Western pressures, the Chinese government began even in the eighteenth century to try to limit sexuality in the public culture, discouraging both literature and art with sexual, including homosexual, themes. Early in the eighteenth century over 150 titles were banned, with efforts to burn reproved books and the printing blocks that manufactured them and with stiff penalties for anyone caught selling this kind of material. Nevertheless, erotic themes continued to appear, often by anonymous authors. Several novels and compilations detailed homosexual practices. The novel *Precious Mirror of Boy Actresses*, late in the nineteenth century, contained explicit descriptions of sexual arousal and intercourse, but also operations on male organs damaged by sexually transmitted diseases. The government for the first time tried to ban homosexual intercourse with a law of 1740, but it was not widely enforced and even in the imperial court homosexual relations flourished well into the nineteenth century. Popular stage performances featured men dressed as women but also men and boys simulating sexual activity. Official Chinese attempts to define and defend sexual respectability probably helped limit Western criticisms—certainly in comparison with Africa or India—though, of course, some hostile commentary surfaced.

The rise of nationalism and communism, particularly by the early decades of the twentieth century, generated new vigor for efforts to redefine sexual standards—including the mounting attacks on concubinage. "New women" were praised, and the notion included greater freedom from parental dictates in selecting a mate. Many revolutionaries wrote of the connection between romantic passion and the zeal needed for political change. Yu Dafu wrote in the late 1920s: "The emergence of a revolutionary career is possible only for that little passion, the cultivation of which is inseparable from the tender and pure love of a woman. That passion, if extended, is ardent enough to burn down the palaces of despots." Whether this rhetoric had much relationship to sexual realities, at a time when engaging in protest was serious and demanding activity, is not clear.

Change and external pressure were clearer themes for the Ottoman Empire where, as we have seen, hostile Western commentary developed early on. Educated Arabs and Turks were quite aware of Western criticism, including the belief that Muslims were excessively lustful and the widespread exaggerations concerning harem practices. Some became deeply offended, particularly because in their view Western women seemed far too free in public, far too little concerned with sexual honor. In French-conquered Algeria, some Muslim writers turned European criticisms right back at the source, arguing that Westerners were the ones who were too lascivious, too unconcerned with protecting women from sexual exposure. Even more efforts were directed—without great success—at correcting Western misimpressions. Several women authors, often writing in a European language, tried to dispel exaggerations about the harems while also indicating changes that were occurring among women themselves. All of this contributed to a widespread discussion in educated circles within the Middle East about women's status and role, and the need to reconsider the structure of marriage. In 1873, for example, Namik Kemal mocked Turkish marriage practices in a play, urging the importance of mutual love as the basis for marital relations and the need to discuss issues of this sort more openly—though the authorities did not look kindly on his efforts. In the 1890s an important debate arose in Egypt over whether women should continue to be veiled—some arguing that change was essential because the West saw veiling as a sign of backwardness, others arguing that the practice was vital both to Middle Eastern identity and to the protection of female purity. Obviously, debate about what women should be like in the modern world, and how this related to older sexual restrictions, was lively here as in China at the same point in time.

Considerable discussion also focused on homosexuality. Many Western observers focused strongly on Islamic tolerance for homosexual relations, greatly exaggerating in the process. Author Richard Burton thus noted, "There is another element in the *Thousand and One Nights* and that is one of absolute obscenity utterly repugnant to English readers, even the least prudish." Homosexual themes in literature, and actual relationships particularly between older men and teenage boys, undoubtedly continued in the Middle East. Love poetry, for example, frequently praised "beautiful boys." Ironically, while these practices drew fire in the West, they also, by the late nineteenth century, began to attract some prominent Westerners interested in homosexual practices and eager either to describe or participate in them—with an openness impossible in the West itself. Writers like T. E. Lawrence and Oscar Wilde; painters like Delacroix all explored these issues through travel to the region (an early example, it has been suggested, of sex tourism). Of course, the general erotic reputation of the region drew others interested in heterosexual contacts, as in India or Africa, but the homosexual twist was unusual.

In the Middle East itself, however, comments on homosexuality became increasingly unfavorable during the period, doubtless in part because of the dominant Western hostility to the practice. Al-Tahtawn, in 1834, criticized the French for being too much under women's control, but added, "One of the better things among their traits … is their lack of predilection for the love of male juveniles or for writing rhapsodies for them." By the 1880s a Lebanese writer could denounce homosexuality, particularly with young boys, as "one of the ugliest forms of debauchery." Another author, in 1922, urged reforms to "strengthen what exists between men and women of natural inclinations," so that, "we would not complain about women's infatuation with women and men's love of youthful boys." Here was an important, and quite specific, version of the larger debate over how widely to apply Western standards in the sexual field.

Along with new discussions, largely at the elite level, other conditions for sexuality in the Middle East maintained great continuity with the past, at least until after 1900. Islamic law remained constant, in terms of attitudes toward adultery, the rules of divorce and so on. Polygamy persisted, though probably at lower levels than before; major rulers had large harems—with 400–500 female slaves in the imperial harem alone, mainly from outlying regions of the empire. Abortion and birth control were still supported, with far less reproval than developed in the West—the *Sharia* clearly sanctioned *coitus interruptus*, but other methods could be used. Slavery did decline in the

region, though without yet disappearing, but many female slaves became domestic servants and were still vulnerable to being treated as concubines. Harem slaves were often
abused by slave traders before reaching the royal court; slave owners also frequently
provided drugs to abort children if the women became pregnant, because open knowledge of their lack of virginity would reduce their value. Some owners even claimed that
venereal diseases could be cured by having sex with young virgin slaves—with no
regard for their health or possible future fertility.

The combination of ongoing traditions, Western critique, and growing reform
impulses increasingly led various leaders to contemplate more fundamental change.
Medical training improved by the later nineteenth century in places like Egypt, providing better gynecological and midwife services. In 1917 a new family law in the Ottoman
Empire placed family issues under more secular authority, with greater rights to
divorce and monogamy. Only a minority of educated women could take advantage of
the law, and polygamy and repudiation of "fallen women" continued, but there was
some movement away from religious norms.

The nationalist regime of Kemal Attaturk, in Turkey, began a more systematic
reform effort in the 1920s. Veils and concealing costumes were banned, because, as
Attaturk argued, they "made the nation an object of ridicule." Polygamy and repudiation of wives were outlawed, replaced by civil marriage and divorce procedures.
Villages, to be sure, clung to older habits, but polygamy did largely disappear in all
social classes, and the marriage age increased. Attaturk had every interest in supporting
the family; his moves were not designed to heighten sexual freedom but rather to provide new protections for women in a familial context. Reforms of this sort nevertheless continued a now well-established debate about changes in gender relations and
adjustments to the Islamic tradition, with significant implications for key aspects of
sexuality. Even though Attaturk harbored a rather conservative family ethic, his
changes significantly altered a number of key institutions in Turkish life, with potential
influence on other parts of the Middle East as well. As in China and elsewhere, nationalism combined reactions to Western critiques with reassertions of sexual propriety,
capping over a century of lively discussion.

Latin America

Key developments in Latin America in the two centuries after 1750 were in some ways
less decisive than those in Asia and Africa, if only because the crucial interaction with
Europe had already occurred. Trends shaped in the colonial period continued in many
ways, even amid the formal achievements of national independence. But here, too, a
new reform current emerged around 1900 that had some additional implications for
sexual change.

Catholic standards officially were meant to define sexual activity, with the emphasis
obviously on marital sex and a strong focus on reproduction. In fact, many of the colonial patterns of informal liaisons and no small amount of violence and exploitation
continued. Until abolition, female slaves often remained fair game for their masters: in
1814 a 17-year-old Peruvian slave, Manuelita, was raped by her master and filed suit in

court, but was found guilty of lying and forced to return to the owner, who ultimately got her pregnant. While rates of rape generally are impossible to determine, they involved more than the slave population; in some cases a vendetta against another family was expressed through rape of a wife. As before, the tensions between religious norms and actual behavior tended to create a vast gulf between decent and presumably virtuous women and others, including not only prostitutes but any women who indulged in sex outside of marriage—a gulf exacerbated by racial factors, with white, European origin often exclusively equated with sexual honor and respectability. Rates of illegitimacy remained high, in a situation in which many people, even in durable relationships, simply did not bother with marriage—though Catholic campaigns against lewd behaviors did gradually push the rates of marriage up. Respectable women were expected to maintain their virtue during courtship, at least until formal engagement occurred. A number of lawsuits reflected problems here, with promised brides surrendering their virginity only to find that the marriage did not occur. In Mexico, Rosa de Pedra sued Antonio de Zarate for breach of marriage promise, but Antonio arranged for many witnesses to testify that she had been with other men before their intercourse and Rosa was ruled a *mujer inquieta*—a woman of loose morality. Effective double standards made it hard for women to navigate relationships successfully. Correspondingly men were often excused for adultery, despite official Church disapproval, whereas women might be punished severely by the families involved.

Changes did develop from the late nineteenth century onward, particularly around new concerns about venereal disease and the growth of urban prostitution, and amid efforts to respond to international pressures against white slavery. Police harassment of prostitutes increased in several cities during the 1870s and 1880s, as prostitutes were scapegoats for the more general disease problem. Feminists—including some women doctors once women began freely to enter medical schools by the 1890s—and public health advocates urged new kinds of sex education, not only to help curtail exposure to disease but also to reduce the stigma of illegitimacy. Catholic control for the most part limited the effectiveness of these efforts. But the calls for increased regulation of prostitution hit home, among feminists as well as other groups, particularly given growing public concerns that the growth of sexually transmitted diseases jeopardized the vigor of future generations. Argentina tried to outlaw prostitution in 1936; Chile mandated blood testing before marriage two years later.

Most other regulatory activity worked at defending marriage and reproduction. Artificial contraception was either illegal or disapproved, though people continued to use herbal preventatives quite widely. Several countries jailed women for having abortions—in Chile this did not change until the 1940s. Argentina, in 1921, granted exceptions for abortions to save a woman's life or for pregnancies resulting from rape, but otherwise mandated four years in prison. In fact, abortions continued—a doctor in Uruguay claimed a 40 percent increase in procedures in public hospitals between 1898 and 1924, as actual sexual habits confronted the problem of too many children or children out of wedlock. But the dominant official attitudes remained forbidding. Most legal systems also made divorce quite difficult, sometimes amid arguments about the importance of marriage in controlling male sexual impulses.

On the margins, mainly among feminists, certain voices were raised on other topics. A magazine article in 1892 talked of marriage as something that "brings the satisfaction of sexual desires, [which have a favorable] effect on women's health and contribute to lengthening her life"—a rare comment about women's sexual interests beyond protection against violence or unwanted pregnancy. Arguments about the need for more available birth control devices and information surfaced more strongly by the 1920s. Another article argued that, "a woman will never be the mistress of her own body if she cannot choose the moment she wants to become a mother." But these were still minority views amid mainstream official insistence on the importance of virginity before marriage, reproduction within it. Feminists themselves, concerned about double standards and the challenge of prostitution to women, marriage, and health, tended to express greater interest in sexual regulation—even urging repression of references to female sexuality in the public media—than in new forms of female expression.

Overall, Latin America participated in a number of the key global trends of the nineteenth century, including signs of growing promiscuity but also some more novel efforts at reform. Less sense of fundamental innovation followed because of the previous encounters with colonial compulsion. There was also little need to discuss disparaging Western views, since the public standards applied to sexuality, derived from Catholicism, were Western as well. Criticism of lower-class behavior, however, did contain an element of worried apology for groups that did not seem to measure up to more Victorian norms and that might therefore seem uncivilized, and some of the regulations imposed—particularly against prostitution—had as one aim the cultivation of international approval.

Japan and Russia: revisiting industrialization and sexuality

Japan and Russia, unlike most of the rest of the world outside of the West itself, began directly to experience an industrial revolution by the end of the nineteenth century, and with this the kinds of disruptions in established sexual patterns that had begun to occur earlier in Western society during the sexual revolution of the eighteenth century. In some ways the result simply intensified patterns in other places around growing urbanism and dislocations of women's economic lives, including the apparently inevitable expansion of prostitution. But the challenge to sexual traditions was greater because of much more substantial displacement, and it extended more directly into the countryside than was true, for example, in India. The notion of a sexual revolution in these two countries would not be entirely displaced.

At the same time, these societies shared with other parts of the world the need to react to complex Western standards and examples. Japan, particularly, newly in contact with global trends, undertook some serious adjustments to try, at least officially, to measure up to standards of respectability. These issues were less acute for Russia, already part of the Western cultural orbit in key respects. Russian sexual traditions were not, in fact, the same as those of the West, which meant that several key developments were quite distinctive; but there was direct participation in some Western trends, particularly by the later nineteenth century. The Russian revolution of 1917, however, ushered in a truly challenging period in which sexual issues were open to new debate, at least for a time, after which a new set of differences from the contemporary West was enshrined for several decades.

The first take on major changes in Japanese sexuality mirrored the wider patterns of exposure to Western imperialism: Japan remained proudly independent, but after 1853, and particularly with the advent of the Meiji era in 1868, the nation encountered growing pressure from Western commentary. Considerable attention focused on the traditional *geisha* houses, which many Westerners viewed as dens of iniquity and essentially lascivious. In fact, the geisha houses involved wide-ranging entertainment, with strong sexual overtones but not necessarily outright sexual contact. The geisha tradition did involve positive assumptions about the validity of male sexual pleasure and an appreciation for female sexuality that undeniably ran counter to contemporary Victorian ideas. Artistic representations associated with the geisha themes frequently featured sensual poses, including the work of Utamaro Kitagawa in the early nineteenth century who depicted women half-clad and wet, resting after a dive—and Western opinion readily dismissed this as outright pornography. This whole aspect of Japanese tradition invited that distinctive combination of exaggeration of explicit sexual content and harsh critique that so often characterized the Western approach in this period. Other commentary disparaged traditions of tolerance for homosexuality—Japan had continued to accept homosexual acts as occasional behaviors, not expressions of exclusive homosexuality—and the vigor of Japanese manhood (this last particularly galling to a country with a highly masculine emphasis in fact).

Japanese official response was exceptionally direct and vigorous: new measures must be taken to counter these Western perceptions. Regulations of geisha houses stiffened. Government bureaucrats reasserted the Confucian emphasis on the importance of family, a combined effort to appeal to traditions of stability while also countering Western concerns. In 1873, an unprecedented law, clearly designed to show Japan as civilized by Western standards, declared homosexual intercourse illegal—and though it was rescinded just seven years later, Japanese official and public attitudes toward homosexuality continued to express new levels of hostility, with one result an increasing effort by participants to conceal any homosexual behavior from the public eye and also from families.

Emphasis on family morality bore particularly keenly on women, who were urged to remain faithful and channel their sexual interests toward childbearing. Thus, without, of course, referring to sexuality directly, the minister of education in 1909 argued that the object of the education of women "is to fit girls to become good wives and wise mothers." Popular magazines urged women to suppress their own needs to uphold the interests of the family. Messages were a bit mixed: there was also some new discussion of sexual desire as part of the ideal women and new praise for Western standards of female beauty. Between 1910 and 1930, media outlets debated the sexuality of what was termed the "new woman," picking up both on new Western standards of more open sexuality and on interests of Japanese youth in less restrictive behavior. One essay, talking about youth culture, simply headlined: "Onward! Dance! Legs! Legs!

Legs!" Some new feminist leaders also talked about greater sexual liberation for women, as against Japanese traditions that kept them as "caged birds" or "fragile flowers." But again, substantial reaction returned to the family theme, urging women to maintain sexual restraint even in the home in the interests of decorum and a concentration on the conception and rearing of children.

One result, apart from the clearly mixed signals being sent to women, was a Japanese variant on a theme that had also emerged in the Victorian West: a sense that the family, though vital, was not the place to seek sexual satisfaction. Given Japanese traditions, this could encourage continued male interest (where wealth permitted) in patronizing the geisha houses or maintaining mistresses. Another result, rather different from the West in the Victorian heyday, was a substantial amount of open, public discussion of sexual issues and a great deal of attention, at least by the early twentieth century, to sex scandals involving people in high places. Both literature and art devoted considerable attention to sexual themes.

More important still were the signs of growing interest in sexual pleasure on the part of the growing populations in the cities—male pleasure at least, and sometimes female as well. Steeply rising divorce rates often reflected male sexual dissatisfaction with their wives, along with the sheer disruption and family dismemberment resulting from rapid urbanization. Large numbers of women now headed into the growing silk sweatshops and textile factories, where they were deprived of traditional community protection and often subjected to sexual harassment—as had been true in the Western factory experience earlier. Sexually suggestive fashions—some of them derived from the West—spread among working women, particularly in occupations like waitressing, where women were encouraged to flirt with customers, sell kisses for tips, and generally project an erotic image. Large "pleasure zones" grew up in cities, including dance halls and theaters in addition to the sex trade—recalling some geisha themes but with less customary nuance and more blatant sexuality. Many observers worried about this kind of more open sexuality because it did not seem confined simply to prostitutes or even to the lower classes alone; inevitably, some blame centered on what were seen as disruptive Western influences, particularly by the 1920s when Western fashions began to project a less Victorian image: thus a lament about moral decline, where because of "frivolous Western influence, young men and women put on airs and rampantly swagger. ..."

The new quest for pleasure combined with severe dislocations in the rural economy, particularly for women, to generate rapid growth in prostitution. Many poor women were essentially abducted (what we now call trafficked), promised factory jobs but then forced into prostitution, often in China or other parts of Asia. Expansion of the occupation in Japanese cities was considerable in its own right: by the 1920s it was estimated that over 50,000 prostitutes were in operation, servicing an average of two to three men daily. As in other societies, though at some cost to the strictest family morals, prostitution was tolerated as an outlet for male desire that thus protected decent women; older Japanese tolerance for a long tradition of female sex service contributed to these attitudes. A law of 1872 emancipated prostitutes, to guard against Western claims that the Japanese treated women as sexual slaves; but it had little impact in practice. And

Japanese patterns had some unusually extreme features. In 1866 a law forbidding Japanese prostitutes to travel abroad was rescinded, leading to a major increase in the export of young women for sex work By the late 1870s a systematic industry existed to gather and ship prostitutes. In 1901 a woman reported being told by a recruiter: "If you go to work abroad, every day is like a festival, you can wear nice kimono, and every day you can eat as much white rice as you want. Won't you come with me?" These recruits ended in Singapore, a British colony, in Japanese-run brothels that had particular local prestige compared to Chinese or Korean counterparts. By the early twentieth century, some of these patterns began to be reversed, as the Japanese themselves began to expand the importation of foreign women. In particular, the Japanese military, after the occupation of Korea, began to bring in "comfort women," over 85 percent from Korea: these were teenagers mainly either kidnapped or promised factory jobs in the same manner earlier employed in Japan itself. These women were often brutally used, and then on return to Korea unable to marry because of the stigma of their experience. By the end of World War II, comfort women were also serving allied soldiers in "recreation and amusement centers," and when these were banned by the allies as violations of women's rights the occupying military set up privately run brothels in their stead. The tradition was hard to break, and would indeed survive into the contemporary era in slightly altered form.

The Japanese sexual experience during early industrialization was clearly contradictory in many ways. Some particular Japanese precedents fed into the growing gap between recommended standards and widespread new behaviors, including the earlier open commendation of sexual pleasure. And the perceived need to react to Western assessments was a complicating factor, shared in this case with most other regions of the world. All this said, the parallels between the Japanese experience and earlier Western industrial patterns were striking: early industrialization obviously created new needs and opportunities for the pursuit of sexual pleasure, including new limitations on older community controls; but it also apparently generated a need to insist officially on greater levels of sexual restraint than ever before, as part of the larger reaction to social change. That the result was deeply confusing is undeniable, but not uniquely Japanese.

Russia would generate its own version of tighter sexual standards and new interests in sexual expression—another version, that is, of a standard early industrial pattern—in which the aftermath of the great 1917 revolution would play an unexpected role.

First, the key changes in sexual behavior, by now predictable enough from the experiences of other early industrial societies. Russian peasants, that vast majority of the population before the 1860s, had long struggled with the controls over sexuality necessary to keep population growth down, given constraints on available land—guided of course by Orthodox Christian morality. Primary focus rested, as usual, on regulating sexual activity before marriage. Strong emphasis on virginity, particularly female virginity before marriage, vied with a certain degree of tolerance for premarital sex in some peasant regions; early marriage ages helped reconcile this dilemma. With the emancipation of the serfs in 1861 and growing mobility, including rapid urbanization, peasant habits changed. Premarital sex increased, and with it—as in Western Europe before—rates of illegitimacy. One writer in the Vologda province noted about the local peasantry, "Before he marries, a bachelor has two or three children from different mothers ... in most parts of the province, no one pays strict attention to a maiden's chastity." Extramarital sex, though morally reproved, increased as well. So did prostitution. Catherine the Great in the eighteenth century had brought prostitution under police supervision, with severe punishments for unregulated activity; but in the 1840s the police began issuing official permits for "comfort houses," including medical inspections, and the other legal constraints stopped being enforced. By the 1890s it was estimated that there were 2,500 brothels across the empire, and cities like St. Petersburg matched the rates of prostitution of other European capitals. Brothers or friends often took boys to be sexually initiated in these houses. And, of course, sexually transmitted diseases began to increase as well. Abortion rates were another sign of change, as people sought to counter the unwanted pregnancies that resulted from heightened sexual activity: between 1897 and 1912 the number of abortions in St. Petersburg increased tenfold, though technically the operations were a crime. Homosexuality may also have gained ground, particularly in colleges and universities. A 1903 law eased the official punishments for homosexual intercourse, which were rarely administered in any event, without making it legal. A popular student song around the turn of the century joked that sex with one's friends was more fun than sex with women.

Against this backdrop of behavioral change, cultural reactions varied. A conservative group lamented the decline of the family, which many observers agreed was now in crisis. Nationalists often blamed Western novels, like *Madame Bovary*, for excessive eroticism, and urged censorship. Jews were another target, often criticized as responsible for the spread of brothels. Writers like Tolstoy railed against sexual preoccupations as animal-like, capable of ruining men—a focus on sex "is an aim unworthy of human beings." Some doctors joined the chorus, lecturing about the health dangers of sexuality for youth. As in the West, many resisted contraception: one commented in 1893 that contraceptive devices were spreading, openly advertised and available in drugstores; but, because they facilitated increased sexual activity, they were seen as damaging health. Masturbation also drew comment, seen as a sign of decadence.

With all this, however, a full Victorian mood did not take hold, if only because sexual issues were so openly and diversely discussed. Newspaper ads appeared with themes like "how to quench your sexual thirst" and "any woman can have an ideal bust," sometimes with pictures of naked women attached. Pornography spread, and intellectuals like Chukovsky endorsed the trend: "People should enjoy love without fear and prohibition ... and this word *should* is a vestige of former intellectual habits, a vestige of a former moral code which is disappearing before our very eyes." Reformers also urged that abortion be decriminalized, because of the dangerous methods used in surreptitious procedures. Poets and painters turned to more erotic themes by the early twentieth century. Bryusov wrote in 1904 that, "passion is that lush color for which our body exists. ... Our time, which has illuminated passion, has for the first time enabled artists to portray it, without being ashamed of their work.... The one who sins is he who has a simple-minded attitude toward passionate feeling." Fascination with sexual violence and with homosexuality—including openly gay and lesbian poets—formed part of this cultural current.

In this climate of cultural diversity and behavioral change, the impact of the Russian revolution first seemed to confirm the sexual liberality of the society. Communist attacks on religion obviously encouraged many people to rethink attitudes toward institutions like marriage—as Claire Zetkin commented, "In the area of marriage and sexual relations, the revolution is nigh, in keeping with the proletarian revolution." Civil procedures replaced church weddings, and divorce was liberalized. Homosexuality was entirely decriminalized in 1917, a move which Bolsheviks touted as a sign of their modern, scientific attitudes. Behavioral trends intensified in this environment, with a great growth in prostitution and venereal disease; the divorce rate exploded by 700 percent by the 1920s. A law in 1920 itself legalized abortion as a means of reducing mortality resulting from infections in clandestine operations—this was the first legalization in all of Europe. Premarital sex increased, particularly in the cities, with the average age of first sexual experience for men falling to 16. Much discussion focused on the sheer physical pleasure of sex, and the need to experiment, as against earlier, outdated ideas about morality or even love. Adultery almost certainly increased, with participants claiming sexual dissatisfaction within marriage as their rationale.

The free mood of the post-revolutionary 1920s did not last. Obviously, some of the problems of the new approach toward sexuality almost required response, for example concerning venereal disease. Communism itself could easily lead to a critique of sexual interests both as too purely individualistic and as distracting people from the true, collective goals of building an industrial economy and a socialist society. Officials even by the mid-1920s were writing that: "Sexual life is permissible only insofar as it encourages the growth of collective feelings, class organization." Increasing concern developed over what was seen as a moral crisis. And, given the huge losses in World War I, there were practical reasons to encourage a greater focus on family and reproduction. Finally, actual popular attitudes had not changed as much as the sexual radicals might imply: many people remained deeply anxious about masturbation, homosexuality, and even heterosexual activity outside marriage.

The result, by the 1930s and the rise of Stalin, was an almost complete reversal of tone and policy, and an increasing association of communism, at least in its Russian version, with a latter-day Victorian ethic on sex. Attacks on "sexual depravity" mounted. Accusations of sexuality and eroticism became part of virtually every ideological campaign against real or imagined opponents of the state. New laws attacked pornography and officially banned prostitution—communism, it was now argued, should make these kinds of deviant sexual activities unnecessary. Schools introduced sex education courses emphasizing moral behavior. Officials attacked homosexuality—one claimed in 1934, "Annihilate homosexuality, and fascism will disappear." By 1936 homosexuality was again outlawed, tied to decadence and counterrevolution. Divorce laws became more complex, as part of the defense of marital sexuality and reproduction. Open discussions of sexual issues became increasingly taboo, even though Stalin himself was mythologized (in traditional leadership fashion) as highly sexual, with many wives and an impressive physical apparatus. Experts touted sexual sublimation and control as a key to productivity, creativity and socialist solidarity—a communist version of the same virtues that Victorians had emphasized during the industrialization decades in the West.

How much this affected behavior is open to question. Precisely because communists developed such a stake in claiming the relationship between revolutionary advance and sexual purity, data on activities like prostitution disappeared—the official claim was that no problem existed. Leaders delighted in contrasting communist sobriety with the decadence they saw increasing in the capitalist West. Abortion rates definitely remained high, despite official encouragement to population growth—abortion became the standard Russian birth control device, a clear sign of continued change, of a new separation between sex and procreation, beneath the surface of public rhetoric. But the asexual tone of Soviet society was unquestionable, down to restrained, even dowdy styles of dress. By the 1950s sexual claims would play some role in the Cold War, with Westerners touting their increasingly open attitudes and alluring costumes with what they saw as a drab uniformity in the communist state, while communists continued to hammer at the theme of sexual decadence. For a time, at least, Soviet Russia's public culture seemed to carve out a distinctive response to the blend of sex and industrialization.

Global themes: new and old constraints

Cutting across regions and diversities, three key factors shaped and constrained world history in the decades between 1750 and 1950. None of them was entirely new, but all of them incorporated some novel elements.

Outside of the Western world, birth control methods did not change greatly—as we have seen, even in the West their full impact was slow in coming. Most people continued to rely on *coitus interruptus* plus herbal contraceptives and abortions. Botanical concoctions varied from one region to the next, but the basic reliance was widespread. In Africa some women used chopped grass or cloth to block their cervix, a distinctive embellishment. Nowhere, however, were methods particularly reliable. Only as industrialization spread, as in Russia, or more haltingly in Latin America, did growing opportunities emerge either for manufactured contraceptives or surgical abortions. Elsewhere, lack of contraceptive innovation was an ongoing fact of sexual life.

This was, of course, old news. What changed, now, was increasing sexual promiscuity in the cities and, in many regions, significant population growth. Particularly toward the latter part of the nineteenth century, improved public health measures began to cut down traditional mortality levels, causing more people to live to childbearing age. The result could be significant pressure on land availability and jobs—a key reason in turn for growing rates of migration and movement toward cities. All of this raised new issues for sex and restraint. As in Europe, many couples doubtless depended increasingly on prolonged periods of abstinence when the risk of having excess children was simply too great. But for those who could not generate this kind of restraint, and for the many women servants and prostitutes often pregnant entirely against their will, other methods were essential. We have seen that in some places, like China, infanticide increased as a result. So did rates of abortion. Reconciling sexual activity and the burdens of children was a classic problem in agricultural societies, and the problem tended to intensify in this period.

Venereal disease was a second issue, not fundamentally new, but reaching new dimensions. Various partial remedies had long been available for sexually transmitted diseases. Until the mid-nineteenth century in Europe, a mercury compound—in ointment form—was normally applied to the skin lesions caused by syphilis, hence a saying "A night in the arms of Venus leads to a lifetime on Mercury." Treatment of course depended on awareness that the disease needed to be addressed, and the results were palliative; there was no cure, and later in life other ailments, including heart disease and dementia, could result. Growing rates of the disease prompted new attention, both in policy and research. Philippe Ricard in France first showed that gonorrhea and syphilis were separate diseases, in 1838; his work also led to new treatments by arsenic compounds, taken as pills—the medicine did reduce symptoms but it was also toxic, causing energy-sapping side effects. Concern also focused on contagion, as officials increasingly realized how important it was to try to prevent transmission. In Britain a new Contagious Diseases act in 1860, though widely criticized as interfering with private matters, led to compulsory health inspections for prostitutes. Military authorities also began to regulate women available to soldiers, and warned soldiers themselves to use caution and/or to employ prophylactics—the result was an actual decline in syphilis among Western military forces between 1860 and 1910.

Most of these developments, of course, focused on Europe and North America. Europeans claimed to be shocked at how Asians tended to ignore the diseases, neglecting possibilities for therapy. But even in Europe, ignorance and the limited effectiveness and side effects of treatment long constrained care. Here and elsewhere, widespread beliefs that the disease was the result of irresponsible behavior also limited attention and sympathy. Women, in Europe, Africa, and in other regions, were less likely to gain any sort of treatment than men, again partly as a result of social shame; in Africa, white colonists had much better access than black Africans, among whom authorities mainly focused on quarantines and containment. Latin American doctors began to worry greatly about the spread of venereal disease by the late nineteenth century, but treatments were sketchy; use of arsenic began only in the 1920s, and it was not very effective. Governments in this situation tried to criminalize the spread of disease, insisting on the responsibility for self-control. Research continued, increasingly on an international basis. The German government established a research institute in 1883 that ultimately focused primarily on curing syphilis. The first diagnostic test for syphilis emerged in 1906. Experiments on gonorrhea focused on using the pus of infected men as a possible vaccine, along with use of bleeding and heavy washing. A blood test for syphilis was developed in the 1920s, and Japanese scientists soon followed with a skin test.

But the real breakthrough did not occur until the 1930s, again first in the West, with the introduction of antibiotics. Antibiotics, soon including penicillin, actually derived from earlier uses of lead, but unlike all the earlier, poisonous compounds these drugs actually cured the leading forms of venereal disease, portending a new (if rather brief) period in the history of sexuality and contagion.

Through most of the period 1750–1950, however, sexually transmitted diseases were a vital downside in the changing sexual climate, prompting growing concern but relatively ineffective response in most societies, with huge differentials in therapy by gender, social class, and region. Rising rates of disease were an important indication of key changes in sexual practice, beneath the surface of moral preachments. Awareness of the disease was also, of course, an important constraint on actual behavior, as not only military and civilian authorities but also ordinary parents and sex educators in the schools urged caution on young people for the sake of basic health, whatever the moral connections—with, of course, mixed results in practice.

A final constraint on sexuality, and this was quite novel on a global basis, involved homosexuality. Homosexual activity had been treated quite variously in particular regions through world history—until the nineteenth century. At this point, however, Western pressure plus some additional factors—like imperial decisions in eighteenth-century China—began to create much more uniform hostility to homosexual practices than had ever been the case before. Western observers claimed to find rampant homosexuality in virtually every other part of the world—it became a standard part of the attack on loose morals and inferior masculinities. In the West itself, as we have seen, new scholarly theories about homosexuality led to more restrictive definitions and harsher attitudes by the later nineteenth century. Direct Western regulation became part of the wave of imperialism in many other regions. Article 377 of the British-sponsored Indian penal code outlawed homosexual intercourse, and was extended to all British colonies—in large stretches of Africa, in Southeast Asia, and in the Caribbean, as well as in New Zealand, Canada, and Australia; homosexuality was outlawed in British-controlled Iraq after World War I—the list was a long one. At the same time, it was revealing how widely other, independent governments also concluded that new levels of hostility to homosexuality were a crucial part of the response to the pressure of Western standards—hence the unprecedented Japanese law on the subject. Soviet Russia made homosexual intercourse illegal in 1936, extending the provision to the republics in the Islamic regions of the empire; this formed part of Stalin's crackdown on sexual license. Many regimes clearly found measures on homosexuality culturally more palatable than action on some other kinds of sexual issues—most societies had looked down on aspects of homosexuality in some respects, so tightening restrictions might seem a particularly feasible step. Furthermore, in a climate in which Western criticisms of effeminate masculinities in Asia, Africa, and Latin America became widely known, many local leaders—as in the Middle East—might easily decide that a new look at tolerance for homosexuality was a crucial response. Here was not only a probable reason for the new and far-ranging changes in policy, but for the passion with which new, anti-homosexual laws would be defended into very recent times, even in societies that had traditionally been far more tolerant. The result, again, was a real change in global history, an unprecedented uniformity of concern, in a key aspect of human sexuality.

Homosexual activity did not, of course, disappear; regulations were not always fiercely enforced. But increasingly homosexual activities had to be conducted in greater concealment—as had long been true in the West; and it became harder for people to maintain a bisexual approach, as opposed to committing either to a hetero-sexual or a homosexual framework—another highly untraditional result for most of the world's regions.

*   *   *

Change, but also continuity, formed the dominant theme in the world history of sexu-ality during the two centuries after 1750—hardly a surprising finding. Reactions to Western standards, plus more general shifts, began to close down some key sexual options, particularly at the upper end of the social scale. Growing foreign disapproval, plus the collapse of great empires like the Mughal and Ottoman, began to end long-standing traditions such as the keeping of harems or the recruitment of eunuchs (cas-tration is now seen as a barbaric mutilation, save perhaps in restraining sex criminals). Upper-class men might seek some partial alternatives for concubines, through mis-tresses or the expanding reaches or prostitution or simply multiple, serial marriages, but some specific sexual institutions were passing from the scene. Even polygamy began to decline in certain societies.

For most people, of course, distant from the world of harems, the most important changes involved the growth of some opportunities for sex before or outside marriage, particularly through prostitution but also through more casual sex in some urban set-tings. At the same time, older standards, such as hostility to adultery or efforts to pre-serve female virginity before marriage, were fiercely defended in many quarters. And the absence of any sweeping changes in the contraception available in most regions continued to constrain marital intercourse with the threat of unwanted numbers of children.

Explicit sexual reforms, backed by some colonial administrators and missionaries, but also local leaders including early feminists, mainly worked to protect women against some forms of sexuality now widely regarded as abusive—as in trying to limit sexual access to child brides by raising the marriage age and also by the more general movement to abolish slavery. Clearly also, in many societies and in many ways, unprecedented concerns were being raised about double standard sexuality. However, rising prostitution, based in part on women's deteriorating economic position in many societies, and the surge of sexual violence to underscore masculine power, pushed clearly in the other direction. The balance sheet here is hard to draw. Although this was not a period that witnessed global freedoms in sexual culture, given not only Victorian but also Chinese and other attempts to hold the line on blatant sexuality, the rise of more available pornography, often with global themes, again suggested new methods in the sexualization of women. And the essentially global efforts to define and attack homosexuality constituted another new kind of constraint in many societies.

On ultimately a global basis also, the two centuries after 1750, and particularly the decades around 1900, established a growing divide between clear signs of increasingly promiscuous sexual practice, among key groups, and strenuous efforts to define stan-dards of restraint often more rigorously than ever before. Gaps between moral recom-mendations and actual response were hardly new to this period, but the space was widening. This was a tension built into trends in the West, at least until after 1900, with the gap between the sexual revolution and Victorianism. Western pressures and reactions to them created similar impulses elsewhere, as governments and officials sought new ways to define a family morality that would measure up to Western standards and perhaps preserve some key traditions as well—as in attempts to find new ways to shore up family morality in Latin America or glorify reproductive sexuality as part of the Japanese Confucian tradition. The decrease in tolerance, at least in public rhetoric, for earlier patterns of more expressive sexuality was part of this trend toward greater rigor. As against this, signs of looser popular behavior were unmistakable. A key question by the twentieth century, in many societies, was whether the gap between norms and practice was sustainable, or whether some new juncture between standards and behavior would become essential.

Key sexual trends in the decades between 1750 and 1950 clearly set the stage for additional changes to come. Reform efforts, with international backing, would continue, even as the age of imperialism receded. More open interest in sexual pleasure, as part of urban consumer culture, would gain ground as well, spurred further by massive changes in media and with the decline of Victorianism in the West. Opportunities to redefine the relationship between standards and behavior arose as a result, at least in a number of regions. However, nothing around 1950 fully foreshadowed the substantial redefinition of sexual issues that would take place during the next sixty years. Popular movies, issued from Hollywood but also regional centers like Egypt, remained sexually sedate in the 1950s—Hollywood still resisted showing even a married couple in the same bed, much less with clothing in any disarray. New statements of human rights, issuing in the late 1940s from the United Nations, scarcely touched on sexual themes even implicitly. Dominant global issues were the Cold War, postwar economic recovery, and decolonization—not sex. But as sexual changes and challenges did emerge more prominently, certainly by the time of the heralded sexual revolution of the 1960s, they did build on the trends of the previous centuries—on reform goals, on urban sexuality, but also on some new attempts to roll back some recent themes as well, for example where homosexuality was concerned. The stage was set for another burst of change, and diverse reactions to change.

Further reading

On China, see J. Fitzgerald, *Awakening China: Politics, Culture, and Class in the Nationalist Revolution* (Stanford, CT: Stanford University Press, 1996); C. Mackerras, *Western Images of China* (New York: Oxford University Press, 1999); K. McMahon, *The Fall of the God of Money: Opium Smoking in Nineteenth-Century China* (New York: Rowman and Littlefield, 2002); G. Rozman, ed., *The Modernization of China* (New York: Free Press, 1981); and S.S. Thurin, *Victorian Travelers and the Opening of China, 1842–1907* (Athens: Ohio University Press, 1999).

For information on Japan, see E. Ben-Ari, B. Moeran, and J. Valentine, eds., *Unwrapping Japan: Society and Culture in Anthropological Perspective* (Honolulu: University of Hawaii Press, 1990); R. Benedict, *The Chrysanthemum and the Sword: Patterns of Japanese Culture* (Boston, MA: Houghton Mifflin, 1946); A. Gordon, *A Modern History of Japan* (New York: Oxford, 2003); H. Harootunian, *Overcome by Modernity: History, Culture, and Community in Interwar Japan* (Princeton,

NJ: Princeton University Press, 2000); and Y. Tomoko, *Sandakan Brothel No. 8: An Episode in the History of Lower-Class Japanese Women*, trans. K. Taylor (Armonk, NY: M.E. Sharpe, 1999).

On the Middle East, see W.G. Andrews and M. Kalpakli, *The Age of Beloveds: Love and the Beloved in Early-Modern Ottoman and European Culture and Society* (Durham, NC: Duke University Press, 2005); B. Lewis, *The Emergence of Modern Turkey*, 3rd ed. (New York: Oxford University Press, 2002); J.A. Massad, *Desiring Arabs* (Chicago: University of Chicago Press, 2007); and E.R. Toledano, *Slavery and Abolition in the Ottoman Middle East* (Seattle: University of Washington Press, 1998).

Resources on Africa include: W.B. Cohen, *The French Encounter with Africans: White Response to Blacks, 1530–1880* (Bloomington: Indiana University Press, 1980); D.L. Hodgson and S.A. McCurdy, eds., *"Wicked" Women and the Reconfiguration of Gender in Africa* (Portsmouth, NH: Heinemann, 2001); and V. Kiernan, *The Lords of Humankind: European Attitudes to other Cultures in the Imperial Age* (London: Serif, 1995).

On Russia, see L. Engelstein, *The Keys to Happiness: Sex and the Search for Modernity in fin-de-siecle Russia* (Ithaca, NY: Cornell University Press, 1992) and I. Kon, *The Sexual Revolution in Russia from the Age of the Czars to Today*, trans. J. Riordan (New York: Free Press, 1995).

Good surveys on India include: P. Banerjee, *Burning Women: Widows, Witches, and Early Modern European Travelers in India* (New York: Palgrave Macmillan, 2003); I. Chowdhury, *The Frail Hero and Virile History: Gender and the Politics of Culture in Colonial Bengal* (Delhi: Oxford University Press, 1998); E.M. Collingham, *Imperial Bodies: The Physical Experience of the Raj, c. 1800–1947* (Malden, MA: Blackwell, 2001); M. Feldman and B. Gordon, eds., *The Courtesan's Arts: Cross-cultural Perspectives* (New York: Oxford University Press, 2006); L. James, *Raj: The Making and Unmaking of British India* (New York: St. Martin's Griffin, 1997); and A. McClintock, *Imperial Leather: Race, Gender, and Sexuality in the Colonial Contest* (New York: Routledge, 1995).

Part III

Sexuality in the age of globalization

In 1959, on a visit to Los Angeles, Soviet Premier Nikita Khrushchev was taken to the Hollywood set of the movie *Can-Can*, in which a variety of actresses were dressed in showgirl costumes presumably reminiscent of Paris around 1900. He professed great shock at so much female flesh being exposed on the screen (he was already annoyed to be dragged to a film studio rather than an aerospace plant). The episode was a minor part of Cold War tensions and had no lasting aftermath, except to confirm to Soviet leaders that American society was sexually decadent, and to the American public that the Soviet system was dreary and repressive and not sexy at all.

In 2003, an Islamic court in northern Nigeria sentenced Amina Lawal, a Muslim woman, to death for the crime of adultery. She was to be buried waist-deep and then stoned by villagers until she died. World opinion was immediately outraged, as human rights organizations like Amnesty International used the Internet to contact individuals in Europe, the United States, Japan, and many other places to urge the Nigerian government (which had not passed the sentence) to intervene. Thousands of individuals and groups petitioned Nigeria, arguing that the punishment was barbaric in any event, and particularly inappropriate for a real or imagined sexual offense. The campaign worked: the villager was spared.

In 2008, two child actors in Afghanistan, who had participated in the movie *The Kite Runner* and its simulated rape scene, had to be flown out of the country because of fears that their involvement with this kind of sexual representation might endanger their lives.

Sex was going global. International film companies, like the sponsor of *The Kite Runner*, could rouse local protest. A remote religious court could generate literally global response for its attempt to enforce longstanding aversion to adultery. In a variety of ways, international standards and local reactions developed complex and unprecedented interactions. The obvious innovation was the creation of a sexually tolerant world opinion that could be mobilized against local actions. But almost as obvious, given the actual history of sexuality, was the exaggerated local response that contemporary conditions seemed to generate: after all, while Islamic hostility to adultery was highly traditional, the idea of killing a participant, with exemplary cruelty, was not characteristically traditional at all; the Quranic punishment had been 100 lashes and then, hopefully, a family reconciliation. Change, in other words, was very real, but highly complex. It involved global standards and activities but also a stiffening of sexual norms associated with the virtually global rise of various kinds of religious fundamentalism. Sexuality became a new kind of battleground in the process.

*   *   *

Historians and social scientists have written a great deal about globalization in recent years, arguing that new levels of contact are recasting key aspects of human history. The results show in the generation of novel global standards in a number of areas but also new varieties in regional response, some welcoming the new cosmopolitanism, some deeply opposed. The historical place of globalization must still be debated: some argue that current interactions are just the latest phase of a long history of accelerating human contact; others contend that it was the mid-nineteenth, not the mid-twentieth century that introduced a new global age.

From the standpoint of the history of sexuality, however, a contemporary global-ization argument is helpful in staking out a distinctive phase in sexual culture and (to a lesser degree) sexual behavior, on a worldwide basis.

Three factors are involved: first, in Europe, the United States, and Japan, and soon other parts of the world, a new and more open culture toward sexuality began to take shape in the 1950s and 1960s. It involved legal changes, allowing, for example, American movie makers to become increasingly explicit in their sexual representations without fear of censorship. It involved new types of birth control and an increasingly open commitment to recreational sexual pleasure. In various ways, particularly in media expressions, sexual openness became increasingly associated with global con-sumerism. There were inevitable and often quite nasty downsides: sex tourism and a new level of international sexual exploitation of women accompanied the surge, as did a new level of sexually-transmitted disease. In general, however, standards and values associated with sexual conservatism came under new attack in what was often hailed as a sexual revolution.

This linked, as factor number two, to the globalization movement. Less reticent public culture in the United States, new European interests in topless public sun-bathing, were not simply regional changes—they had worldwide implications thanks to new international media companies, an unprecedented wave of international tourism, and the general pressure of consumerism. Highly sexualized beauty contests, to take an obvious example, gained ground almost everywhere, even though they were initially purely Western in origin. But consumer sex was not the only global movement: new human rights concerns and a semi-global feminist movement also influenced sex-ual standards, sometimes in sympathy with the advocacy of sexual pleasure, but some-times more hesitant. New efforts to define and stigmatize rape as a war crime were just as much a part of globalization in the sexual field as were the ubiquitous Miss World contests.

The third factor was quite simply the diverse regional response and the innovations that defenders of more traditional standards thought were essential to guard against the more open culture and the new global pressures. Some innovations were violent: the unprecedentedly severe punishments of sexual crimes in certain societies or the new uses of rape as a weapon in civil strife. Other innovative reactions were perhaps equally passionate, but more purely political, like the efforts to write constitutional restrictions on homosexual couples in many American states. Sex in the global age was hardly a uniform phenomenon: change was the one consistent theme.

Earlier themes persisted, of course. Some of the cultures traditionally open to ideas of sexual pleasure, as in India, adapted to some of the changes distinctively—because tradition helped prepare adjustment. New medicines to enhance sexual potency for older men caused and also reflected real change, but it is important to remember that many societies had worked on performance enhancement before—the change was not so much the goal as the new chemicals available and the new openness of advertisement.

This final section deals with a host of specific issues, from the rise of abortion, to AIDS, to the unprecedented discussions and controversies around homosexuality. It offers new sets of comparisons, not only in cases where violent reactions can be con trasted with relatively placid adjustments, but also to the odd, and somewhat unexpected, differences between the United States and other advanced industrial societies in approaches to issues such as public nudity or premarital sex. Amid diversity of response and diversity of issues, however, the basic framework should be clear: increasingly, on a worldwide basis, sexuality was substantially reshaped by the new pressures toward recreational pleasure and an expressive public culture, the unprecedented contacts described as globalization, and the various kinds of regional reactions that answered these pressures for change, reactions that were often themselves quite novel.

What was happening, it can be argued, now on a worldwide basis, was the painful intensification of a movement away from the agricultural framework for sexuality and toward the creation of an industrial framework. Promotion of the birth rate receded in importance, as region after region, family after family, realized that traditional reproduction rates had to come under new control—but there were also new mechanisms to do this by means other than abstinence. With this, and with changes in women's work and educational patterns, traditional attempts to monitor female sexuality became more difficult, or less easy to justify—though this could generate impassioned resistance in the name of older values. The new round of changes also forced many societies to confront the gap between rigorous official standards and actual behaviors, that had opened up in the decades before 1950 in the first reactions to the challenges to agricultural norms—though here, too, responses varied. Inevitably, if the agricultural framework, buttressed as it had been by religious standards, was now giving way, the transition was both confusing and contested. It was not clear what the end result would be.

Chapter 8

Sex in contemporary world history

The dominant theme of sexuality in the last 60 years of world history involves an increasing commitment to sex for recreation and pleasure, with reproductive sex, though hardly disappearing, becoming a subordinate theme. This was the big shift away from the characteristic patterns, and many of the prevailing moral codes, of the agricultural periods in world history. It was a shift that also partially—not entirely—resolved some of the tensions that had arisen in the two centuries before 1950, when often increasingly stringent definitions of sexual respectability warred with actual behavioral changes. Public culture became steadily more sexualized. Both new practices and new cultures clearly fed a new, industrial-age definition of sexuality that was in many ways unprecedented. And all of this happened amid the global opportunities for cultural dissemination and behavioral imitation, with innovative sexuality becoming a central feature of globalization itself. In the process of redefinition, some new attention was also paid to reconsidering women's sexual role, though changes here were vigorously disputed.

Obviously, interest in and achievement of sexual pleasure were not new in world history. But what was happening now was an intensification of focus and a reduction of other definitions of sexuality and sexual restraint. Victorian culture and, soon, communist culture both passed from the scene, at least as far as sexuality was concerned, leaving only partial remnants to complicate the pattern of change.

The global thrust was unmistakable, but of course it also embraced important regional differences based on prior culture and degrees of urbanization. Some societies adopted the new sexual codes more wholeheartedly than others. It was also true that the new patterns had a number of obvious drawbacks, including a recrudescence of disease problems—here too, complexities arose that might deflect the dominant trends and also create another set of regional distinctions. Sex was changing, but it hardly shed some serious dispute or complexity.

*   *   *

Contraception and disease: a new framework

The most dramatic development regarding sexuality in contemporary world history was the literal explosion of a more highly sexualized public culture, affecting virtually every society—a triumph (if that is the proper word) of new media, new consumerism, and globalization combined. Here was a major encouragement to the widespread pursuit of recreational sexual pleasure. But a more basic contribution to the same change involved a variety of breakthroughs concerning birth control and surgical sterilization, which also had global implications though amid great regional variety. An important, though briefer, respite from the most common traditional forms of sexually transmitted disease added to the implications of more widespread birth control. The key shift, however, was in the growing ability to separate sex from procreation, and the growing interest in doing so.

The most striking single change occurred in the industrialized regions, initially particularly the West. The early 1960s saw the introduction of dramatic new birth control methods, notably a pill that could be taken by women that would prevent conception; a new intrauterine device (IUD) also won some attention though it had side effects that quickly limited its utility. The pill, however, was a magic bullet for many—complicated for some by concerns about potential health risks, by the need to remember regular dosage, and certainly by the need to obtain a doctor's prescription, but increasingly widely used nevertheless. Later developments around the turn of the century added to the available contraception, notably a "morning after" pill (emergency contraception) pioneered in France that could prevent conception even if taken soon after intercourse rather than before. These major innovations built on increasing familiarity even with older devices, like the diaphragm and the condom, including a growing engagement by previously reluctant groups (like American Catholics, who began to practice birth control quite widely despite official disapproval by the Church). By the final decades of the twentieth century, though more fully in Western Europe than in the United States, availability of various methods extended even to teenagers, facilitating premarital sex without significant risk of conception. Finally, though mainly for adults, surgical procedures, including vasectomies for men and tying of the fallopian tubes for women, fostered sterilizations that prevented conception with unprecedented reliability.

The fact was, particularly from the 1960s onward, that most Westerners could and did engage in sex quite independent of procreation, simply interrupting whatever methods were used when there was a desire for a child and sometimes accepting sterilization when the interest in reproduction ended altogether. The number of unwanted or unanticipated children, correspondingly, dropped sharply, and the basic birth rate remained far lower than had been the case in the agricultural age. But the most striking result was the separation of most sexual activity from any thought of conception: sex for pleasure, at least in principle, was more widely available than ever before in human history. The change was probably more significant for women than for men, because of the inescapable female involvement in dealing with pregnancy, but there were implications for both genders.

Of course complications entered in, even in the Western world. The baby boom, which extended from the late 1940s to the early 1960s, showed that reproductive sex was still important—though baby boom families moved up only to three to four children on average, hardly a traditional figure. The end of the baby boom, when birth rates dropped toward two per couple or even below, more starkly revealed the decline of procreative sex. By 2000, several societies, like Greece and Italy (and also Japan) were dipping below population maintenance levels, save insofar as they were bailed out by immigration.

The dramatic surge in birth control inevitably raised objections. Many religious authorities were particularly hesitant, worried about the loss of souls through population restraint and the new emphasis on unrestrained sexual pleasure. Concerns in the United States, particularly with a revival of religious interest from the 1970s onward, outstripped those in Europe—leading to some clear limits on policy commitments to birth control, particularly for teenagers at home and for population control efforts abroad. American funding for international family planning efforts plummeted in the 1980s and again after 2000, as authorities insisted that people should be able to restrain their sexual impulses without artificial assistance. This paralleled a distinctive reliance on "just say no," or sexual abstinence campaigns among American teenagers—which gained some popular support, even including public pledges by some teenagers, but also generated a higher adolescent pregnancy rate than prevailed in most other industrial societies.

Still, for most American adults, and certainly for the Western world more generally, the combination of new birth control availability and range, and new levels of acceptability, created a dramatic new context for sexuality.

Broadly similar developments took shape elsewhere, though with different specifics. The variations on a theme were striking, as material conditions and cultural attitudes shaped very different choices (and timing) concerning birth control—almost always, also, amid some debate and acrimony. But the growing global involvement was impressive as well, as efforts to limit the birth rate and, at least in some cases, to increase opportunities for recreational sex took on international proportions.

Japanese commitment to Western methods of birth control was surprisingly complicated by hostilities to many of the specific devices involved, and particularly to ingesting pills, as well as by official concern about promoting promiscuity through reducing the reproductive constraint on sex. The Ministry of Health approved the pill only in 1999, after a three-decade campaign by women's rights organizations. But use of the rhythm method and of condoms had spread widely before that point, and Japan also developed one of the highest per capita abortion rates in the world (building on an older national tradition of reliance on this procedure). Birth rates plummeted to 1.34 children per woman by 1999, and, as we will see, commitments to recreational sexual activity, even among teenagers, rose dramatically, even though, at least until the early twenty-first century, the contraception methods continued to differ from Western standards.

Several other societies relied on rising rates of abortion for reasons of cost: artificial devices seemed more expensive than recourse to cheap procedures when unwanted pregnancy actually ensued. In some cases the reliance was also encouraged by official policies that limited information about other devices in interests of population growth. Abortion had been well established in the Soviet Union even earlier, and in the second half of the twentieth century it burgeoned still further: by the 1990s the average woman had three abortions during her reproductive life. While condoms were available in some urban markets (though often in short supply), abortion on demand, at any local hospital, was a readier recourse (when rhythm methods failed)—and many women also welcomed the fact that they could bypass male objections when they adopted this option. Contraception debates surfaced in the 1960s and 1970s, with the balance of opinion opposing oral contraceptives because of cancer fears. In 1991, however, with more openness to the West and rising middle-class prosperity, a Russian Family Planning Association formed, launching extensive educational campaigns; and condoms became more widely available, though still stigmatized as unmasculine. Abortion costs rose at the same time, leading to more back-alley procedures.

South Korea was another case where growing reliance on abortion gradually yielded, with greater economic prosperity, to more reliance on artificial devices. Condoms, however, continued to be mainly imports; the pill had been available since the 1960s but was often used ineffectively; IUDs were limited because only doctors were authorized to insert them and access was difficult. High rates of abortion abated, but only gradually.

China offered yet another story. The early years of the new communist regime, through the 1950s, saw great official emphasis on population growth, seen as a vital asset to the state; so birth control gained little ground, at least in public. The state mounted intense pro-birth campaigns. With policy change in the late 1970s came a dramatic reversal of field, with the state beginning to enforce strict limits on the number of children per family—one child in the cities, two in the countryside. This in turn forced a variety of behaviors on ordinary people. Some were quite traditional, including a resurgence of infanticide and child abandonment, mainly designed to get rid of unwanted girls—if there was to be only one child, many parents still wanted to make sure it was a boy. Herbal remedies and rhythm methods were widely employed; and so was abortion. Gradually, however, though particularly in the cities, artificial devices made some headway. Married couples were using IUDs and pills fairly widely by the 1990s, and sterilization was common as well; the use of pills was constrained because of women's anxieties and (by Western standards) overemphasis on side effects. Unmarried couples relied heavily on abortion and condoms, and condom use gained by 2000 amid new disease fears. China represents a case where the movement away from reproduction was quite marked, but the measures that would allow more unrestrained recreational sex developed slightly more hesitantly than in the West, Korea, or Japan, at least until very recently when much clearer overlap emerged. In Hong Kong, however, 65 percent of all families were using contraception methods by the 1990s, mainly by means of condoms, secondarily by sterilization (after one or two children) or abortion—despite vigorous urban campaigns to urge larger families.

Thailand, another Asian case, had a more straightforward record, varying a bit with political climate. Midwives were allowed to insert IUDs and distribute the pill, meaning rising access for rural women. Overall, the pill was most widely used, followed by female sterilization; condom use was low. Religion—Catholicism in one case, Islam in the other—impeded new methods of birth control in the Philippines and Indonesia. But people in the larger Philippine cities defied the Church and turned to new methods, while in Indonesia injected contraceptives and the pill have gained popularity in the last ten years. Massive birth control efforts in India, backed by extensive foreign funding, promoted sterilization (particularly vasectomies) but with limited effects; urban upper classes however increasingly turned to the familiar range of artificial drugs and devices, while rural and poorer elements remained more immune to change.

Both Latin America and the Middle East present fascinating cases of quiet adaptations amid great diversity. Birth control advanced rapidly in the more secular parts of the Middle East. Egyptians relied heavily on the IUD and the pill, but the lower classes had yet to make major change. Oral contraceptives and the IUD gained in Tunisia, while in Turkey about 71 percent of all married or cohabiting women used contraception—particularly the IUD or the condom, with the pill less popular. Turks turned to abortion in over 10 percent of all pregnancies. Urban Iranians used the pill widely in the 1970s, but with revolution and war came new promotion of population growth and backlash against modern methods (though for a time in the 1990s the Ministry of Health offered free contraceptive and planning services to all married couples). Withdrawal, or *coitus interruptus*, became the most popular method, consistent with a rising birth rate by the 1990s. In many other strict Islamic areas, opposition to abortion and birth control actually increased over traditional levels, with many fundamentalists arguing that abortion was actually child murder and with widespread claims that family planning was a Western conspiracy to hold Muslim populations down. Yet individual countries, like Bahrain, offered quite open access to birth control, and, in general, the advance of education for women (quite striking in the Middle East as a whole, despite traditional barriers) coincided with increasing awareness of birth control options.

Many Latin Americans faced massive barriers to change through a combination of laws, Catholic policy, and male machismo that might be particularly hostile to the use of condoms but might also maintain some delight in frequent pregnancies for women. Colombia was an early exception, where the government launched family planning in the 1970s and generated widespread use of oral contraceptives and female sterilization. In Chile and Guatemala, by contrast, information about new methods was limited and abortion was strictly outlawed—which meant in practice that illegal abortion provided major recourse, with one Chilean estimate in the early 1990s claiming that almost 40 percent of all pregnancies were ending in abortion. Cuba also, in characteristic communist fashion, urged reproductive sex, while in Nicaragua the revolutionary Daniel Ortega declared abortion reactionary and unpatriotic. Condom use was widely disdained, despite some feminist efforts to promote it. Brazil established many family planning clinics but found it difficult to persuade women to use them. Yet, despite all the hesitations and variety, change did occur, particularly from the 1970s onward. A rural Mexican woman describes how both her priest and her husband tried to limit her knowledge of birth control options, but radio broadcasts, local doctors, and family planning clinics provided new options: "They say terrible things about women who want to practice birth control. Some say, 'The only reason you want birth control is so you can go with other men.'" When a radio program urged men that small families live better, the woman's husband only laughed. But the woman persevered, beginning to take the pill when the second of her "only" two children reached eight months (probably, when she stopped breastfeeding): her husband was unaware, believing that she was still trying to have a son. "The only thing I don't do is go to confession, because then I would have to confess that I take the pill, and the priest would say 'Leave the church.'" And indeed, building from hundreds of thousands of cases of this sort, Latin American birth rates began to fall dramatically.

Sub-Saharan Africa—poorer than other regions on average, with lower rates of education—turned to change slowly. Many rural people still relied entirely on herbal contraceptives. Male resistance to condom use was extremely high, and other measures remained unfamiliar or too expensive or both. Oral contraceptives and IUDs did become more widely available in the cities—though still a 2008 estimate held that only 19 percent of all Africans were using any modern form of contraception.

Regional diversity, major gaps among social classes and between rural and urban populations, huge variations of preferences for methods, holdovers from tradition— the complexities in the patterns of birth control were huge—quite apart from the fact that birth control interests at some level were hardly new in the later twentieth century. In some cases—as when new techniques were used to determine the sex of a fetus— modern methods simply facilitated older preferences, as when Chinese, Koreans, or Indians disproportionately aborted female fetuses. As against change, many men held out for customary sexual patterns because they found certain new methods incompatible with their definition of pleasure and because they actually valued demonstrations of reproductive prowess and the controls frequent pregnancies facilitated over women. Many women were ignorant of options, browbeaten, or actually lured by the high valuation of motherhood still provided in numerous cultures. Even when change occurred, as in the Mexican case cited above, it often had far more to do with prevention of customary numbers of children than with any new appetite for sexual pleasure. Deep reliance on abortion in many societies might have little to do with inclinations for recreational sex, and complications from abortion might constrain sexuality directly.

Still, certain basic patterns of change were developing quite widely. Through various methods, increasing numbers of people were able to cut birth rates without relying on abstinence and by using methods more reliable than those of the past. International conferences—like the 1994 Population and Development Conference in Egypt— though resisted by some Islamic states and the Catholic Church (and sometimes the United States government as well), also helped to create more global awareness of birth control options. In some cases, as in Mexico, the new options also helped facilitate a larger women's voice over the consequences of sexuality—even when husbands had to be kept in the dark. By 2008 it was estimated that 61 percent of the world's population was involved in some modern forms of birth control (surgical abortions and sterilizations included)—a huge contrast with just a century before.

Here, in turn, was a vital context for new sexual behaviors that might increase the frequency of sex, loosen the links between sex and marriage, and promote new thinking about what the purposes of sexuality were. These changes were contested and uneven, but by the early twenty-first century it was clear that they were no longer tentative. Key elements of the agricultural framework for sexuality were being remade.

Briefly, the birth control context was further abetted by the spread of modern methods of combating traditional sexually transmitted diseases. Research on diseases like syphilis in previous decades plus the introduction of new anti-bacterial drugs by mid-century allowed effective treatment of several of the most important traditional venereal diseases, often at relatively low cost. Though available most widely in industrial countries (including Soviet Russia), where government programs were particularly effective in encouraging treatment, even some other urban centers were benefiting from the new options by the 1960s. Where condom use spread (a very uneven pattern, as we have seen), further protections against infection emerged. Briefly, in the 1960s, it looked like some of the traditional biological constraints on sex, in the form of diseases that were hard or painful to treat, were easing, along with unwanted pregnancies. This was only a moment in world history, as viral infections, from genital herpes to the new disease of AIDS, quickly moved in to provide a new set of threats.

A culture of sexuality

The second major contributor to the new context for sexual behavior, and an important development in its own right, involved the striking emergence of a more erotic public culture, affecting all areas of the world to some degree and literally inundating certain regions. Historical perspective remains important amid change, even more than with birth control. Cultures had highlighted erotic themes before, particularly prior to the rise of the world religions. Literary eroticism and how-to handbooks had survived even the religious surge. Pornography actually gained ground in several regions in the early modern period and again in the nineteenth and early twentieth centuries. The sexualization of public culture was thus not entirely new, and it built on some important recent precedents.

Still, it remains true that changes in the decades after 1950 brought explicit sexual themes and innuendos to wider public attention, in more graphic and provocative fashion, than had ever before been true. Opportunities to see sexual poses, to watch other people having or simulating intercourse, to read about sexual methods were more extensive than at any previous point in human history. All of this developed amid a clear value system that argued for the validity of sexual pleasure, for the importance of pursuing sexual enjoyment as part of a happy life—including, but not confined to, a happy married life. The sexual tide virtually swept away Victorianism and its communist analogues, a few surviving fragments aside, and it pushed back older religious strictures as well.

Three changes were particularly salient in preparing the new culture. First, of course, were a series of innovations in media. Movies were not new in the 1950s, but, increasingly, movies could be exchanged more widely than ever before, thanks to video stores and hotel services (in both of which sexually explicit fare loomed large). Sexual exploits of movie stars, widely publicized in the tabloid press (particularly, but not exclusively, in the West) added to the pleasure-seeking implications of the racier films, as life imitated art and vice versa. Television and then the Internet created additional possibilities for visualizing sexual themes and disseminating them widely. Improved print technology played a role as well, in facilitating a new series of sexually-oriented magazines. Second, huge alterations in regulations were crucial. Religious objections to sexual materials remained strong, but religious organizations, in many regions, were less capable than before of enforcing their values. Many governments simply withdrew from the regulatory field, except perhaps for mounting certain protections against child viewing. Changes in Western laws were vital here, but the collapse or the consumer transformation of communism was at least as important on an international scale. Finally, there was the global element itself: cultural innovations in one region—often, but not always, the West—readily spread to other societies, eager to keep up with modernity and aware that sexually-relevant fare was easy to transport across borders. The spread of beauty contests, initially (in the 1920s) an American innovation, to enthusiastic participation in India, Africa, and elsewhere, with swimsuit poses a core element, was one of many signs of the emergence of new global standards of public stimulation focused, obviously, on the female form above all. Sexually explicit magazines spread widely on most global newsstands, and Western or Japanese entries were even more widely copied in cheaper, sometimes slightly adapted local versions. By the 1990s, the Internet, though open to some censorship and control, was a global commodity by definition.

All of these changes, of course, were predicated on a primary spur: sexual culture sold, and helped sell other goods. Here, the rise of a sexually explicit culture interacted closely with changes or at least new articulations in popular values, and it was impossible fully to sort out which came first, the culture or the appetite. A wide array of goods—for example, automobiles—could now be presented as relevant to sexual appeal, complete with models in revealing poses ready to illustrate how this particular product might turn them on. Women's magazines focused increasingly heavily on sexual advice and a cultivation of the body. Sports might add buxom cheerleaders or swimsuit issues to make it clear that sex was relevant here as well. The interconnections between public sexuality and consumerism, again on a global scale, became increasingly intricate.

Upheavals in American legal rulings help explain why the 1950s created something of a dividing line in public culture. Supreme Court decisions permitted circulation of materials that had once been censored, essentially on grounds that censorship efforts had interfered with freedom of expression and imposed arbitrary standards of literary or artistic merit. As a result books that had been written earlier, such as D. H. Lawrence's *Lady Chatterley's Lover*, could now be freely sold in the United States. This opened the door to new efforts as well, such as the formation, in 1953, of *Playboy Magazine*, frankly devoted to sexual pleasure and featuring what came to be known as "soft core" pornography. Restrictions on circulation of materials in the United States mail were largely dropped. Hollywood standards began to shift, allowing much franker representation of sexual scenes including (usually just female) nudity. Residual constraints remained: certain kinds of materials, for example those involving child pornography, could still be banned as against the public interest. Hollywood accepted a rating system intended to prevent minors from access to the raciest movies. In the main, however, the traditional barriers crumbled, and American (and by export other) audiences had increasing access to more and more vivid expressions of sexuality and sexual titillation.

Thus *Playboy* was followed by even more explicit magazines, such as *Penthouse*. Adult sex shops and movie houses proliferated, offering a variety of products designed to stimulate pleasure (and serve a wide range of sexual interests). Pornographic movies became more widely available thanks to film rental outlets with carefully designated but widely popular adult sections. The advent of cable television allowed access to pornographic channels in the home, as well as in hotel rooms—and again, extensive popularity ensued. By the 1990s a substantial minority of movie rentals fell in the pornographic category. Television shows were a bit more restrained, as federal regulations continued to ban certain kind of sexually-provocative words and outright nudity, but sexual references and the approving portrayal of casual sexual relationships became part of some of the most popular dramas and situation comedies. The widely-popular *Sex and the City*, on cable outlets, showed clearly how television could move into this field, dramatizing frequent and varied sexual encounters and clearly indicating that sex and romance should often be separated. Never before had sexual fantasies been so widely served by public fare.

American developments were matched and surpassed in Western Europe. Magazines for teenagers, like *Bravo* in Germany, increasingly assumed that sexuality was a normal part of teenage relationships. European advertisements and television began to feature nudity outright, not confining the efforts to movies. By the early twenty-first century even daily newspapers, of the more tabloid sort, might feature photographs of bare-breasted women. Sex shops were even more pervasive than in the United States, in countries like the Netherlands or Sweden. In Australia, the women's magazine *Cleo* pioneered a male centerfold, while also advising women on "how to be a sexy housekeeper." Throughout the Western world and beyond, the advent of the Internet provided yet another, unprecedented, varied and personal, opportunity for receipt of various forms of pornography and sexual solicitation, with pornographic sites one of the leading uses of the new medium.

Music also participated in the trend. Rock music, particularly, introduced more graphic and provocative lyrics. Some popular music also veered off into praise for sexually-related violence.

Media were not the only outlet for public expressions of sexual stimuli. Styles of dress continued to change, extending a theme launched earlier in the twentieth century, though amid frequent oscillations. The 1960s featured the miniskirt. By the early twenty-first century exposure of midriffs and (shortly thereafter) cleavage became part of daily wear on the street, and not just the stuff of celebrity parties. In Western Europe (but not the United States) topless beaches became increasingly pervasive. And while the most important costume changes involved women, Europeans also turned to swim suits for men that were both skimpy and clinging. Particularly, but not exclusively, in leisure wear, in other words, bodies were on display as never before. And where bodies seemed inadequate, relevant parts could now be redone: breast enlargement, through silicon injections, became one of the most popular forms of plastic surgery in the Western world, despite some health concerns, while new kinds of penile augmentation surgeries were also available for men.

Not surprisingly, sex manuals changed as well, though here important themes—including a new emphasis on female pleasure—had been launched earlier. New books increasingly dropped or reduced older emphasis on the importance of love and marriage in sexuality, in favor of more fulsome endorsement of enjoyment. Thus a new American book in 1958, called *Sex without Guilt*, openly endorsed masturbation and premarital intercourse, and urged that each individual be free to pursue whatever path to pleasure was available:

> Every human being, just because he exists, should have the right to as much (or as little), as varied (or as monotonous), as intense (or as mild), as enduring (or as brief) sex enjoyments as he prefers—as long as, in the process of acquiring these preferred satisfactions, he does not needlessly, forcefully, or unfairly interfere with the sexual (or nonsexual) rights and satisfactions of others.

Here, then, was the new mantra: anything goes, so long as it was voluntarily engaged in; and people were urged to discuss their sexual needs with potential partners as openly as possible. Alex Comfort's *The Joy of Sex*, widely sold on both sides of the Atlantic, urged an attack on the old idea that women should be passive, men active, instead stressing women's role in "getting him excited to start with, or in controlling him and showing off all her skills," "the main dish is loving, unselfconscious intercourse—long, frequent, varied, ending with both parties satisfied but not so full they can't face another light course, and another meal in a few hours." As against some manualists who placed greater emphasis on avoidance of performance standards, Comfort urged the importance of frequency and the desirability of simultaneous orgasm. An even more widely-selling set of authors, Masters and Johnson, made it clear that they were eager to avoid condemning any sexual practice outright, so long as it brought pleasure and involved no compulsion. As yet another manual explained, "It must be accepted that rules have always existed with regard to sexual love .... On examining these rules we find that some of them are entirely arbitrary and irrational."

Similar kinds of sexual advice escaped the print medium, as radio and television shows began to feature gurus like Dr. Ruth, where again mutual pleasure, the validity of masturbation and other contemporary themes were fully aired.

Sexual themes, revelations and advice also spread to other outlets, such as women's magazines. *Cosmopolitan*, most famously, converted to sexual emphases in the 1960s, talking particularly to single women and urging them both to seek sexual pleasure and to learn a growing array of tricks to please the man or men in their lives. *Mademoiselle*, again in the 1960s, urged women to loosen up, noting with approval that men increasingly judged women for their "capacity for pleasure." Important tensions remained in this popular female literature: while pleasure seeking was fine, women were urged not to fall into the trap of assuming they had to accept any male offer or technique that came along, and they were assured that periods of celibacy might be quite valid and that an effort to link sex to emotional commitment was absolutely appropriate. Some commentary acknowledged that, at least for women, sex was not always what it was cracked up to be.

Another important public outlet involved open reporting on sexual habits. Beginning with the Kinsey reports of the 1950s, Americans and others were treated to recurrent discussions of what people actually did in or around the bed. The results provided another support for an understanding of the variety of individual preferences, while more generally making it clear that reticence about sexuality was old-fashioned and repressive. Here was another component of a new public culture that underscored both the appropriateness and the deep significance of sex as a topic.

These various cultural developments obviously stirred controversy, particularly in the United States where religious commitments ran deeper than in Western Europe. Recurrent efforts to re-impose censorship combined with concerted efforts to counter the public culture, particularly where children were concerned. Thus while a few sex education ventures in the United States—for example, one in New Jersey in the 1970s—talked openly of pleasure—"And you can give yourself pleasure, too, and that's okay. When you touch your own genitals it's called masturbating"—most continued to surround sex with a host of warnings and some outright disapproval. Thus an Atlanta middle school program in the 1980s stated its main goal: "to help boys and girls resist pressures to engage in sex." Federal guidelines, inspired by conservative politicians, urged older themes: "a mutually faithful monogamous relationship in the context of marriage is the expected standard of human sexual activity" and, more ominously, "sexual activity outside of the context of marriage is likely to have harmful psychological and physical effects." Efforts to counter the open hedonism of much public culture did not succeed in rolling the culture back—each decade saw new forms of availability for sexually explicit materials and injunctions to pleasure—but they expressed some deep moral concerns and they could sow no small amount of confusion. Even so, the new culture itself remained the dominant development in this aspect of contemporary Western history.

The transformation of Western public culture, though prepared by some previous trends, was dramatic, deeply shocking to some, and because of the West's power and capitalist-consumer outreach, particularly influential on a global scale.

Changes in Western culture famously influenced global standards, but they blended with equally important regional transformations as well. In China, for example, new openness to foreign influence and the official embrace of a more market economy and greater consumerism from 1978 onward had almost immediate implications for sexual culture. The 1980s saw a dramatic emergence of new pornographic novels, sex manuals, medical discussions of sexology, and the widespread translation of Western materials on sex, both scholarly and pornographic. Explicit sex scenes in movies became increasingly common in the 1990s, which was also when beauty pageants hit the mainland (though the Miss Beijing contest in 1993 stressed a "Chinese" focus on brains and talent). Use of sexual suggestion in advertisements became increasingly widespread as well, with both Western and Chinese models freely invoked. Indian movies, which in any event had traditional erotic images readily available, moved toward more explicit suggestiveness in the 1980s. Naked women were featured in advertisements—against vigorous feminist protest—while the film capital Bollywood often highlighted sexual themes—along with direct imports from Western films, magazines and TV shows. Pornographic materials, again often of Western origin or copied from Western or Japanese prototypes, became increasingly available in African cities.

In Latin America, the Western influence was particularly strong, but combined with important regional innovations. Knockoffs of American women's magazines became quite prevalent, though on average they were slightly less racy than ventures like *Cosmopolitan* and more heavily focused not just on how to please men but also how to win their love. Soap operas strongly featured sexual-romantic themes, with women seeking love at any cost, with some acceptance of sexual violence in the process. Beauty pageants were hugely popular, with many poor girls, even in the countryside, seeing beauty queen-dom as an escape from ordinary life. Costume changes were striking, particularly in countries like Brazil, with beachwear increasingly suggestive and with the adoption of more body-exposing costumes even at work. Latin America also featured unusual interest in widely-advertised services for sex therapy and pleasure enhancement, sometimes linked to older definitions of machismo.

In Russia, not surprisingly, the fall of the Soviet Union and the new openness toward the West led to an explosion of more open sexual eroticism. The year 1989 itself saw a major increase in pornographic materials available on the streets, as policing dropped off, and the emergence of video salons highlighting soft-core porn. The 1998 movie *Little Vera* featured the first cinematic sex scene in Russian history, and it was followed by a huge surge of erotic and pornographic films mainly aimed at younger audiences. Beauty contests proliferated in Eastern Europe and central Asia.

Japan became a world leader in the production of sexualized culture. As elsewhere, pornography expanded, and even mainstream magazines adopted standard sexual materials and sensationalism. By the 1990s these outlets even featured pictures showing pubic hair. By the 1990s Interpol reported that Japan had become the largest single source of child pornography on the Internet, though the government moved to ban such productions in 1999.

By the twenty-first century only the Middle East and a few other pockets like Cuba or North Korea stood out as largely exempt from the surge of the sexualization of public culture. Even here, of course, more conventional sexual products were available from more private vendors, and the wealthy could (and often did) seek more up-to-date materials on their global travels. Otherwise, the embrace of sexuality in mass consumerism gained ground steadily, though of course with some regional adjustments and significant differentiations based on standard of living. By 2008 after all, only about a third of the world's population had regular access to the Internet, which meant of course that this potential source of sexual materials, including pornography, faced continued constraints. Still, the reach of the new standards of public sexuality was striking. Many of the most popular cultural exports had strong sexual overtones—at one point in the early 1990s, for example, the American TV staple *Baywatch*, whose main claim to fame involved scantily-clad California beach girls, was the most widely watched show in the world.

The new availability and diversity of sexual themes constituted a significant change in their own right. The culture became an important part of the leisure lives for many people in many places. At one prestigious American university, for example, the only significant student protest to emerge in the 1990s involved reactions to university efforts to block some pornographic Internet sites—many (mostly male) students argued that this deprived them of their main alternative to studying. The sheer sales and audiences for sexualized magazines and media fare made the same point in a general way. So, of course, did the shocked reaction of many conservatives and religious leaders, quite aware that the popularity of the sexual culture undercut key aspects of their message; and many feminists, concerned about the disproportionate exploitation of female imagery and sometimes also protective of selective older family values, joined in as well. For the most part, except in efforts by governments and international agencies to combat child pornography, most of the dismay did little to change the cultural tone. Lots of contemporary people, in lots of places, really liked to watch sex or sexual provocation, and they had unprecedented opportunities to do so.

Behaviors

Even granting the importance of the sexual culture as a new recreational staple, including the genuine concern it caused in many quarters, the key question was what impact it had on behaviors. Opponents widely assumed, but also tended to exaggerate, the link between what people now could watch and what they would be disposed to do directly. It was easy to confuse sexualized media with huge alterations in private life. Changes in birth control raised the same analytical dilemma: it became increasingly possible to separate sex from the constraint of unwanted children, but how many people actually sought to take advantage of this opportunity through radical innovations in behavior?

Three points dominate this aspect of contemporary world history: first, it is harder know about behaviors than about public cultures or contraceptives technologies, so some really important questions cannot be fully answered. Second, behaviors did change, in hardly surprising directions, particularly in the area of premarital sex. But, third, average behaviors changed less dramatically than the culture did—less dramatically in fact than many people assumed to be the case. More traditional elements persisted here, including some important regional variations and some lingering gender differentials, than was true with regard to public culture or even birth control. The combination was fascinating, and truly significant in terms of the way contemporary peoples experienced this vital aspect of life.

In Western Europe and the United States, the 1960s heralded a sexual revolution, widely trumpeted in the media—the claim coincided, obviously, with a growing (if temporary) youth presence in Western culture (the result of the baby boom) and also the new discoveries in birth control and the impact of new cultural outlets like *Playboy*. In fact, careful research suggests that actual shifts in sexual behavior began a bit earlier, and that their range—though meaningful—was less sweeping than media hyperbole, or conservative fears, sometimes projected.

Still, several major alterations did take shape. First, the average age of first sexual intercourse shifted downward, and normally now (though not invariably) preceded marriage. In the United States, by the 1950s about 35 percent of all college women had sex before marriage (and often concealed the fact); by the 1970s, 29 percent of all women had a first sexual experience between the ages of 15 and 19 and by 1980, 42 percent fell in this category; by 1988 the figure had reached 52 percent. Because the average marriage age was simultaneously rising, the rate of premarital intercourse was even higher. Correspondingly, by the 1970s, a growing minority of couples were living together before marriage. Finally, largely but not entirely because of new premarital experiences, the average number of sexual partners encountered during an active life-time went up: by the 1980s a majority of American women had more than one but less than four. Only a minority admitted to committing adultery, though here too the figures may have risen. But premarital sex, frequent divorce often followed by sexual activity and sometimes remarriage, plus some outright infidelity added up to a measurable alteration in patterns. During the 1970s a small group even advocated what was called open marriage, entertaining multiple partners with knowledge and, in principle, approval of the spouse. More widely, efforts to reduce sexual jealousy suggested an emotional concomitant to the new behavior patterns: it became very childish to express concerns about prior sexual partners at the very least. Masturbation, or at least willingness to admit masturbation, also increased. Changes were more striking the higher the educational level, intensifying the social class differential that had begun to emerge earlier in the twentieth century.

Sexual methods also expanded. Particularly striking was the rise of oral sex—by the 1980s a majority of men claimed to have had an oral sex experience. Oral sex might be part of an effort by men to increase women's satisfaction, but it also became a test of women's willingness to innovate, though only 17 percent of all women (well under the percentage actually engaged in the practice) claimed to enjoy giving oral sex.

Changes in Western Europe again moved faster than those in the United States. Premarital sex became more widespread, and was less often associated with teenage pregnancy (at least after the 1960s, when rates went up on both sides of the Atlantic) because of more accessible birth control for adolescents. In several European countries marriage rates declined dramatically—by the early twenty-first century a majority of couples in Sweden and in France, many of them quite stable, remained unmarried.

Behavioral change in many other parts of the world moved in similar directions, though for the most part somewhat more hesitantly, and with some interesting local variants. Rates of premarital sex also increased in Japan, but with more expressions of moral disapproval; as elsewhere, university students were particularly open about premarital sex and also premarital cohabitation. Discussion of sexual issues within families, however, was more constrained than in the West, with even more young people reporting learning about sex mainly from pop culture and peers. Only a small percentage of Japanese youngsters had sex below age 15 (6 percent of boys, 4 percent of girls), a lower figure than in the West; but older teenage boys reported increasing embarrassment if they had not lost their virginity.

By the 1990s, 17 was the average age for first sexual experience in Russia, again constituting a drop, but less dramatic than in the West, along with a continued double standard that disapproved of women's involvement more than men's. Reports also suggested an increase of adultery and extramarital affairs, even by women, though strongly condemned in principle.

The 1970s were the decade of rapid expansion of premarital sex in Latin America, with Brazil leading the way. A 1995 *Isto E* article noted, "Sex is no longer a sin. Loss of virginity is no longer a taboo but is now an option. Teenagers are freer to choose their sexual initiation." Surveys suggested boys often starting sex by age 14, girls more commonly between 15 and 17—though with widespread public disapproval of changes among females.

China maintained lower rates of sex and masturbation among young people than was true in many other regions, according to a 1992 study. In the Middle East, premarital sex probably increased a bit, despite massive concern. And earlier arrangements, like temporary provisions for teenagers to allow them to deal with urges even though they were not ready for formal marriage, may have enjoyed a resurgence in places like Iran and Egypt. African cities experienced a major increase in premarital and extramarital sex, and in pregnancies outside marriage.

Across many regions as well—though the phenomenon was particularly notable in Catholic areas—the popularity of professions that required chastity declined rapidly. Shortage of priests and rapid declines in the number of monks and nuns, though doubtless responding to a variety of factors, suggested how much more important opportunities for explicit sexual activity had become.

Another significant change reflected the growing commitment to sexual expression in practice as well as in culture: the rising sense that older people could and should continue to participate in sexual activities. Even though youth behaviors drew primary focus in defining contemporary sexual revolutions, older people were involved as well—a vital point given the rapid expansion of the elderly segment of contemporary populations. As in other respects, continuities were involved as well as change: many societies had seen some older men seek to maintain sexual prowess and look for ways to maintain their capacity. Now, however, the interest undoubtedly broadened. Particularly important was a growing sense, initially in places like the West and Japan, that women's sexual activity did not have to end after menopause. The general trend of loosening the link between sex and reproduction had crucial implications here, as more and more older women continued to try to look and act more youthful rather than renouncing any claim to sexuality once they could no longer conceive. For men, by the early twenty-first century, new and widely popular products like Viagra, aimed at curing a newly identified and widely-trumpeted disorder called Erectile Dysfunction, made it clear how many people now expected to be able to maintain sexual vitality well into later age. (Viagra might also play into masculine assertions and insecurities by other age groups—in Brazil the typical user was reportedly a 22-year-old male.) Obviously, individual patterns continued to vary—some older women, for example, actually welcomed an excuse to withdraw from the sexual arena; and opportunities were undoubtedly greatest in the more prosperous regions and social classes. The fact that older women far outnumbered older men introduced a gender variable in opportunities as well; as many feminists pointed out, campaigns for the new medications focused disproportionately on male needs, without corresponding attention to the female side of things. But the trend toward greater discussion of sexuality as part of later age was revealing, and showed every indication of gaining ground. The trend was important in its own right, and it reflected of the wider increase in the expectation that greater access to sexual pleasure was a crucial aspect of adult life.

How revolutionary all this was could be debated. Most societies, for example, had indulged a certain amount of premarital sex before; part of the contemporary trend was simply more open acknowledgement of prior behaviors that had previously been kept under wraps. A general tendency toward rising marriage age, because of longer periods of education, also encouraged more premarital sex but not, necessarily, more sex per person. Many regions and many individuals even in the most open regions held back from the general trends, as well, as sexual change became a matter of more individual choice and also more open to dispute. There is no question that, except for a few self-described swingers, actual sexual behavior was far tamer than media representations suggested. For better or worse, many people were watching sexual expressions that did not describe their actual lives. Still, as could be expected from the birth control and cultural trends combined, sexual constraints did alter somewhat, most obviously for the young but also for other age groups, and a number of earlier conventions were challenged in the interest of (real or hoped-for) sexual pleasure.

Changes in culture, behavior and expectations also contributed to other developments, which similarly fused important innovations with ample remnants from prior patterns. Sexual appetites continued to fuel prostitution, where novel elements also emerged. New patterns of disease reflected sexual trends. The shock of change, plus specific concerns about novel contemporary problems, led to new efforts to introduce behavioral controls. Sex and violence and homosexuality represented other areas where change involved complex manifestations. Several threads ran through these various arenas: a measurable increase in the quest for sexual pleasure, but also discomfort with this increase and some of the issues it generated and some real confusion over what contemporary standards involved.

Sex for sale

A key sign of accelerating sexual appetites involved the expansion of prostitution broadly construed. The occupation was not a new one, so there was ample precedent for the contemporary manifestations—indeed, prostitution had mirrored changes in sexual contexts earlier in world history, so it was not surprising that new connections resulted from the contemporary transitions. Furthermore, we have seen that urban dislocations and an increase in recreational interests had already enlarged the field, from the later nineteenth century onward; to a considerable degree, the most recent developments extended earlier trends. There were also some counter-currents: in the Western world and Japan, new patterns of premarital sexual activity among youth, and particularly the growing, if still contested, acceptability of sex for younger women, reduced an earlier pattern in which young men would be encouraged to go to brothels for their initial sexual encounters. In these regions, the continued vitality of prostitution often had more to do with middle-aged men seeking some additional stimulus outside of marriage—again, not an entirely new phenomenon, but one that could expand as expectations of sexual pleasure changed. Finally, and quite obviously, many of the indices of contemporary prostitution had very troubling implications, particularly for many of the women involved—one of the clear downsides of contemporary sexuality in the global context.

Many older themes and controversies persisted. Young men in Latin America still sometimes turned to prostitutes for their sexual initiation. Beliefs about the importance of prostitution to restrain male lust continued as well: a police inspector in Mumbai in 1995 thus argued, "According to me, prostitutes are social workers—if it was not for them, women from good families would not be able to walk on the streets …. Men would attack women to get rid of their lustful impulses." Red light districts expanded in many cities, including in India, building on previous trends. Urban dislocation generated hundreds of thousands of prostitutes in China, some of whom regularly solicited customers by phone in the busier hotels. In Africa, some women essentially served as concubines to wealthy men, including some foreigners, maintaining an older pattern that had declined in some other areas. Different regions oscillated on regulation: prostitution was officially forbidden in Pakistan and condemned by Islam, but a fairly clear, if informal, grading system existed depending on looks, youth, and markings of class, with a major brothel located right below the leading mosque in Lahore. Japan passed an anti-prostitution law in 1958, but this was countered by the development of bathhouses with private rooms. Russia debated regulation after the fall of communism, but inconclusively amid extensive promotion of the industry by organized crime. Several West European countries, headed by the Netherlands, openly recognized prostitution—in some cases, the women were even unionized and allowed to advertise—in return for careful policing in the interests of public order, disease control and protection for prostitutes themselves. Hungary also legalized prostitution—but, in contrast, the practice was punishable by death in Sudan. Debates over this kind of issue reached global levels, at least in rhetoric: in 1986 the Second World Whores' Congress in Brussels urged recognition of prostitution as legitimate work, while a 1998 Taipei Declaration called for decriminalization in the interests of improved public health regulation; in 2005 the informal Declaration of the Rights of Sex Workers in Europe protested new local rules restricting sex work, arguing that this merely drove the sex industry underground and hampered public health measures.

Several factors combined to generate newer kinds of growth in the industry, often regardless of official policy. Enhanced sexual appetites, along with the prosperity of many men in industrialized countries, were one component—new types of prostitution in this sense mirrored the larger changes in expectations. Growing poverty and dislocation for many women was a second factor, not novel, but simply playing out on a larger scale by the 1990s. Rising rural poverty, for example, drove many female immigrants into India from Nepal into prostitution (fueling an Indian tendency inaccurately to blame all sorts of problems exclusively on the immigrants); there were an estimated 200,000 Nepalese prostitutes in India by the early twenty-first century, valued among other things for their light skin. Poverty played a huge role in expanding prostitution in sub-Saharan Africa and Southeast Asia (the latter with Japan as major destination).

Social disorder after the fall of communism, with a reduced welfare network combined with rising unemployment among women, generated new sources of prostitution in Russia and east-central Europe. For a number of years, prostitutes lined the highways leading into the Czech Republic from Germany, for example. As early as 1986, a Moscow newspaper revealed the glamorous lives of upscale urban prostitutes serving foreigners in exchange for dollars or European currencies, but a growing number of very poor women were drawn into the trade as well, at much less luxurious levels. Between 1991 and 2008, an estimated 500,000 women from Ukraine had been trafficked—that is, exported for prostitution—with 400,000 as well from the tiny but impoverished country of Moldova. A final element in some regions involved wars, which not only generated other forms of dislocation but also fed the sexual expectations of soldiers. Thailand began to emerge as a center for prostitution on the heels of American servicemen sent for rest leaves during the Vietnam War; many US solders were quite open about their use of Thai prostitutes as "rented wives." Prostitution in the Balkans increased in service to United Nations peacekeeping forces. Following the 2003 US invasion, many Iraqi refugee women worked, or were coerced into working, as prostitutes in the Middle East and North Africa, with an estimated 50,000 women and children serving in Syria alone. The number of conflicts in recent decades obviously escalated a common push toward sexual service.

In addition to the sheer growth of prostitution in many cities, in various parts of the world, three innovations, or at least innovative extensions of prior practice, were particularly striking. First: International recruitment of sex workers increased rapidly—well beyond the fabled (and exaggerated) white slavery of a century before. Russian women began to be sold abroad in the 1980s, often under the aegis of organized crime; many were sent through several different countries in order to conceal their ultimate destination and purpose. Other women from Eastern Europe and central Asia were heavily involved—by 2008 it was estimated that as many as 500,000 women from these regions (including Russia) were serving as prostitutes in the European Union. The prestige of having white women available for sexual services in places like South Korea (they were regarded as exotic and highly-sexed) helps explain the wide use of east European sex workers in parts of Asia and the Middle East; overall, it was estimated that up to two-thirds of the women in contemporary sex trafficking came from this region. African women, however, were also heavily involved. East African women were frequently promised work as nannies or domestic servants, then raped and drafted into prostitution, including service abroad. Nigeria, in West Africa, tried to crack down on trafficking operations, but met resistance not only from criminal agents but also from women themselves, who either feared retaliation or wanted to keep international service as an option to allow escape from poverty. A 2003 Trafficking in Persons Law Enforcement Administration Act was a pioneering step in Nigeria and the whole region, but its effects were unclear.

Overall, a 2005 report suggested that as many of 600,000–800,000 people were being trafficked each year, over 80 percent of whom were women widely destined for sexual service. The business of international trafficking for prostitution was generating well over $7 billion a year as early as 2000, with levels rising steadily as the industry became one of the fastest-growing criminal activities in the world. International organizations—both United Nations agencies and non-governmental organizations—fought against the trade, out of concern for protection of human rights and health, but with limited success.

Many women involved, of course, were simply coerced or duped or both. Others, given poverty at home, may have been more willing participants, though not always aware of what they were getting into. Some regions offered new terms for prostitute, like "matan zamani," or "modern woman" in Niger, that suggested how some women regarded prostitution as a gesture toward independence from traditional constraints, a chance to gain financial freedom without the burdens of marriage.

Destinations for sex trafficking were in part predictable: Western Europe, North America (including the United States), and Japan. Canada and the United Kingdom were held to be particularly lax in enforcing legal restrictions. Japan, with large numbers of Southeast Asian women working in bath houses (called "soaplands") and massage parlors, had an overall sex industry (pornography as well as sex devices and prostitution) rated at well over 1 percent of the entire gross national product. But industrial countries were not the only recipients, as trafficked women also served new regions of sex tourism—the second, and even more decisively novel, element in the contemporary version of the world's so-called oldest profession.

Travel for purposes of promiscuous sexual activity was not brand new in human history, but its massive deployment, and the designation of particular regions as destinations, awaited contemporary conditions. By the early twenty-first century, sex tours could easily be identified, mainly for men from the industrial regions, with destinations ranging from Thailand to the Dominican Republic, Brazil, and Costa Rica. Particular cities might attract sex tourists, with organized prostitution to match, including Amsterdam and Las Vegas. Sex tours could also be arranged with particular hotels in places like Ukraine (often through American agents who contracted with the women and carefully noted what kinds of sex acts they would or would not engage in). Again, a multi-billion dollar industry was the global result, with particular areas, like Thailand, benefiting so substantially that local opposition was difficult. Sex tours to Thailand advertised "anything goes in this exotic country," along with myths that diseases could not be contracted with Thai prostitutes. An estimated 50,000–200,000 girls had their virginity sold each year in the nation, with particularly eager clients from other parts of Asia and the Middle East where this feature was particularly valued. Parts of Africa also participated in sex tourism—for example, Madagascar, catering to European tourists; even Syria became a cut-rate destination on the strength of the low-priced Iraqi refugees. On the user side, Canadians alone were estimated as spending over $400,000 a year on sex tourism, and figures for the United States or Japan were much higher.

Sex tourism drew young women in with dreams of concubinage to wealthy foreigners. It attracted migrants from other countries, thus blending with sex trafficking more generally. It sometimes followed from legitimate jobs in hotels or the entertainment industry, with coercion applied once the work was underway. In a perverse way, sex tourism served as a revealing example of the quest for sexual pleasure, while also reflecting the huge power differences between wealthy and poorer regions, and between men and women.

The third innovation in sex for sale or coercion involved the growing use of the Internet to lure sexual partners and to advertise both trafficked sex workers and tourism opportunities. Internet inducements measurably increased all forms of the sex trade. It also facilitated solicitation of young girls even within a single country. The United States surfaced many examples of teenage girls, eager to flaunt their sexuality on the Internet, trapped into involuntary sex with strange, and often middle-aged, men. Japan in the 1990s experienced the rise of *enjo kosai*—high school girls paid to sleep with older men. Japan also saw a proliferation of clubs offering sexual stimulus over the telephone, sometimes offered by underage girls eager for the excitement and the extra earnings. Contemporary communications, in other words, helped spread sexual opportunities even beyond pornography, and in some cases encouraged entrapment as well.

Clearly, global conditions by 2000 had considerably transformed the venerable practice of buying and selling sex, with its inevitable concomitant of coercion and abuse. New practices, new numbers, new internationalism, and new, or at least more open and available, sexual appetites in an age that encouraged the legitimacy of pleasure-seeking provided unprecedented stimulus.

Disease

The increase in sexual promiscuity almost inevitably produced new problems with sexually transmitted disease, again resurfacing and expanding trends visible in earlier historical periods including the later nineteenth century, providing both evidence for and reflection of broader new behaviors. Even before the advent of AIDS, a rising incidence of genital herpes in places like the United States in the early 1980s demonstrated that new levels of sexual contact were generating new opportunities for viral transmission, with results that could be controlled by (often rather expensive) medication but that were neither fully preventable, save by abstinence, or curable.

But the big news on the disease front was the emergence of AIDS—Auto-Immune Deficiency Syndrome, caused by the Human Immunodeficiency Virus, or HIV—as an international epidemic and a source of new fears about contemporary sexual practices and about certain social groups. The disease was first identified in the early 1980s, but had begun to spread earlier in Africa and a few other places like Haiti; the first United States report, from Los Angeles, surfaced in 1981. As it initially emerged, its prospects were unusually intimidating, as no known treatments existed and it was typically fatal, after a period of wasting and painful symptoms.

In all regions where it hit, the disease tracked many features of the changes in sexual behaviors: it was transmitted by the exchange of human fluids, with sexual fluids prominent among them, and it was highly contagious. It was thus extremely sensitive to promiscuity, when one sexual partner brought disease previously conveyed from someone else; it could particularly respond to prostitution or sexual tourism. It was also often associated with homosexuality (again, where promiscuity was involved), as well as with drug use, thanks to reused needles.

News of the disease in the Western world caused a veritable panic in the 1980s—out of proportion, as things turned out, to what actually happened. Three characteristic responses emerged, often in some combination. First, obviously, a variety of leaders issued urgent pleas to rethink certain sexual practices, to roll back aspects of the sexual revolution as well as homosexuality in the interests of health. For certain groups, AIDS seemed almost a divine retribution for the abandonment of traditional morality, but even for more liberal segments the disease might call for new kinds of restraint. At the very least, in this first response, countermeasures such as the use of condoms (which restricted fluid exchange, though without absolute guarantees of immunity) were widely urged. Second, eager requests for scientific research signaled a belief in the possibility of medical prevention and cure and a desire to impact actual sexual practices as little as possible. Massive government investments began to go to AIDS research. Third, certain groups began to be stigmatized as particularly dangerous: foreigners might be indicted for particular promiscuity, homosexuals were common targets, and the poor or racial minorities might be highlighted as well. AIDS in this sense exacerbated social tensions on the basis of real or imagined sexual differences. Many Americans thus criticized African Americans, while Indians attacked the Nepalese.

In the industrial world, medical research began to pay off by 1995, with the introduction of new antiretroviral drugs. These drugs neither cured nor prevented the disease, but they did inhibit the development of HIV into AIDS. For most people in the developed nations—the drug package was expensive, and also depended on a willingness to follow instructions and take medicine regularly—HIV increasingly became a lifelong condition, but not a fatal sentence. This did not mean that fears disappeared, and injunctions to avoid promiscuity and/or use condoms continued. But after the great flurry of concern—which had reflected real dangers but also, perhaps, a certain degree of guilt about contemporary sexual indulgence—the actual impact on sexual behaviors retreated considerably, among heterosexuals and homosexuals alike.

In poorer parts of the world, where the most effective treatments were impossibly expensive or complicated or both, as least for wide use, the epidemic had larger ramifications. In Thailand, the spread of AIDS led to new efforts to curb prostitution and even to encourage marriage as a preferable option, though effects were limited. Campaigns to urge prostitutes to insist on condom use, however, had somewhat greater success. Other countries displayed a greater tendency to deny the problem, often by blaming it almost entirely on foreigners—this was long the case in Russia, for example. China and India were slow to recognize the issue, and then hampered both by high levels of prostitution and by limited facilities for sex education. Still, a feared escalation of the epidemic in Asia and Latin America (except Brazil) has not fully materialized.

Sub-Saharan Africa was a special case. High levels of urban prostitution—by the mid-1980s, half of the prostitutes in Kenya were infected—and substantial rates of extramarital sex combined with lack of effective policy response and an incapacity to afford expensive medical treatments. Many governments had few resources to devote to a new public health concern, and the most effective recommendation—condom use—frequently fell on deaf ears, as men resented a device that interfered with their pleasure and women often believed they had to please their men. (Three-quarters of polled South African men refused condom use, deriding it as "dressing up" and Western rather than African.) The result was a rapid disease spread, particularly in southern and eastern Africa, with catastrophic effects not only on adult public health (men's and women's alike) but also on the health of many children born with the disease as a result of maternal transmission. A few partial success stories emerged by the early twenty-first century, where government campaigns produced greater response in terms of more careful behaviors and condom use—Uganda was a case in point. But the disease showed no signs of slackening overall, with well over 20 million people infected by the early twenty-first century.

AIDS was a new problem: it was not initially caused by changes in sexual habits but it certainly spread on the heels of these changes, and to an extent became global because of altered behaviors as well. A vast new worry, the disease did not, clearly, affect sexual activity in any fundamental way, save perhaps for the brief period of anxiety in the West. Western success in developing a medical response (even if addressing symptoms rather than root causes) plus some further steps in condom use (building on earlier readiness to adopt birth control devices) relieved most groups from much actual alteration in sexual activities. African response, though far different, also suggested a reluctance to change current sexual patterns. AIDS or other diseases might still prompt greater adjustments in the future, but to date the new problems have suggested the depth of commitment to sexual expression even in the face of unexpected obstacles.

Resistance: tradition and innovation in restraint

New forms of sexual behavior, and the more open sexual culture, inevitably produced a variety of discontents, from people who believed older standards remained valid and vital and from people who, while not traditionalists, worried that contemporary sexuality damaged other, more fundamental goals. The result was a flurry of reaction, some of it with global and not simply regional implications. The obvious downsides of contemporary sexuality, in the form of abuses of sex workers and the rise of disease, created additional incentives for more effective regulation or self-restraint or both.

Traditionalists could be found everywhere—men who thought women's new sexual freedoms, real or imagined, were menacing and inappropriate; American conservatives who believed that birth control for adolescents would encourage sexual license and so insisted on the abstinence—"just say no"—campaigns instead; a segment of Islamic clerics who blasted women's athletic costumes as inventions of Satan because of the amount of body they exposed and the resultant temptation they created. The collapse of Russian communism led to a religious revival that in turn generated a minority eager to restore older sexual standards. Chinese conservatives attacked masturbation as unwholesome, echoing earlier Victorian concerns. In Latin America and elsewhere, Catholic leaders stood out against key aspects of contemporary sexuality. Focal points for debate included, of course, the controversies over not only birth control but also abortion, which pitted opponents of undue sexuality but also people who sought to maintain a greater link between intercourse and reproduction against a variety of more liberal interests. Many Western European countries managed to reduce tensions by allowing abortion but under rather strict limits; and in other countries, for example in Asia, the importance of abortion overshadowed any significant debate. But in the United States and Latin America, political battles around these aspects of sexuality were fierce, and resolution seemed difficult.

Conservative uses of sexual traditions had a number of goals, not always directly relating to sexuality. In Pakistan, for example, accusations of adultery were sometimes used to discipline wives or daughters, whose gestures of independence had nothing to do with sexual behavior. The accusations were often disproved, but only after considerable effort and expense in court, and with resultant shame that permanently damaged women's reputations in any event. Here was one of many instances, and not only in Islamic areas, where sexual debates focused wider concerns about gender and change.

Special concerns about children helped bridge between conservatives and other groups. Many societies and international agencies tried to protect children from sexual exploitation; regulations against the use of children in pornography stiffened, though it proved hard to counter new media accessibility. In the United States, fears about child molestation increased, arguably beyond the actual incidence of problems; this signaled the tension between the values applied to children and the new sexual culture. Laws against sexual "predators"—some of whom were serious offenders, but others guilty of nothing beyond teenage sex with an underage partner—became more rigorous. Great anxiety surrounded the relocation of sex offenders after prison time served. In the same vein, many therapists urged adults to recall childhood abuse, sometimes encouraging false memories in the process. Behaviors within the family, where older relatives showed particular interest in physical contact with children, once regarded as eccentricities, were now singled out and, at least technically, might be considered crimes. Traditional hopes for children's innocence, challenged by modern culture, combined with new levels of concern about some very old practices.

Extensions of rules also applied to adults, with the United States leading the way but with growing echoes elsewhere. Feminists, particularly after the first blush of enthusiasm for the sexual revolution of the 1960s, often urged new boundary lines. Most accepted in principle the importance of sexual expression for women, and to that extent could support the main lines of behavioral change. But increased exploitation of women, for example in the media and advertisements, where women's bodies were far more prominently displayed than men's, and worries about coercion within private relationships, prompted second thoughts. New areas of legal regulation included more precise definitions of what became known as date rape, including situations where women might participate in the first stages of a sexual encounter but then change their minds, and the even wider area of sexual harassment. An initial definition of sexual harassment appeared in a *Ladies Home Journal* article in 1976, focusing on work situations where a job superior—usually, though not always, a male—tried to use the power advantage to compel intimacies that the subordinate did not wish to experience. As the first sally suggested, "The woman victimized ... can suffer great personal anguish, depression, and physical stress symptoms such as nausea, headaches and severe body pain. If she's seen as a tool for sexual pleasure, she knows her work won't be taken seriously." Large numbers of women responded to this new concept, which in principle imposed new levels of restraint on men, despite increasingly close interactions with female colleagues in a highly sexualized culture, which sometimes included provocative styles of dress.

Regulations about sexual harassment, and court cases designed to implement the new balance, spread not only in the United States but also Western Europe and elsewhere. The issue was also discussed in Japan. This was hardly a global movement at this point, and it focused primarily on white-collar or professional job settings in industrial societies where the sexualized public culture was particularly advanced. Nevertheless, the effort to define new sexual boundaries, in addition to conservative attempts to reassert tradition and public health efforts to curb practices conducive to disease, constituted a significant complexity in the larger trends of sexuality in contemporary world history.

Sex and violence

Sex and violence were hardly new companions. In many contemporary societies older attitudes continued to support the notion that men could and should use violence as part of their sexual approach to wives and other partners. While it is impossible to measure violence rates against prior levels—we know too little about present realities and far too little about the past—it is likely that, beyond sheer traditionalism, violence rates increased. Against this, another new movement, global in aspiration, called for new rules and enforcements against sexually related violence.

Several factors pushed toward greater abuse in a number of different regions of the world and a number of different situations. To the extent that the new culture of sexuality promoted an "anything goes" attitude, it might seem to authorize greater assertions of masculine force. In 2008, for example, it was reported that traditionally-clothed women in Cairo, Egypt, were being subjected to new levels of harassment by men who wondered "what they looked like underneath" or "what were they trying to hide." Much of the purpose of concealing garb was to protect from masculine gaze, so the new intrusions were both unexpected and unprecedented—a possible sign of the permissiveness some men claimed to find in the contemporary context.

Sheer confusion between tradition and modernity was another source. Women who did not conform to conventional dress codes in some societies, whether of local origin or foreign, might seem to be inviting aggressive sexual approaches that could lead to violence. A number of men clearly believed that modern women were becoming too defiant and that a new level of intimidation was essential to keep them in their place. A similar impulse might increase the amount of violence in penalties for sexual misbehavior: in Jordan for example husbands not infrequently killed wives caught in adultery, and then suffered only light punishments in return—the basic perception of the crime was not new, for adultery had long been reproved, but the temptation toward violent response may have risen because of new levels of uncertainty about women's fidelity, and suspicions about modern women more generally.

Rising levels of prostitution and the power imbalance this involved also occasioned violence. Attacks on prostitutes were reported in many societies.

Rape surfaced in a number of situations, not necessarily new, but newly visible, amid growing international concern. In some regions, beliefs surfaced that raping a virgin could cure HIV. Rates of rape apparently increased in Russia in the 1990s, though whether this resulted from more actual cases or better reporting was not entirely clear. Russian society divided over what constituted rape—for example, some believed that if a woman was drunk and a man attacked her, it was really her fault and did not constitute rape. Rape within marriage was another disputed category. In some Latin American countries a rapist would not be prosecuted if he persuaded his victim to marry him. Rape in India was fairly widespread, but again definitions were disputed: in 1987 a book entitled *How to Rape* was published in Mumbai with graphic details, including how to evade prosecution. Rape within marriage was not regarded as a crime amid beliefs that a good wife would be submissive no matter what. Rape also provided a way to coerce women—including foreign women, like the Nepalese contingent in India—into prostitution. In New Delhi, where the problem was particularly severe, over 750 rapes were reported in 2007—and many more went unrecorded; the effort to use rape to protest educational and job gains by women was quite explicit in this instance. Depending on the region, it was estimated by the early twenty-first century that between 6 and 59 percent of all women encountered sexual violence from a husband or intimate partner. The incidence was widespread and varied.

The most widespread instances of rape involved actions by men during war and civil strife. Conflicts in Haiti often involved rape, and the same held true for the Shining Path rebellion in Peru. Mass rape campaigns were positively encouraged in Rwanda in 2001 as part of genocide: the frequent indulgence in rape by armed men was exacerbated by beliefs that forcing sex on a different ethnicity would weaken and dishonor their group by humiliating women and defiling their ethnic purity. Similar developments occurred in Sudan a few years later. Beliefs about ethnic categories, in other words, may have provided an additional motive for sexual violence, making an older historical problem worse than before.

Along with sexual violence, and to an extent because of it, a variety of international groups mobilized for preventive or remedial action. The clearest innovation in the field of sex and violence in the past half century have been a growing number of international resolutions and agencies concerned with defining sexual violence as a crime. During the 1990s, conflict-based rape was declared a war crime, with some prosecutions resulting both in the former Yugoslavia and in Rwanda. Amnesty International increasingly turned to sex crimes against women as one of the leading human rights issues. A United Nations resolution in 2000 recognized the vast amount of rape in armed conflict, and urged the Secretary General to involve more women in peace processes and to take more explicit measures to protest women's rights; a 2006 resolution noted wide persistence of the problem of sexual violence. Obviously, this new level of awareness and disapproval has yet to win striking results, and in some regions the whole human rights effort in the area of sexuality is viewed as a colonial-type Western intrusion and is ignored or even flaunted accordingly. Still, there is some evidence that, over time, well-meaning global standards can encourage some change in attitudes toward more disapproval of violence. The interaction between this aspect of global standards and actual behaviors deserves continuing attention in the future.

Homosexuality

In 1998 a group of Wyoming teenagers seized a gay University of Wyoming student, Matthew Shephard, and beat and tortured him so severely that, after having been tied to a post and abandoned, he died. His attackers were imprisoned, one without possibility of parole, and the case led to national discussion of firmer measures against hate crimes. In 2007 a French gay man was badly beaten by a group in Dubai, and authorities, rather than prosecuting the attackers, arrested the badly-injured foreigner and ultimately deported him.

Homosexuality was a final area in which global trends emerged haltingly, though in clear relation to some of the larger developments in sexuality, with massive controversy, new regional divides, and periodic violence developing in the wake of novel developments.

The main lines of change were clear enough. Earlier shifts, pioneered in the West but increasingly affecting other societies, had redefined homosexuality to mean a person's permanent sexual orientation rather than an occasional behavior. In fact, of course, bisexuality persisted, and many people, if often secretly, had sexual experiences with both genders at least at some point in their lives. But the focus, particularly for men, increasingly depended on a definition of basic sexual orientation, and by the early twenty-first century some scientific studies added confirmation through research suggesting that for many, if not all, homosexuals their brain wiring was different from that of the majority. Hostility to homosexuality, thus redefined, continued strongly through the 1950s. The Cold War led to prosecutions of homosexuals as security threats in the United States and Britain. Communist China reversed traditional Chinese tolerance and attacked homosexuals as bearers of Western decadence, even executing some.

Homosexual cultural products, however, began to gain new ground, particularly in Japan and the West, with many prominent novels, on the high culture side, and a new line of popular male body books that in fact catered to gays. In the 1960s, a strong gay rights movement emerged, initially in the United States. It flowed from the larger civil rights effort but also attached to the broader trends of sexuality: if the main purpose of sexuality was pleasure, and if each individual should define his or her own enjoyment (so long as partners consented freely) then a new sexual logic could apply to homosexuals as well as others. In 1969, New York police raided the Stonewall Inn, a gay center, and violent protests ensued. A more public gay liberation movement resulted, that had wide impact in encouraging homosexuals to assert their claims in public and in altering some public attitudes as well. In 1973, after massive debate, the American Psychological Association removed references to homosexuality as a mental disorder, though treatments of patients unsure of their sexual orientation continued into the late 1980s. By the early twenty-first century, popular media fare included greater openness toward homosexuals and even portrayals of some homosexual behaviors (such as kissing), while easily-accessible pornographic outlets included homosexual fare for interested audiences.

Global echoes quickly emerged. In 1978 an International Lesbian and Gay Association emerged, based in Northern Europe but with adhesion from member groups in over 70 countries. In the 1990s, homosexuals mounted successful law suits against discrimination in Japan, and in 1997 the Tokyo High Court ruled that the government must treat homosexuals as a respected minority. The World Health Organization deleted references to homosexuality as a disease in 1992. Chinese attitudes began to ease, and a new condom designed particularly for gays appeared on the market. The South African constitution banned discrimination based on sexual orientation in 1994. Early in the twenty-first century, several countries, and a few American states, legalized gay marriages: Spain, Belgium, the Netherlands, and Canada headed the list of nations, while in 2005 the United Kingdom introduced protections for gay unions.

Concern about AIDS generated new hostilities to homosexuality, particularly in the West, where promiscuity among some gay men unquestionably helped transmit the disease. On the other hand, the legal rights effort helped other groups—bisexuals, trans-gender individuals—to express their sexual orientations and concerns about acceptance more openly. Gay leaders themselves continued to press against both formal and informal discrimination, and the movement in several countries to urge a right to marry capped this trend.

The push for tolerance, if not more, stirred deep feelings and massive debate. Within countries like the United States, deep divisions opened over homosexuality and the demands of advocacy groups. Many fundamentalist Christians continued to regard homosexuality as a sin, and also focused on this issue wider fears about permissive sexual trends. Many states saw successful political efforts against any acceptance of gay marriage, even as some other states, in some cases by popular vote, actually approved legalization. Polls suggested that, on the whole, tolerance was increasing, but the process was hardly uniform.

Global developments were in some ways predictable, reflecting the same halting but discernable process of globalization expressed in other sexual trends. Many regions moved gradually toward greater openness. Actual homosexual encounters, even by married men, may have been more common in Latin America than in the United States; in some definitions of masculinity, a homosexual experience was built in. But acceptance of homosexual identity was more halting, particularly amid the culture of *machismo*; stigmatization in communist Cuba was particularly intense. Still, gay rights groups did begin to emerge in several countries. Mexico opened gay pride days by 2008, while a glossy gay magazine appeared in Colombia. But violence, including murders, against homosexuals continued at a high rate, reflecting the kinds of passionate divisions the contemporary framework for homosexuality generated so widely.

Limited efforts toward recognition of gay rights occurred in Africa, but there was also massive resentment of international movements toward liberation, viewed as offensive Western intrusions. In combination with Christian or Islamic concern, the result was a widespread rejection of homosexuality as both sinful and foreign. Again, violence, including rape, was common, even as more traditional versions of homosexuality—for example, male-identified women in Namibia called "Damara lesbian men," or marriage between two women in Uganda—persisted in some areas.

Russia continued to arrest some homosexuals into the early 1990s, sentencing as many as 800 men a year under sodomy laws, though a gay subculture was implicitly tolerated. While great public hostility persisted, the situation eased a bit with the fall of communism. India, with legislation on the books from colonial days, but with an older culture of homosexuality based on the *hijras*, the "third sex" group, also saw significant gay rights movements develop along Western lines, with many grassroots gay and lesbian organizations. A more open gay culture separate from the *hijras* also emerged, including fairly open acceptance of lesbianism as a sexual identity.

The greatest tensions emerged within Islam, though they echoed some of the bitter divisions in other societies. Here was the most striking case in which long prior traditions of tolerance were almost entirely reversed, at least in terms of official outlook and policy. Earlier efforts to fend off Western disapproval contributed to the harsher stance. Many Muslims also reacted to the Western-inspired redefinition of homosexuality that emphasized durable identity rather than occasional behavior—the new emphasis proved much harder to accept. Finally, as with other groups, attacks on homosexuality allowed expression of hostility to Western cultural influence and Western sexual licentiousness more generally; here was one source of the new intensity of public reactions. A complex variety of factors, obviously, generated a major departure not only from trends in the West but from the hints of a global pattern more generally—and from earlier latitudes within Islam itself. A variety of subcultures persisted, but amid great anxiety and tension. Hints of gay rights advocacy emerged only in Beirut, Lebanon, with scant echo elsewhere in the region. Upper classes came to define homosexuality as a psychiatric disorder and often urged treatment. But widespread public hostility and repression formed the most obvious theme. Whippings of homosexuals in Iran; police attacks on gay gatherings in the otherwise-tolerant Dubai, an Egyptian raid on a floating gay dance club in 2001, which generated dozens of arrests—this created a framework of impassioned, possibly growing opposition that defined a distinctive regional approach.

The local and the global

Globalization as a general phenomenon must always be balanced against regional patterns and reactions, and this is certainly true with sexuality. The contemporary history of sexuality, building on trends that had begun to emerge by the later nineteenth century, reveals not only some unusual regional diversities, but also an intriguing shift in balance. A century and a half ago, the West might be criticized for many things in the sexual arena, including intolerance of local customs and abusive coercion of colonial women, but leadership in liberality would not have been one of the charges. In scarcely a century, the West, along with Japan and a few other highly industrial regions, has become the global leader in the open pursuit of sexual pleasure, as measured by public culture, reasonably tolerant acceptance of premarital and non-marital sex, and embrace of diverse forms of recreational sex. It has also led in the new prominence of medical evaluations of sexuality and sexual health. Caught in this rapid transition, many other regions find themselves suspicious of the West's new standards and, in some cases, less committed to tolerance of varied sexual practices than had been the case traditionally.

Huge diversities result in part from differences in levels of prosperity. Capacities to afford expensive medications in cases of sexually transmitted disease constitute a major variable. Female poverty and dislocation in some regions contrast with eagerness to absorb foreign prostitutes or participate in sex tourism in others. Variations result also from the timing of transitions to greater commitments to birth control and the devices available to accomplish this.

Cultural differences, however, also loom large. Highly religious regions and groups simply move far more slowly to accommodate some of the leading forms of sexual change. In parts of Africa, religiously-linked traditions continue to inspire defense of female circumcision, despite growing efforts by international agencies and Western governments to uproot the practice. Even immigrants to the West, from places like Somalia, maintain the tradition, either illegally on site or by returns to the homeland. Open defense of this tradition continues, as with Haji Sasso, head of the National Council of Muslim Women in Sierra Leone, who said in 1997, "I am defending circumcision to protect our culture. I don't want to see this ceremony eradicated because it binds us, we the women, together."

Religious commitment even more directly helps explain key differences between the United States and Western Europe, despite many shared cultural and behavioral trends. West Europeans, in the main, accepted the implications of new levels of birth control and the changes of the 1960s far more widely than their American counterparts. Restrictions in the cultural sphere, for example in the fare that can be shown on television, are far less severe in Europe than in the United States. Promotion of birth control devices for teenagers, with resultant low levels of adolescent pregnancy, contrast with American efforts to support abstinence. Americans are urged to worry deeply about the sexual behavior of political leaders, an area that most Europeans view as politically irrelevant. The contrasts are intriguing, and where they inform larger policies—for example, in support of or opposition to family planning efforts internationally—they gain additional historical significance.

Islam, particularly in its Middle Eastern versions, correlates with yet another set of distinctive responses. Attacks on abortion and birth control, as well as the level of hostility to homosexuality, actually diverge from earlier Islamic and regional patterns. Extreme efforts to control women's sexuality and insist on concealing costumes, as with the Taliban in Afghanistan, suggest that sexual behavior and symbolism have become battlegrounds for the preservation of regional identity as against the intrusion of Western and modern values—even when the standards being defended are far stricter than tradition would call for. Divisions over sexual issues play a serious role in mutual regional disapprovals, with Westerners easily attacking Islamic prudery or punishments for sex crimes, Islamic leaders eagerly returning the favor as they note Western promiscuity and decadence.

Diversities within regions, however, reflect similar factors. Americans divide, often bitterly, over sex education, abortion, and sexuality outside marriage. Countries like Turkey or Morocco, with more secular cultures and less experience with direct Western control (and therefore, presumably, fewer defensive identity concerns) differ in their range of sexual tolerance from stricter regimes like Saudi Arabia within the Middle East. Rural–urban and social class divisions mark most regions, at least to some degree.

All of this is to be expected. Sex has always produced disputes over standards and over how strictly to apply standards in practice. A time of deep change—in media representations, in birth control devices, in disease issues, in types of commercial sex— inevitably finds some groups and areas moving faster toward acceptance than others, others pulling back in appalled resistance. Where sexuality entangles with other issues, like identity versus Western influence, divisions widen even more than actual sexual changes might predict.

The result, however, seriously complicates any sense of prediction. It is tempting to argue that global patterns will move more fully in the future toward tolerance, acceptance of sex for pleasure rather than reproduction, and enjoyment of a sexualized culture, along lines already suggested by Japan and the West and (increasingly) by urban China and Russia. Just as agricultural economies generated some basic characteristics in sexual forms, around emphases on reproduction combined with control against too many offspring and on female subservience, so industrial economies will produce characteristic pleasure-seeking forms around which regional variations add more superficial distinctions. But we don't know that the whole world will in fact industrialize, and we don't know that, if it does, a modern sexual pattern will triumph over deeply-rooted cultural diversities. Among other things, contemporary sexual change has encouraged so many new problems that a larger backlash might not be surprising.

History, here, cannot forecast. The global history of sexuality does, however, suggest how certain kinds of change will continue to challenge older patterns. It suggests some of the reasons for comparative differences in response. It provides a framework through which the coming decades can be evaluated. And the global history of sexuality certainly shows why and how changes in sexuality matter, in the individual human experience and in wider social interactions.

Further reading

For additional resources on birth control, see Grant, L. Juggernaut, *Growth on a Finite Planet* (Washington, DC: Seven Locks Press, 1991); W.C. Robinson and J.A. Ross, eds., *The Global Family Planning Revolution: Three Decades of Population Policies and Programs* (Washington, DC: World Bank, 2007); and the International Planned Parenthood Federation (www.ippf.org).

On HIV and AIDS, see J. Engel, *The Epidemic: A Global History of AIDS* (New York: HarperCollins, 2006); C. Farber, *Serious Adverse Events: An Uncensored History of AIDS* (Hoboken, NJ: Melville House Publishing, 2006); and J. Iliffe, *The African AIDS Epidemic: A History* (Athens: Ohio University Press, 2006). www.avert.org/ecstatee.htm contains current statistics on HIV.

On Africa, refer to T. Falola and N. Afolabi, eds., *The Human Cost of African Migrations* (New York: Routledge, 2007); B. Freund, *The Making of Contemporary Africa: The Development of African Society since 1800*, 2nd ed. (Boulder, CO: Lynne Rienner, 1998); Y. Hernlund and B. Shell-Duncan, eds., *Transcultural Bodies: Female Genital Cutting in Global Context* (Newark, NJ: Rutgers University Press, 2007); D.L. Hodgson and S.A. McCurdy, eds., *"Wicked" Women and the Reconfiguration of Gender in Africa* (Portsmouth, NH: Heinemann, 2001); and R. Morgan and S. Wieringa, *Tommy Boys, Lesbian Men and Ancestral Wives: Female Same-Sex Practices in Africa* (Cape Town, South Africa: Jacana Media Ltd., 2005).

On sexuality and Japan, see S. Fruhstuck, *Colonizing Sex: Sexology and Social Control in Modern Japan* (Berkeley: University of California Press, 2003); J. Kingston, *Japan in Transformation, 1952–2000* (New York: Longman, 2001); A. Ueda, *The Electric Geisha: Exploring Japan's Popular Culture*, trans. M. Eguchi (New York: Kodansha International, 2005); and T. Norgren and C.A.E. Norgren, eds., *Abortion Before Birth Control: The Politics of Reproduction in Postwar Japan* (Princeton, NJ: Princeton University Press, 2001).

On Russia, see I. Kon, *The Sexual Revolution in Russia from the Age of the Czars to Today*, trans. J. Riordan (New York: Free Press, 1995); and I. Kon and J. Riordan, *Sex and Russian Society* (Bloomington: Indiana University Press, 1993).

Good surveys on India include F. Agnes, et al., *Woman and Law in India* (New York: Oxford University Press, 2004); T.L. Brown, *The Dancing Girls of Lahore: Selling Love and Saving Dreams in Pakistan's Ancient Pleasure District* (New York: Fourth Estate, 2005); G. Gangoli, *Indian Feminisms: Law, Patriarchies and Violence in India* (Burlington, VT: Ashgate, 2007); and W.R. Jankowiak, ed., *Intimacies: Love and Sex Across Cultures* (New York: Columbia University Press, 2008).

On the sex trade, see I.D. Gaon, and N. Forbord, eds., *For Sale: Women and Children* (Crewe, UK: Trafford Publishing, 2005); C. Ryan and C.M. Hall, eds., *Sex Tourism: Marginal People and Liminalities* (New York: Routledge, 2001); and S. Skrobanek, et al., eds., *The Traffic in Women: Human Realities of the International Sex Trade* (New York: Macmillan, 1997).

On Asia, see L. Edwards and M. Roces, eds., *Women in Asia: Tradition, Modernity and Globalization* (Ann Arbor: University of Michigan Press, 2000); J. Farquhar, *Appetites: Food and Sex in Post-Socialist China* (Durham, NC: Duke University Press, 2002); G. Gangoli and N. Westmarland, eds., *International Approaches to Prostitution: Law and Policy in Europe and Asia* (Bristol: Policy Press, 2006); M. Jolly and K. Ram, eds., *Borders of Being: Citizenship, Fertility and Sexuality in Asia and the Pacific* (Ann Arbor: University of Michigan Press, 2001); P. Massonet, *The New China: Money, Sex and Power* (Boston, MA: Tuttle Publishing, 1997); and P. Van Esterik, *Materializing Thailand* (New York: Berg, 2000).

On Latin America, see M. Leiner, *Sexual Politics in Cuba* (Boulder, CO: Westview Press, 1994); M. Melhuus and K.A. Stolen, eds., *Machos, Mistresses, Madonnas: Contesting the Power of Latin American Gender Imagery* (New York: Verso, 1996); M. Mendible, ed., *From Bananas to Buttocks: The Latina Body in Popular Film and Culture* (Austin: University of Texas Press, 2007); M. Padilla, *Caribbean Pleasure Industry* (Chicago: University of Chicago Press, 2007); and S. Paternostro, *In the Land of God and Man: Confronting our Sexual Culture* (New York: Dutton, 1998).

On the Middle East, see Y.Y. Haddad and J.L. Esposito, eds., *Islam, Gender, and Social Change* (New York: Oxford University Press, 1998); S. Joseph, *Gender and Citizenship in the Middle East* (New York: Syracuse University Press, 2000); S. Joseph, *Intimate Selving in Arab Families: Gender, Self, and Identity* (New York: Syracuse University Press, 1999); D. Kandiyoti, *Woman, Islam, and the State: A Comparative Approach* (Pittsburgh, PA: Temple University Press, 1991); N. Keddie, *Woman in the Middle East: Past and Present* (Princeton, NJ: Princeton University Press, 2006); L. Welchman, *Women's Rights and Islamic Family Law: Perspectives on Reform* (New York: Zed Books,

2004); and B. Whitaker, *Unspeakable Love: Gay and Lesbian Life in the Middle East* (Berkeley: University of California Press, 2006).

Other good surveys include D. Altman, *Global Sex* (Chicago: University of Chicago Press, 2001); B. Bailey, *Sex in the Heartland* (Cambridge, MA: Harvard University Press, 1999); K. White, *The First Sexual Revolution: The Emergence of Heterosexuality in Modern America* (New York: New York University Press, 1992); E. Freedman and J. D'Emilio, *Intimate Matters: A History of Sexuality in America* (Chicago: University of Chicago Press, 1998); S. Ullman, *Sex Seen: The Emergence of Modern Sexuality in America* (Berkeley: University of California Press, 1997); J. Burnham, *Bad Habits: Drinking, Smoking, Taking Drugs, Gambling, Sexual Misbehavior, and Swearing in American History* (New York: New York University Press, 1993); P.N. Stearns, *Battleground of Desire: The Struggle for Self-Control in Modern America* (New York: New York University Press, 1999); R. Gurstein, *The Repeal of Reticence: A History of America's Cultural and Legal Struggles over Free Speech, Obscenity, Sexual Liberation, and Modern Art* (New York: Hill and Wang, 1996); and E. Laumann, J. Gagnon, R. Michael, and S. Michaels, *The Organization of Sexuality: Sexual Practices in the United States* (Chicago: University of Chicago Press, 1994).

Epilogue
Sexuality from past to present

Sexual behavior is determined by a combination of factors. Basic drives vary from one person to the next, but they obviously contribute to sexual activities in any period of history. Even on a purely physical basis, however, they are also conditioned by historical variables such as nutrition—which is why changes occur in phenomena like age of puberty or age of menopause. Sexual behavior is also shaped by fundamental economic frameworks, particularly as these stipulate numbers of children sought by societies and families alike. We have seen that three basic human frameworks have played major roles in defining reproductive sex and the kinds of social and personal constraints that affect sex beyond reproduction. Finally, partly translating the economic frameworks but also exercising independent influence, cultures shape sexuality as well—religions first and foremost, but also other cultural systems related to science and medicine, or magic, or consumerism. Considering sexuality as a product of three interlocking systems: basic, biological impulses; economic imperatives; and cultures; helps sort out major points of historical change and also the varieties of social formulations within each principal historical period. The same interlocking systems also help explain varieties and changes concerning sexual preference, including homosexuality, and the ways these play out in social systems as well as personal preferences.

Humans have also long used sexual expressions to provide additional outlets, usually in relationship to actual behaviors, but for other purposes as well. At all points, since artistic records exist, sexual cultures have reflected beliefs about gender, about the natural world, and about divinities, going well beyond regular sexual activities. At many points, and certainly from the classical period onward, sexual expressions have also served as entertainment. The history of sexual spectatorship, as people heard stories, read manuals, or looked at erotic art, is an important topic in its own right. Here, too, change over time reflects a variety of factors, from the nature of available media to moral codes (or ways to protest these codes when they seem too rigid) to recreational needs. Sex as a source of problems has a history as well. Sex is often a way to express, and abuse, power relationships. Its link with violence ties sex to war and crime alike. The association between sex and disease connects some of the downsides of this human activity to wider changes in rates and ranges of sexual contacts. Globally, and in most individual societies including our own, sexuality currently is undergoing a transition between deeply-rooted systems that derived from agricultural needs and attendant cultural definitions—these mainly emanating from religious formulations—and a still-not-fully-charted situation shaped by reduced needs for reproduction and a new kind of consumer culture. The transition challenges many established traditions, and it also creates new problems that require response. While elements of contemporary innovation began to take shape more than two centuries ago, for most groups the pace of sexual change has accelerated considerably over the past several decades. This means, among other things, that many people face sexual patterns for which their own upbringing did not fully prepare them—which is what change means in such a profoundly personal area. The results are exhilarating, confusing, or deeply offensive, or some mixture of all three, depending on the observer. Because so many of the factors shaping contemporary sexuality are new—as both economic frameworks and cultures shift ground—and because reactions are so varied, clashes over sexuality are unusually sharp, predictions of future patterns unusually uncertain. The past still shapes many behaviors and even more reactions to behaviors, serving as the baseline from which the transitions emerge. Knowledge of the past—of sex's history—while it cannot generate precise forecasts, provides the basis for understanding key trends and controversies in this vital aspect of the human experience.

Index

Childhood in World History

Peter N. Stearns

Childhood exists in all societies, though there is huge variation in the way it is socially constructed across time and place. Studying childhood historically greatly advances our understanding of what childhood is about and a world history focus permits some of the broadest questions to be asked.

In *Childhood in World History* Peter N. Stearns focuses on childhood in several ways:

- Childhood across change – the shift from hunting and gathering to an agricultural society and the impact of civilization and the emergence of major religions
- New and old debates about the distinctive features of Western childhood, including child labour
- The emergence of a modern, industrial pattern of childhood in the West, Japan and communist societies, including a focus on education and economic dependence
- Globalization and the spread of child-centred consumerism

This historical perspective highlights the gains but also the divisions and losses for children across the millennia.

Hbk: 978–0–415–35232–1   Pbk: 978–0–415–35233–8

Food in World History

Jeffrey M. Pilcher

Providing a comparative and comprehensive study of culinary cultures and consumption throughout the world from ancient times to present day, this book examines the globalization of food and explores the political, social and environmental implications of our changing relationship with food.

Including numerous case studies from diverse societies and periods, *Food in World History* examines and focuses on:

- how food was used to forge national identities in Latin America
- the influence of Italian and Chinese Diaspora on the US and Latin America food culture
- how food was fractured along class lines in the French bourgeois restaurant culture and working class cafes
- the results of state intervention in food production
- how the impact of genetic modification and food crises has affected the relationship between consumer and product.

This concise and readable survey not only presents a simple history of food and its consumption, but also provides a unique examination of world history itself.

Hbk: 978–0–415–31145–8   Pbk: 978–0–415–31146–5

Available at all good bookshops
For ordering and further information please visit:
www.routledge.com

Consumerism in World History
2nd Edition
Peter N. Stearns

Reviews of the first edition:
'This is a clever book.' – *Business History*

The desire to acquire luxury goods and leisure services is a basic force in modern life. *Consumerism in World History* explores both the historical origins and world-wide appeal of this relatively modern phenomenon. By relating consumerism to other issues in world history, this book forces reassessment of our understanding of both consumerism and global history.

This second edition of *Consumerism in World History* draws on recent research of the consumer experience in the West and Japan, while also examining societies less renowned for consumerism, such as Africa. Every chapter has been updated and new features include:

* a new chapter on Latin America
* Russian and Chinese developments since the 1990s
* the changes involved in trying to bolster consumerism as a response to recent international threats
* examples of consumerist syncretism, as in efforts to blend beauty contests with traditional culture in Kerala.

With updated suggested reading, the second edition of *Consumerism in World History* is essential reading for all students of world history.

Hbk: 978–0–415–39586–1   Pbk: 978–0–415–39587–8

Available at all good bookshops
For ordering and further information please visit:
www.routledge.com

Gender in World History
2nd Edition
Peter N. Stearns

From classical times to the twenty-first century, *Gender in World History* is a fascinating exploration of what happens to established ideas about men and women, and their roles, when different cultural systems come into contact. This book breaks new ground to facilitate a consistent approach to gender in a world history context.

This second edition is completely updated, including:

- expanded introductions to each chronological section
- extensive discussion of the twentieth century bringing it right up to date
- new chapters on international influences in the first half of the twentieth century and globilization in the latter part of the twentieth century
- engagement with the recent work done on gender history and theory.

With coverage right up to the present day, *Gender in World History* is essential reading for students of world history.

Hbk: 978–0–415–39588–5   Pbk: 978–0–415–39589–2

Available at all good bookshops
For ordering and further information please visit:
www.routledge.com

Poverty in World History

Steven M. Beaudoin

Poverty is a perennial problem in world history, but over time its causes have shifted from local issues like natural disasters or warfare to more global economic issues which impact on available resources, systems of distribution and potential solutions. Poverty in World History focuses upon the period from around 1500 onwards when poverty become a global issue, and uses the process of globalisation as the chief lens through which to study and understand poverty in world history.

The result is both a tying together of significant strands of world history and an examination of changing attitudes towards poverty and poor relief throughout the world. This wide ranging study underscores a major consequence of increased cultural and economic interaction among the world's societies, highlighting the similarities and differences in impacts and responses to the resulting 'smaller' globe. Topics include:

- Innovations in Early Modern Poor relief
- The causes of trends towards a globalisation of poverty after 1500
- Poor relief since 1945 to the present
- Poverty, morality and the state

A genuinely global survey of world poverty from 1500 to the present day, Poverty in World History is essential reading for students in World History.

Hbk: 978–0–415–25458–8   Pbk: 978–0–415–25459–5

Desire
A History of European Sexuality
Anna Clark

'Provides a valuable overview of the history of sexuality in Europe since classical antiquity, synthesising as it does a mass of studies of specific regions and periods which have appeared during the last two decades.' Lesley Hall, *Wellcome Library, UK*

Desire: A History of European Sexuality is a survey of sexuality in Europe from the Greeks to the present. The book traces two concepts of sexual desire that have competed throughout European history: desire as dangerous, polluting, and disorderly, and desire as creative, transcendent, even revolutionary. Following these changing attitudes through the major turning points of European history, Anna Clark concludes by demonstrating that western European sexual culture is quite distinct from many other cultures, and asks whether the vision of sexual desire as revolutionary, even transcendent, has faded in the modern secular era.

While *Desire* builds on the work of dozens of historians, it also takes a fresh approach. Explaining how authorities tried to manage sexual desire and sometimes failed, the book introduces the concept of 'twilight moments' to describe activities seen as shameful or dishonourable, but which were tolerated when concealed by shadows. Other topics addressed include:

- Sex in Greece and Rome
- Divine desire in Judaism and early Christianity
- New attitudes toward sexuality in the seventeenth and eighteenth centuries
- Victorian twilights.

Written in a lively and engaging style, this new survey contains many fascinating anecdotes, and draws on a rich array of sources including poetry, novels, pornography and film as well as court records, autobiographies and personal letters. *Desire* integrates the history of heterosexuality with same-sex desire, focuses on the emotions of love as well as the passions of lust, and explores the politics of sex as well as personal experiences.

Hbk: 978–0–415–77517–5   Pbk: 978–0–415–77518–2

Available at all good bookshops
For ordering and further information please visit:
www.routledge.com